The American Ship Building Company's Lorain, Ohio, Plant,
American Ship Building Company.

LAMAR UNIVERSITY-BEAUMONT
0 00 01 0163491 3

FRESHWATER WHALES

FRESHWATER

WHALES

A History of
The American Ship Building Company
and Its Predecessors

By Richard J. Wright

The Kent State University Press

*To my wife, Martha, for her patience and forbearance,
and to Captain Frank E. Hamilton for his inspiration and guidance,
this book is sincerely dedicated.*

Acknowledgements

The historian must know where to go for research material, but knowing where to go is of negligable value without the cooperation of those who possess or control that information. In every case the author received enthusiastic and overwhelming support from everyone he approached. For this he is indebted and indeed grateful.

Captain Frank E. Hamilton of Kelleys Island, Ohio, belongs at the top of the list of acknowledgements. He lured the author into the field of Great Lakes history and spoon-fed him for years. Without the spark and guidance that Captain Hamilton generated, this book would have been impossible. He not only supplied information and photographs but read the manuscript to pull out the inevitable errors.

Father Edward J. Dowling, S. J., of the University of Detroit, also bears special mention. He spent hours of discussion with the author, generously supplied photographs, and painted the illustration of the World War I blockade runner that was never built.

Within the American Ship Building Company, President George M.

Steinbrenner III furnished the necessary faith and interest to make the project possible and tuned a distant but interested ear as the manuscript progressed through its various stages. Most of the grief fell on the shoulders of Vice-President Gordon Stafford who accommodated every request and considerably lightened the author's burden. Great assistance from the firm's Lorain office came from Robert Bartlome, George B. Ramsayer, Joseph Lanasa, Walter Humphrey, Daniel S. Connelly, John Smutko, and Jean Graham. The Toledo yard of the company proved to be a gold mine of information thanks to the assistance of W. B. Clevenger, B. F. Majo, and William F. Gerhauser. The same was true of Jerry Thoman, John Krezman, J. A. Skodny, and Jack Pillon at the company's Chicago yard. Edgerton B. Williams, retired company vice-president, relayed some enlightening experiences by telephone from his Winter Park, Florida, home.

Professors James M. Gidney and Lawrence S. Kaplan of the Kent State University Department of History provided the professional guidance for a doctoral dissertation and kept the author within stylistic bounds. Robert B. Wright, of the Cleveland-based M. A. Hanna Company, deserves credit for opening many doors in the shipping industry that might otherwise have been closed.

Much research was done in various government agencies. In Washington, D.C., at the Industrial Records Division of the National Archives, Miss Jane Smith, Albert Blair, and especially Kenneth Hall were most helpful. John K. Tennant of the Maritime Administration set the author on a true course in those uncharted seas, and grateful acknowledgements go to Charles J. Cookson, William L. Nesbitt, Mrs. Virginia C. Wilson, Mrs. Nellie C. Borngesser, and James White of the same staff. The Navy Department Library personnel were also most cooperative.

James M. Babcock and Mrs. Alice Dalligan of the Burton Historical Collection, Detroit Public Library, were very helpful, as were Robert E. Lee and C. Patrick Labadie of the Dossin Marine Museum on Belle Isle. David T. Glick and J. Albin Jackman, individuals dedicated to lake history, lightened the load considerably through their shared knowledge and loaned materials. The staff of the U. S. Lake Survey Office provided valuable access to their chart vault, where several mysteries were solved. Also in the Detroit area, the author wishes to thank Mrs. DeWindt of the Wyandotte Public Library for her assistance, particularly in searching local newspaper materials.

In Bay City, Michigan, Donald Comtois shared his newspaper findings with the author. Mrs. Betty Sporman of the Bay County Historical Society and Alfred R. Kraig and his staff at the Bay City Public Library were exceptionally cooperative. Ralph Roberts of Saginaw, Michigan, took a full day to drive the author up and down the banks of the Saginaw River.

Edmund Fitzgerald and Harry C. Brockel answered the author's call for assistance in Milwaukee, as did Paul Sotirin and his staff in the Marine and Local History Room of the Milwaukee Public Library. Christian J. Stellrecht of Orchard Park, New York, dug deep into his basement store of material on the Buffalo Dry Dock Company. Erik Heyl was another engaging and valuable source of information in Buffalo. Both the Buffalo and Erie County Historical Society and Public Library staffs were very helpful.

Wesley R. Harkins spent several years collecting material on shipbuilding history in the Duluth-Superior region. He did not hesitate to open his files, generously, to the author. Kenneth E. Thro, of Superior is one of the few people who can identify the individual whaleback barges. He graciously shared his findings. Arvid R. Morken and Barney B. Barstow were very cooperative and Richard D. Bibby contributed his enthusiasm and hospitality to the project.

In Toledo, George L. Merrill gave access to the papers and notebooks of his grandfather, John Craig. Mrs. Irene M. McCreery, of the Toledo Public Library, also deserves thanks for her assistance and suggestions pertaining to the local scene.

Many people in the greater Cleveland area were of much assistance. Alexander McDougall gave the author access to his grandfather's notebooks. Norman E. Borowske related his experiences in rebuilding the U.S.S. *Wolverine*. Others who rendered much aid were W. G. Bartenfeld, a well-known lake naval architect; Janet Coe Sanborn, editor of *Inland Seas*, the publication of the Great Lakes Historical Society; and John W. Manning of the M. A. Hanna Company.

Sam Meader of St. Louis, Missouri, telephoned his World War II experiences with the company. At the author's request, Norman L. McKellar, of Tamworth, New South Wales, Australia, sent his valuable study of U. S. Shipping Board vessels which had appeared in *The Belgian Ship Lover*. Mrs. Earl O. Wright, librarian at the Morley Library, Painesville, Ohio, performed the laborious task of indexing the book.

Last, but certainly not least, a special thanks to Captain H. Chesley Inches, the grand old man on the bridge at the Great Lakes Historical Society Museum in Vermilion, Ohio. He opened the museum's fine documentary files to the author and was always willing to sit and chat about his own experience in and observations about the lake trade.

Again, sincere thanks for the invaluable assistance rendered by those innumerable people not mentioned whose help and added interest made this book possible.

Richard J. Wright

Bowling Green, Ohio
March, 1969

Contents

Introduction

Many authors have devoted thousands of pages to studying the development of the railroads that crisscross our nation. A lesser amount of time and space has gone into the study of American seaborne commerce, though this area has been much neglected by the serious historian. But almost nothing has been brought to light about the vast amount of commerce that has been conducted on the almost landlocked Great Lakes for the past two hundred years. *The Harvard Guide to American History* lists exactly one book devoted exclusively to this topic, and it is long since out of print. Yet there is a richness and excitement generated by the freshwater seas that is diffierent and should be set apart from the saltwater.

This volume deals with the history of a shipbuilding company that has played a basic role in the development of freshwater commerce. But it is more than the story of a shipbuilding company with a tradition that is just now being revitalized. It is the story of the development of a specialized floating tool, the steel-hulled bulk freighter. It is the story of steel shipbuilding on the lakes as mirrored by a single giant corporation. Unusual circumstances dictate the setting in that since the turn of the century, The American Ship Building Company has maintained a position of leadership in its field. This situation has been preserved by the huge amount of capital and technical skill required in the building and repairing of large steel ships. Overhead costs are great and profits are slight. But the business is indispensable to the overall lake shipping industry.

In order to discover the shadowy forerunners of The American Ship Building Company it has been necessary to dig deeply into the musty basements and hot attics of private individuals and local libraries as well as the great archives of the nation. Much of the early history had to be pieced together as though it were a broken family keepsake vase being glued together. The first six chapters deal with that broken vase—the predecessor companies. Each of the six chapters is devoted to a particular locale and follows the shipbuilding history through to just before the incorporation of the present firm. A genealogical chart has been included in those areas where the reader—and the author—is likely to be swamped by the profusion of background or secondary companies coming together.

The spotlight has been focused on ships rather than men. Because of local situations, personalities still glitter brightly before the incorporation was achieved. But with the increased scope of operations afterwards, few personalities slip through. Yet the technical skills of a Jim Wallace or the business aplomb of a Merton E. Farr cannot be denied. Nor can the quick, resolute mind and organizational ability of a Harry Gerhauser be submerged. But for the most part, the skilled artisans who designed and built the ships after the turn of the century are swallowed up in a sea of faces. Only their monuments—the ships and the memories of ships—remain.

1.

The Early Years, 1880-1898

~~~~~~

The American Ship Building Company, with its main offices located in Lorain, Ohio, celebrates its seventieth anniversary in 1969. This, in business history, is not particularly noteworthy. But the fact that this corporation's history is essentially the history of steel shipbuilding on the Great Lakes is noteworthy. Its pre-eminence can further be appreciated when viewed in relation to the national picture.

The economy of the nation is tied basically to the steel industry. The rise of this industry was made possible through geological and geographic conditions. The three basic components of the steel industry—iron ore, coal, and limestone—are linked together by the Great Lakes and their connecting channels. Without the relatively inexpensive bulk transportation of these materials by water, such a rapid development might not have been economically feasible. Thus the role of the shipbuilder fits into the total steel industry at the very outset and at the bottom rung of the productive ladder. Hulls had to be provided before the mineral components could be brought together on a scale large enough to be profitable.
~~~~~~

But long before the iron ore fields were developed, the seeds of American Ship Building's predecessor companies were planted. Those companies, and the corporation into which they evolved, traverse almost the entire history of the lake shipping scene. The story is characterized generally by a practical conservatism. This is perfectly logical, because the men involved with the predecessor companies and with the early years of the corporation were well schooled by "on the job training" in shipbuilding. They enjoyed an attractive position in the shipbuilding trade because of limited access to salt water from the lakes and, in turn, did not have to face the type of domestic and foreign competition which bred progressive innovation. Rather, they were limited by geographic features, by a local or regional trade and, as the iron ore fields developed, by the peculiarities of bulk transportation.[1] The predecessor companies also furnished the link between the building of wooden and steel ships.

Therefore, in order to form a comprehensive developmental picture, it is necessary to explore the local situations in the lake cities where American Ship Building Company plants evolved. The genealogical pattern takes on a web-like appearance, and yet it is from this pattern that the tradition and heritage of The American Ship Building Company was born.

The pre-twentieth century shipping and shipbuilding industry can be divided roughly into two parts. The various factors that influenced naval architecture—*i.e.*, ship design—occupy one half, and shipyard methods occupy the other half.

A factor that was critical to lake shipping as the growth of industry increased the size of cargoes was the need for deepened waterways. Former Michigan Senator Thomas W. Palmer, in an address before the Deep Waterways Convention in 1891, focused attention on the need for congressional appropriations. He called for a concentration "in the improvement of the different harbors, of the little streams that men say cannot float a sand barge; because . . . they have been of vast benefit to every portion of the . . . Great Lakes."[2]

1. Bulk transportation refers to raw commodities such as iron ore, coal, and grain. This is in contrast to finished, or "packaged" freight, such as barrels or other containers; hence the terms "bulk" freighter and "package" freighter.
2. Remarks of Hon. Thomas W. Palmer, Detroit, Michigan, December 17, 1891,

But vessel owners knew that shallow harbors were only one problem that eventually had to be conquered. The demand for more congressional appropriations to provide deeper channels became more insistent with the shifting in emphasis from grain to iron ore in the carrying trade. The new Weitzel Lock, at Sault Ste. Marie, provided a sixteen-foot channel in 1881. But as new iron ore deposits opened in the Lake Superior region, vessel owners issued the call for a twenty-foot channel. By 1885, and with the realization of what a small appropriation would mean to the building of a larger Sault lock, the business men of the northern region were "aroused . . . to strenuous exertions that Congress may be fully informed of the situation and induced to act promptly."[3]

When the Vermilion and Gogebic iron ranges opened in 1886, the need for a twenty-foot waterway became more apparent. A government survey showed the possibility of cutting such a channel through the Hay Lake portion of the St. Marys River that would not only shorten that sixty-mile waterway by eleven miles, but would also provide for possible night time navigation. The extra four feet of water would permit an estimated increase of one-third in the carrying capacity for the Lake Superior trade.[4]

The resulting demand for tonnage brought every resource of wood and iron shipbuilding on the Lakes into use. In 1887 alone, sixteen steamers costing $200,000 each, and nineteen costing $135,000 each, were under construction. This provided an additional investment in lake shipyards for that single year of $5,765,000.[5] Five years later, the commissioner of the Bureau of Navigation, William W. Bates, a former Manitowoc, Wisconsin, shipbuilder, pointed out that "it has cost

---

Deep Waterways Convention Held at Detroit, Mich., December 17 and 18, 1891 (Detroit: Free Press Printing Co., 1892), pp. 17-18.

3. Ralph W. Baker (comp.), *Annual Report to the Duluth Board of Trade of the Trade and Commerce of Duluth for the Year Ending December 31, 1885* (Duluth: Rossiter & Evans, 1886), p. 21.

4. *The Sault Ste. Marie Canal and Hay Lake Channel: Necessity of their Speedy Improvement: Proceedings of the Waterways Convention Held at Sault Ste. Marie, Michigan, July 20, 1887* (Duluth: Daily News Print, 1887), p. 25.

5. *Ibid.*

the farmers of the . . . Northwest an hundredfold in lower prices . . . , because Lake vessels could not be built large enough to do their work economically." He then applauded his fellow shipbuilders:

> There is nowhere in the world a higher skill or better
> judgment in proportioning and modeling vessels to carry
> great loads on light draught of water, than on these Lakes; . . .
> It is not their fault in the least degree that Lake transportation
> cost too much for so many years. It is the fault alone of a
> mistaken idea of the expenditure of public money.[6]

The pressures that the lake region brought to bear on Congress bore fruit with the passage of the Harbors and Rivers Act of July 13, 1892. This act provided for the critical twenty-foot waterway connecting Chicago, Buffalo, and Duluth. The vessel owners were guaranteed deep water not only in the St. Marys River, but in the Detroit River and St. Clair Flats as well.[7] The way was now open to build longer and deeper vessels, but lake shipbuilders were already considerably ahead of congressional appropriations.

The great change in ship construction on the lakes is graphically illustrated in statistics from a most unexpected place—the floor of the House of Representatives. In 1886 there were twenty-one steamers on the lakes having over 1,500 net registered tons; in 1890 there were 110 such steamers. In 1886 the lakes could boast of six steel-hulled ships; in 1890, there were sixty-eight steel-hulled vessels on the lakes.[8] The above figures undoubtedly included the iron hulls on the lakes as well.

Iron was no novelty on the lakes scene by 1880. The first iron-hulled ship in the United States Navy, the U.S.S. *Michigan*, was put together at Erie, Pennsylvania, in 1843. The package freight steamer *Merchant* was built at Buffalo in 1868, and several more package freighters were built at Buffalo in the 1870's. Steel was not used in ship construction that early.

6.   William W. Bates, "Deep Water Navigation Through the Lakes and to the Sea," *Proceedings of the Deep Waterways Convention . . . at Detroit . . .*, p. 62.
7.   J. B. Mansfield (ed.), *History of the Great Lakes* (2 vols.; Chicago: J. H. Beers & Co., 1899), I, 248.
8.   Speech of Theodore H. Burton, of Ohio, February 5, 1891, U.S., *Congressional Record*, 51st Cong., 2d Sess., 1891, Appendix, XXII, Part 4, 142.

The first hulls designed specifically for the iron ore trade were the steamer *R. J. Hackett*, in 1869, and the consort *Forest City*, in 1870. Both were built by Peck & Masters of Cleveland, Ohio. They were the first lake vessels to have continuous holds with hatches spaced twenty-four feet between centers with machinery aft.[9] They were constructed of wood and set a pattern in lake vessel design that has been followed basically down to this day. In spite of the success and durability of the iron package freighters, the first iron bulk carrier, the *Onoko*, was not built until 1882. Her angular lines did not create a picture of symmetry or nautical beauty. In fact she was variously described as a "floating boot box" designed along the lines of the "canalboat style of naval architecture."[10] Regardless of looks, she was still a money-maker when she was lost in 1915.

Iron and steel offered the dual benefits of strength and durability that were needed to combat the rough loading and unloading methods required in the iron ore trade. In 1886, the first steel-hulled ore carrier, the *Spokane*, was built in Cleveland. Steel was easier to work with and cheaper to produce, and it soon replaced iron in the building of lake vessels.

The new steel hulls were subjected to rigorous examinations, particularly after the disastrous season of 1892. The Inland Lloyd's agent in Cleveland, Captain F. D. Herriman, declared that some of the earlier steel steamers were stronger-built than later ones. His greatest criticism was that many of the newer steel vessels were out of proportion. Vessel owners took immediate action to correct possible design deficiencies and Herriman noted that those vessels whose keels were laid during the winter of 1892-93 included, among other safety features, double thickness of shear strakes and increased weight of stringers.[11]

Yet in the spring of 1894, the Lake Carriers' Association tabled a

9.   "Freight Carriers of the Great Lakes," *Marine Review*, XXIX (June 2, 1904), 53. Hatches were measured from the center of one hatch to the center of the next hatch.

10.   John Chamberlin, "Situation at Buffalo," *Ibid.*, XXXI (May 18, 1904), 19; J. B. Mansfield (ed.), *History of the Great Lakes*, I, 413.

11.   *Marine Review*, VII (February 9, 1893), 8.

measure to confer on construction rules for insurance evaluation with The American Shipmasters' Association, though for reasons other than hull strength.[12] Despite this, the more expensive open hearth steel was fast becoming the rule for use in hull construction.

The question of strength in steel hulls also brought about changes in the outboard profile of vessels. The basic design initiated by the *Hackett* and followed by the *Onoko* was still predominant. However, vessels' lines became more refined. For a period of about eight years, their lines changed with the frequency of the hem lines in modern female fashions, as innovations appeared.

The most drastic departure from the angular *Onoko* and her immediate progenies was the whaleback design introduced by Alexander McDougall in 1888. The whaleback hull was cylindrical to the waterline and gave the appearance, especially when loaded, of a water-logged cigar. The bow had a sharp rake, was cylindrical, and came to a blunt end or snout; hence the nick-name "pig-boat." The whalebacks carried a round turret forward to house necessary deck winches, and the after cabins, which housed the crew and machinery, were supported by round turrets. Both steamers and barges were constructed on this design, and the steamers also had their pilothouses perched on the after cabins. They never were popular with lake men, perhaps because of their appearance, but they were strongly built and rugged. As one old lake captain remarked, "If I had money enough to build a ship, I'd build a ship, and not one o' those blame scows!"[13] Another vessel man, upon seeing the barge *104* lying off Buffalo with a load of iron ore, remarked, "Doesn't she look for all the world as though a section of the Dunkirk pier had broken off and drifted down the lake?"[14]

12.   The reason for such action by the Lake Carriers' Association lay in the relationship of Commissioner of Navigation William W. Bates to The American Shpmasters' Association. A few years before, Bates almost succeeded in gaining congressional approval for a load-line bill that would have been harmful to the lake vessel owners. "Third Annual Meeting of the Lake Carriers' Association, Detroit, Mich., January 18, 1894," *Ibid*, January 18, 1894, 8-9.

13.   "The Spectator on the Great Lakes," *The Outlook*, LIV (September 26, 1898), 544.

14.   *Marine Review*, I (May 8, 1890), 7.

Though ungainly and much-ridiculed, the whaleback was the basis for most design changes that occurred between 1890 and 1895. The first whaleback barge was launched in 1888, and by 1890 freighters appeared with a rounded forecastle. They were promptly called "turtlebacks." They created a very pleasing picture with their rounded forward decks, gracefully-curved hulls, refined forward quarters, and rakish stacks. Prominent among these vessels were the Menominee Transit Company's *German, Grecian, Roman, Saxon,* and others. But by 1892, the turtleback was falling into disfavor with vessel owners and masters. They were slightly more expensive to build and captains voiced strong objections, claiming that visibility ahead was reduced and that sound was different, particularly during thick weather.[15]

The "monitor," a direct descendent of the whaleback, appeared in 1892. This design had a conventional bow, but the ship's side slanted outward from the main deck to the waterline at almost a forty-five degree angle. The stern was spoon-billed, and all cabins were aft. The stack was straight up and down. The monitor never became popular and only three were built, the *Andaste, Choctaw,* and *Yuma.*

Another innovation that appeared in the first half of the 1890's was the "straightback." This design carried a high forecastle, with the hull running in a straight line all the way to the stern. The pilothouse was located about a third of the way back from the bow. Again, the design failed to catch the fancy of vessel owners and only three, the package freighters *Codorus, Mahoning,* and *Schuylkill,* were built.

One other variation in ship design bears mention. Naval architects began to re-evaluate the "hogging" and "sagging" qualities of vessels on the lakes in the 1890's. The problem in question was one of weight distribution spread over the length of a vessel. With a given set of circumstances, including the length of a wave, the point or points of greatest weight stress, and the speed of the ship, a vessel can theoretically—and sometimes actually—buckle or break in half.

An analagous situation would be created by moving weights of varying degrees along a steel girder. If the weight is too great at either

15.　*Ibid.,* V (June 30, 1892), 7.

end, the girder will bend skywards, or "hog"; if too great towards the center, the girder will bend earthward, or "sag."

In 1893, the F. W. Wheeler & Company of West Bay City, Michigan, launched three bulk carriers with their boilers and machinery amidships. The idea here was that by moving the heavy machinery away from the after extremity, the maximum bending moment could be extended. Within a few years, all three vessels, the S.S. *Curry*, *Merida*, and *Centurion*, were reconstructed along traditional lines. The major fault with this design was that the propeller shaft tunnel interfered with the ore unloading machinery. One package freighter, the *Mohawk*, was also built of this design in 1893, even though she would not be subjected to the great stresses encountered in the iron ore trade.

In 1894 the Chicago Ship Building Company launched the bulk freighter *Kearsarge*. She was the first lake steamer built on the channel system of construction. This system, invented by Sinclair Stewart, a surveyor for the United States Standard Register of Shipping, was designed for giving greater strength to hull construction, while at the same time reducing weight and facilitating repairs. This was of particular interest to vessel owners because their ships were built heavy to withstand the strains of frequent groundings and the carrying of heavy cargoes. The lake ships were double-bottomed, and the space between was used for water ballast. This system was used even more extensively the following year on the steamers *Yale*, *Zenith City*, and *Victory*, and the barges *Marcia*, *Malta*, and *Aurania*.[16] Ultimately the channel-shaped steel supplanted angle iron and plates riveted together to form the same shape provided by the stronger channel steel.

Another factor that influenced naval architecture on the lakes was the development of machinery to handle heavy bulk cargoes, especially iron ore. The loading process remained virtually unchanged throughout the nineteenth century. Trestles were constructed so that vessels could tie up alongside. Chutes dropped into the open

16. *Ibid.*, IX (May 31, 1894), 7; XI (April 25, 1895), 7; XI (May 2, 1895), 6. Channel construction referred to the use of I-beams in ship construction. Prior to this innovation, brackets or angles were rivetted to straight lengths of steel to achieve a joint.

hatches of the vessel and iron ore dropped from railroad cars atop the trestle, down the chutes, and into the vessel. The actual time that a vessel spent at the dock depended more on the arrival of the ore from the mine than on the loading process.

But the unloading procedure at the lower end of the lakes was the time-consuming bottleneck. The first method used to unload iron ore was with the time-honored shovel and wheelbarrow. On a good day, perhaps 100 tons would be unloaded. A good-sized cargo amounted to 400 tons. A schooner captain could plan on the loss of four or five days while his vessel was unloaded—if he had a clear dock. To the vessel owner, time spent at the dock was money lost.

In the middle 1860's, the firm of Bothwell & Ferris, which operated the "Nypano" ore docks in the Old River Bed at Cleveland, began to employ horses to unload vessels. Steel drums, sawed in half, and, later, iron tubs, made specifically for the task, were lowered through the hatches by means of ropes passed through snatch blocks in the vessel's rigging. When filled, they were pulled back up.[17] The tubs were filled in the cargo hold by shovelers, and as many as forty horses were employed on shore pulling on the ropes. After the filled tub came up, it was dumped into wheelbarrows and the barrows were pushed across a narrow gangplank to shore. By using horses, the unloading time was reduced by about half.

In 1867 J. D. Bothwell was struck with the idea of replacing horses with a portable steam engine. He approached Robert Wallace, of Wallace, Pankhurst & Company of Cleveland, and they built a small portable steam engine. The machine cost Bothwell & Ferris $1,200, but it proved an immediate success as their contract was based upon a fixed percentage of the tonnage they handled.[18] Again, unloading time was cut in half, and a 400-ton cargo could be unloaded in one day.

The small steam engine also made Wallace, Pankhurst & Company a success. As Robert Wallace recalled later, "I remember what a mighty big thing those contracts seemed to us—and to have nine of

17.   *The Pennsylvania Railroad's Cleveland Docks* (Cleveland: Ohio & Western Pennsylvania Dock Co., 1946), pp. 14-19.

18.   Ralph D. Williams, *The Honorable Peter White: A Biographical Sketch of the Lake Superior Iron Country* (Cleveland: Penton Publishing Co., 1907), p. 179.

them, one right after the other. It literally put us on our feet."[19] The engine performed the same task the horses had done, except that it handled three ropes and tubs simultaneously. Two shovelers and two helpers manned each hatch in the cargo hold and a dumper and three wheelers moved the ore to the dock. This meant that a minimum of eight men plus the engineer were involved in the operation.

In 1880, another Cleveland man, Alexander E. Brown, invented an improved hoist. This was a single cable-worked rig nick-named "Tom Collins." The back piers of the cable supports were permanent, but the front piers were movable. The cables replaced wheelbarrows, but tubs and shovelers were still required. Brown soon improved on his design and the "Tom Collinses" were replaced by Brown hoists with three working legs. Through the use of a tramway, dock operators now loaded directly from vessels to railroad cars, from vessels to the storage area, and from storage area to railroad cars. Individually, the machines would not have saved much time, but by nesting or grouping them, several hatches could be worked simultaneously.[20] Tubs were still filled by hand.

Lake Michigan received its first ore unloading machines in 1883. Robert Aspin, their inventor, installed the Champion ore hoists at the docks of the Illinois Steel Company at South Chicago.[21] The Champion ore hoists' design was considerably more simple than that of the Brown machine. This design consisted of several hoists, built on the derrick principle, lined up side by side on a permanent basis. The tub on each machine emptied into a trough from which the ore was loaded directly into railroad cars passing beneath it.

Near the turn of the century, the Hoover & Mason Company, of Chicago, found a solution to replace the time-consuming method of filling tubs by hand. They designed a bucket that partially penetrated the ore pile on its first closing motion. Then the bucket swung toward the horizontal, giving a scraping action for almost the entire reach of the bucket. The bucket had a reach of about eighteen feet and a capac-

19.   *Ibid.*
20.   *Ibid.*, pp. 189-90.
21.   *Ibid.*, pp. 190-93.

ity of five tons of ore.[22] The bucket was incorporated with the improved Brown hoists at Conneaut, Ohio, in 1898. By using four nests of three machines each, or twelve buckets, the Conneaut dock averaged about 6,300 tons in seven hours.[23]

The greatest concern of the shipbuilders were hatch openings designed to accommodate the unloading machinery. The hatches were centered principally to accommodate the loading chutes. From the steamer *Hackett* and the barge *Forest City* to those vessels built just prior to 1900, the standard measurements were eight foot hatches with twenty-four foot centers. Most of the freighters engaged in the ore and coal traffic had wooden decks in the cargo hold, whether they were steel or wooden-hulled ships. The conversion of wooden to steel tank tops came at about the same time as the channel system of construction was adopted.

All of the bulk carriers built prior to 1900 were supported internally by a web-like framework of stanchions. As the unloading machinery improved and became larger, the shipyards received more and more repair jobs because the unloading buckets bent, weakened, or broke the internal stanchions. The wooden tank tops also had to be replaced at frequent intervals as the machinery smashed them in.

The length of the bulk carriers increased as channels became deeper, as unloading time was reduced, and as steel became stronger and more reliable. The *Onoko*, a giant in 1882, was 2,164 gross tons and 287-feet long. When the *Victory* was launched in 1895, she was the largest ship on the lakes: 3,774 gross tons and 387-feet long. By 1897 shipbuilders were drawing plans for 500-footers.

It would have been an arduous and expensive proposition for lake shipbuilders to construct a four or five hundred foot steel-hulled freighter in 1882. The iron and steel ships of that era were literally hand-made. Most of the skilled workmen, such as architects, superintendents, and foremen, received their early training on the Clyde in Scotland. Hence the Clyde influence on the lakes was great.

Under the old method of ship construction, many of the bottom

22.   *Ibid.*, p. 202.
23.   J. B. Mansfield (ed.), *History of the Great Lakes*, I, 562-65.

plates were wedged and blocked into position and held there in a temporary fashion until they could be permanently riveted. If the plate was intended for the side of the ship, a temporary derrick was raised to lift and hold the plate in place until it could be bolted preparatory to riveting. Then the derrick was torn down and put up in another position for another plate. This process required from fifty to one hundred men per boat to supply the riveters with material. Thus the speed with which a ship was built was severely limited by the number of men employed in handling material. All of the riveting was done by hand. As the demand for more steel ships increased, lake shipbuilders gave more thought to shipyard methods and techniques. The two innovations that made the large volume of construction on the lakes possible were the gantry crane and pneumatic tools.

In 1887, Henry D. Coffinberry, president of the Cleveland Ship Building Company, was alarmed at the huge amount of manpower needed to move material from the machine shop to the building ways. He contracted with Alexander E. Brown, of the Brown Hoisting and Conveying Company, of Cleveland, to build an appliance to fit the special needs of the Cleveland Ship Building Company's yard. The result was a hand-powered traveling crane with which two men could lift 2,000 pounds at the rate of fifteen feet per minute, and could travel the trolley across the crane's bridge 150 to 250 feet per minute. The entire crane moved along the tramway at the rate of eighty to 120 feet per minute with a full load.[24] The Cleveland Ship Building Company officials were astonished at this show of efficiency. In fact, the crane was so efficient that another crane was not needed until the company contracted for a boat whose beam was too wide for the first crane to accommodate it.

The reputation of the two cranes soon spread to other shipbuilding plants. By 1890, the F. W. Wheeler Company, in West Bay City, Michigan, could boast of a steam-powered crane with a cantilever extension capable of carrying plates to the river side of the vessel under construction. No outboard supports had to be raised to support the river side of the crane, as was the case in Cleveland. The Wheeler

---

24. *Marine Review*, III (January 8, 1891), 3-4.

people claimed that the crane more than paid for itself in six months through savings in time and labor.[25]

When the Chicago Ship Building Company was organized in 1890, a Brown Hoist travelling crane was constructed which could supply two building berths. It was a balanced cantilever type with a span of 110 feet and had a working capacity of from 6,000 to 20,000 pounds. The only piece of machinery that could not be placed in a newly-constructed vessel prior to launching was the boiler.[26]

In 1898, the Wellman-Seaver Engineering Company of Cleveland manufactured two shipyard cranes. One was for the American Steel Barge Company at Superior, Wisconsin, and the other for the Union Dry Dock Company, of Buffalo, New York. The former was a cantilever type crane and covered two building berths. The latter covered only one berth, but was designed to serve the entire yard. Both cranes were high-speed and were operated by electric motors.[27]

The addition of cranes to the lake shipyards had several important effects upon shipbuilding. One of the most obvious benefits was the cutting down of a large unskilled working force. Another was the time-saving factor—both in the movement of material and in the placing of material for riveting. From the construction standpoint, larger plates could be used which cut down the number of rivets and increased the strength of the shell of the vessels.

The pneumatic riveter compares favorably with the gantry crane in revolutionizing shipyard methods. Prior to the invention of pneumatic tools, most of the work was done by hand. Ordinarily, the riveters were organized into gangs. A gang consisted of a heater, a holder-on, and two riveters. They drove from 300 to 500 rivets per day. A plate was bolted into position. The heater threw a red-hot rivet to one of the riveters who inserted it into the hole with tongs. The holder-on, using a large sledge-hammer suspended by a hook in the center, kept the rivet in place. Then the two riveters pounded down the head of the rivet. The whole process took about a minute.

25. *Ibid.*, p. 4.
26. *Ibid.*
27. *Ibid.*, XVII (March 3, 1898), 13.

The driving of a single rivet cost about three cents and the rivet gang made an aggregate of about ten dollars per day.[28] Riveting was hard but indispensable work in the shipyard. As a result, the riveters were inclined to be very independent and demanding. As W. I. Babcock, of the Chicago Ship Building Company, described them:

> The riveters have always been a troublesome element in the ship yards and have been at the bottom on nine-tenths of the strikes we all have had. . . . They made big wages and were deserving of a full return for their labor, but they did about as they pleased and we had to put up with them as best we could.[29]

Pneumatic riveting machines made their appearance in lake shipyards about 1896. Most of those used on the lakes were manufactured by the Chicago Pneumatic Tool Company, although machines made by John F. Allen of New York also enjoyed some popularity. In a test run, a riveting machine drove 340 rivets which, by the old method, would have cost $11.90. The actual cost was "$5 for the gang and perhaps 50 cents for the power, or at the outside less than $6, ..."[30]

The yoke-type riveter was introduced in 1898. It proved most adaptable to inside work on the ships, such as girders and brackets, and was an immediate success. The Babcock-Gunnell riveter, developed at the Chicago Ship Building Company, but manufactured by the Chicago Pneumatic Tool Company, was used on the shell work. Superintendent F. A. Kirby, of the Detroit Dry Dock Company, devised a method to use riveting machines on deck and bulkhead work. He also experimented with an electrical heater which would heat 150 rivets per minute. Kirby even considered putting in a system of pneumatic tubes to deliver rivets to the different parts of the ship, allowing one forge to supply several machines.[31] One of the greatest attributes of the riveting machines was that unskilled labor could be trained to operate them in a short period of time. This would

28. *Chicago Sunday Tribune*, March 24, 1895, p. 41.
29. *Marine Review*, XVII (June 16, 1898), 11.
30. *Ibid.* May 19, 1898, p. 10.
31. *Ibid.*, May 26, 1898, p. 13.

reduce labor expenses and almost eliminate one large managerial headache.

Riveting machines were not the only pneumatic tools that came into common use in the 1890's. The list also included pneumatic drilling machines, caulker hammers, chipping hammers, and reamers. By January, 1898, every major lake shipyard engaged in steel ship construction had "gone pneumatic," with the exception of the Wheeler yard in Bay City.[32] The Wheeler plant had some pneumatic tools, and was experimenting with the pneumatic riveter. The pneumatic riveter was expected to have the same effect on riveters that the type-setting machine had on printers—"deprived them of their occupations and made it necessary for them to seek other employment."[33]

Another factor in lake shipbuilding was the iron ore carrying rate. Large corporate interests became involved with the mining and transportation of iron ore, and the rates gradually fell. As the rates were reduced, the small independent vessel owners were hard pressed to maintain their existence. The orders that were placed with lake shipbuilders were generally placed by the larger shipping lines, or by large financial combinations, for bigger ships that could compete with the lower rates. The rates from Marquette, Michigan, to lower lake docks fluctuated from $2.00 to $2.75 in 1880. By 1897, they were down to fifty cents per ton. Many factors influenced the reduction. Deeper channels, larger ships with more carrying capacity but relatively cheaper operating costs, and improved and faster dock facilities were some of the factors. Cooperation to stabilize the rate at a yearly average by the major steel interests, especially the Rockefeller and Carnegie interests, also had an important bearing.[34]

Ships were more costly to build by 1898, however, only because they were bigger. Actually, they were cheaper to build on a "per ton" basis:

> . . . while the capacity of the Lake freighter has thus been
> doubled during a period comparatively short, the cost of
> building and running it has been reduced at a ratio of from 30

32. *Ibid.*, January 20, 1898, p. 20.
33. *Bay City Times*, January 6, 1898.
34. *Marine Review*, XVII (March 17, 1898), 7.

to 40 per cent. That is to say, the 5,000-ton steamer of to-day costs only $5 per ton to build, while the 2,500-ton steamer of 1885 cost $7 per ton; . . . . It will be perceived that, though the average freight rate on ore is less than half what it was in 1885, there may, for the modern type of vessel at least, still be a sufficent profit in the business.[35]

One reason for this was a reduction in the price of ship steel as the steel industry geared itself for large-volume business. Another factor was that of improved technology and shipyard methods. An illustration of this was the pneumatic riveter, as described earlier in this chapter. In the ordinary lake steamer of 4,000 tons, the saving was from $4,000 to $5,000 over hand work.[36]

The price of vessels was also occasionally forced down by the large corporate interests. While the lake shipyards were still suffering from the aftereffects of the panic of 1893, John D. Rockefeller conferred with Samuel Mather about the possibilities of building twelve ships. Mather took on the task of asking for bids from the builders, knowing that if the news leaked out that a dozen vessel contracts, plus two for himself, were involved, the shipbuilders would be in a position to raise the price per ship. As it stood, each builder thought he was competing with the others for one or two vessels. In December, 1895, on the day before the contracts were to be let, all of the bidders were in Cleveland by Mather's invitation. One by one they went into his office for special conferences covering all of the details prior to the final bid. As each builder submitted his final bid and came out with a smug look on his face, the others suffered many doubts.

When the critical hour for opening the bids arrived, each expectant builder received a note from Mather telling him that he had been awarded a contract. The builders rushed to the hotel lobby to display their good fortune and to console their competitors. The lobby

<hr>

35. John Foord, "The Great Lakes and Our Commercial Supremacy," *North American Review*, CLXVII (August, 1898), 160.

36. W. L. Babcock, "Portable Pneumatic Riveters in Shipbuilding," paper presented before the Sixth Annual Meeting of the Society of Naval Architects & Marine Engineers, New York, November 10, 1898, reprinted in *Marine Review*, XVIII (November 17, 1898), 11.

was a scene of mixed emotion—humor and chagrin—when the builders found that each had been competing only against himself.[37] The combined Rockefeller-Pickands, Mather and Company interests placed orders for a total of fourteen vessels with six different lake ship building concerns.[38] Rockefeller was able to get a low per-ship price and the builders had their yards full of work. The contracts helped the shipbuilders, but the circumstances illustrated the advantages— or disadvantages—that were evolving in the lake shipbuilding business by 1898.

37.   John D. Rockefeller, *Random Reminiscences of Men and Events* (New York: Doubleday, Page & Co., 1909), pp. 124-28.
38.   *Marine Review*, XII (December 12, 1895), 5.

2.

The Forest City Turns to Steel

Logically, the story of the American Ship Building Company begins in Cleveland, Ohio, where the company had its general offices for over sixty years. During the last decade of the nineteenth century, Cleveland was one of the leading steel shipbuilding centers in the United States. In 1891, Cleveland shipyards launched fourteen steelhulled vessels. This placed her second only to the Philadelphia area, which launched twenty-one such vessels. Third place fell to Wilmington, Delaware, with seven vessels.[1] Any other year in the 1890's would show a comparable story.

Had someone mentioned this possibility to Henry D. Coffinberry in 1865, he would have snorted in disbelief. When the Civil War ended, young Henry had more immediate decisions to make. He en-

1. *Marine Review*, V (March 17, 1892), 5, quoting *Report of the Commissioner of Navigation to the Secretary of the Treasury for the Year 1891* (Washington: Government Printing Office, 1891).

tered the navy in 1861, at the age of twenty, as an ordinary seaman. In four exciting years, he rose through the ranks to command the ironclad gunboat *Louisville* in the Mississippi Squadron. He now had an opportunity to become a career naval officer. But with peace restored to the nation, Henry decided that military life was not to his liking. After his war experiences and his position of command, formal schooling held little appeal. Following a short jaunt through the West, Coffinberry returned to the home of his locally prominent father, Judge James M. Coffinberry, in Cleveland. He entered into a partnership with Leavit & Crane, carriage and wagon axle manufacturers. But he soon found that this business required more capital than he could command. So he sold his interest in the axle manufactory and purchased a one-fourth interest in Robert Wallace & Company, a small machine shop in Cleveland.

The other partners were Wallace, Arthur Sawtel, and John F. Pankhurst. Sawtel sold his interest to the others soon afterward.[2] The company prospered with Coffinberry as financial manager and, in 1869, they were able to buy out an older competitor, Cowle, Cartwright & Company, more generally known as the Globe Iron Works.

John B. Cowle, of the older firm, retained his three-eighths interest and joined Coffinberry, Wallace, and Pankhurst in the new firm. They conducted business as the Globe Iron Works, with a shop on Elm Street. Coffinberry continued as financial manager.

Of the quartet, only John Pankhurst had a lake marine background. He had studied engineering in his youth and in the early 1860's sailed as an assistant engineer on lake vessels. He left the water in 1865 to join Robert Wallace in the machine shop venture.[3]

Robert Wallace emigrated to America in 1854 from Ireland. He was then twenty years old. He went to California for a few months, then came to Cleveland, where he obtained employment in a machine shop.

John B. Cowle emigrated with his family from England in 1839 and

---

2.   Samuel P. Orth, *A History of Cleveland, Ohio* (3 vols.; Chicago: S. J. Clarke Publishing Co., 1910), III, 955.
3.   *Ibid.*, II, 500-03.

CLEVELAND SHIPYARD GENEALOGY TO 1898
Cowle, Cartwright & Co. (Globe Iron Works) 1854
Presley & Stephens 1850
Radcliffe & Langell 1872
Cuyahoga Steam Furnace Co. 1834
Wallace, Pankhurst & Co. 1867
Globe Iron Works 1869
Ira Lafrinier 1847
Globe Dry Dock Co. 1876
Presley & Co. 1878
Cleveland Ship Building Co. – 1887
Globe Ship Building Co. – 1881
Globe Iron Works 1886
Cleveland DD Co. 1886
Ship Owners' DD Co. 1888
December, 1897
1897
1898
Lorain Plant
Cleveland Plant
Parent firm
Subsidiary or duplicating stockholder control

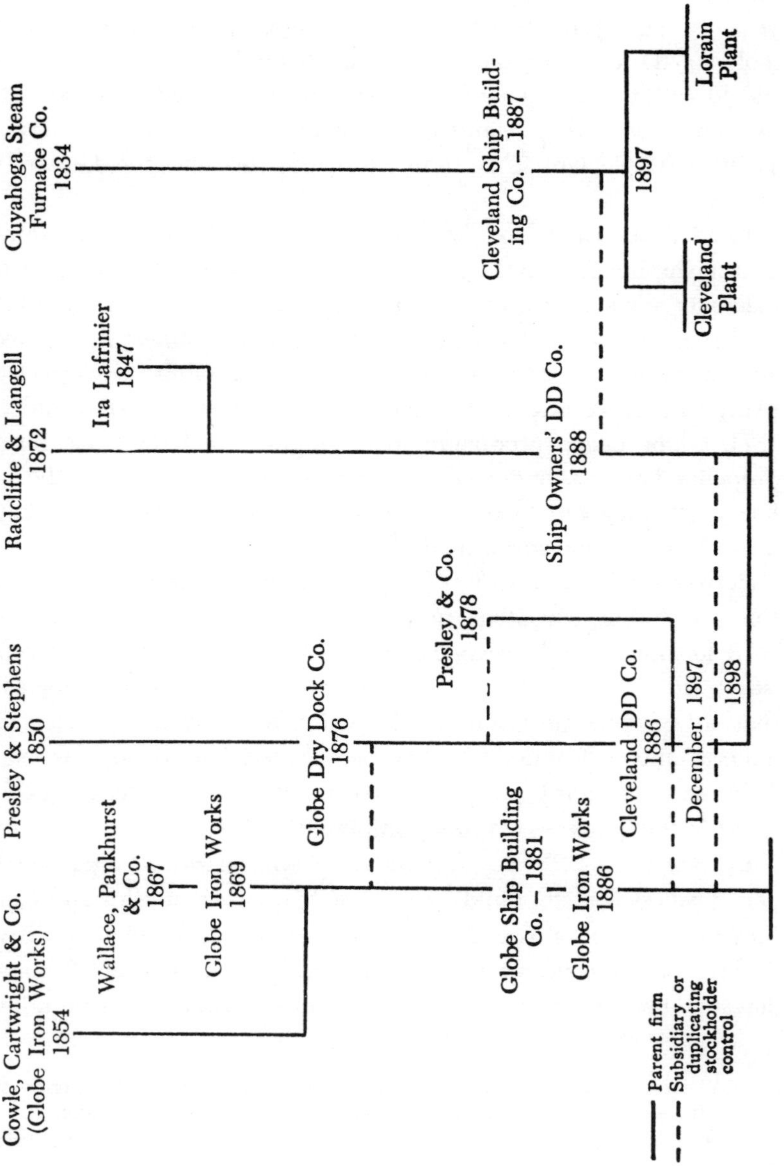

his father opened a marine blacksmith shop in Cleveland. At fourteen years of age, John began serving an apprenticeship to learn the molder's trade at the old Cuyahoga Steam Furnace Company. He stayed with that company for fifteen years. Cowle left it in 1855 when he purchased a three-eighths interest in a machine shop owned by William McClellan. This shop ultimately became the Globe Iron Works.

In 1872, the *Cleveland Leader*, in an appeal for the establishment of iron shipbuilding in the Forest City, pointed out that the necessary elements, coal, iron and capital, were already in evidence—that it only remained "for Cleveland to improve to the utmost her splendid advantages in this respect."[4] By this time, the Globe works was already turning its attention to the potentially lucrative lake trade. In 1871, Globe began producing steam engines, including one for the propeller *Peerless*, under construction by Ira Lafrinier.[5] In the next five years, they turned out over seventy steam engines, including at least eleven marine steam plants.[6]

Between 1871 and 1876, Cleveland shipyards produced forty-five ships, including seventeen propellers. A *Leader* prophecy made in 1873, looking upon the revival of shipbuilding in Cleveland as a promise to the return of their "old time Marine supremacy," suggested that "all things come around to him who cares to wait."[7] Wallace, Coffinberry and colleagues felt they had waited long enough when, in 1876, an opportunity presented itself for them to purchase a half-interest in the Stephens & Presley shipbuilding firm.

In 1850, George Presley and Harvey Stephens formed a partnership and developed a shipbuilding yard at the corner of Elm and Cedar Streets, in Block "R" on the Old River Bed of the Cuyahoga River. Today, the site is occupied by the Huron Portland Cement Company elevator. Presley and Stephens built a horse-powered marine railway

4. *Cleveland Leader*, March 16, 1872. Note that this was exactly twenty-seven years before the incorporation of the American Ship Building Company.
5. *Lafrinier* had many spellings, including *Laffrinnier*, *Lafrinnier*, and *Lifranier*.
6. "Record of Engines Built by Globe Iron Works," hand-written index in possession of author.
7. *Cleveland Leader*, September 16, 1873.

which was replaced by a steam-driven one in 1856. Although their chief source of business was vessel repair, they did average one new vessel a year. In 1875, prompted by the signs of prosperity in the vessel-building business surrounding them, they decided to build a dry dock. They soon found themselves over-extended, and Harvey Stephens decided to drop out. The Globe Iron Works purchased Stephens' interest on May 24, 1876, for $36,000.[8]

George Presley came into the Globe organization with excellent credentials. He served his apprenticeship under George S. Weeks and John Oades in the Clayton, New York, shipyards. In 1843 he came to Cleveland and worked at various times for Sanford & Moses, George W. Jones, and Samuel and Alvin Turner. After five years, he began to make sub-contracts on his own and so became associated with Lafrinier & Stevenson.[9]

The newly-acquired shipbuilding interest operated apart from the parent Globe firm. The dry dock was completed and operated as the Globe Dry Dock Company.[10] In 1878 Presley organized Presley & Company, and in the next eight years constructed five wooden ships. He also built three wooden steamers under the Globe Dry Dock name. Most of the engines for these vessels were built by the Globe Iron Works. At the instigation of Robert Wallace, the custom of "farming out" contracts for various parts of the vessel—*i.e.*, hull, rigging, and fittings—was broken. The first complete Cleveland-built vessel delivered under one contract was the *Republic*, in 1881.[11]

Early in 1880 considerable interest developed in the use of iron for the building of bulk freighters. Iron-hulled vessels were nothing new to the lakes. Though they were few in number, they were proven successes, but none had been built specifically for the iron ore trade.

---

8. *Cleveland Plain Dealer*, May 27, 1876.

9. Samuel P. Orth, *A History of Cleveland, Ohio*, II, 894.

10. Frank E. Hamilton, "Notes and Lists on Shipbuilding in Great Lakes Ports," unpublished manuscript, Kelleys Island, Ohio. The dry dock was 340 feet on the blocks, 360 feet overall, 50 feet wide at the gate, and had 20 feet of water over the sill. In 1892, this dry dock was enlarged to 364 feet overall, 350 feet on the blocks, 52 feet wide, and had 16 feet of water over the sill.

11. J. B. Mansfield (ed.), *History of the Great Lakes*, I, 431; *Cleveland Plain Dealer*, March 8, 1911.

Henry Coffinberry was particularly impressed by the advantages of iron over wood in vessel construction and, after a thorough investigation of the problems, he persuaded his partners to form the Globe Ship Building Company.[12] Coffinberry was elected president and financial manager; Pankhurst, vice president and designing engineer; Wallace, secretary; and Cowle, treasurer.

Globe purchased land to construct a ship yard on the Old River Bed, at the foot of Taylor Street, and hired John Smith, who learned the trade of iron shipbuilding on the Clyde, to superintend construction. Norman Wheeler, inventor of the direct acting steam pump, became engineer.[13] At the same time some prominent shipping men in Cleveland and Northern Ohio developed enthusiasm for the project. George Washington Jones, the retired "dean" of Cleveland's early shipbuilders, was most enthusiastic.[14] Jones, Philip Minch, Isaac W. Nicholas, John N. Glidden, William J. Pringle, and the Globe Ship Building Company formed a stock company and the keel of an iron ore freighter was laid in February, 1881.

In November of that year, the iron-hulled steamer *Brunswick* was holed in a collision on Lake Erie and sank with the loss of three lives. She had no compartmentalized cargo hold and simply filled like a bathtub and went down. Even though the iron-hulled freighter that was well along on the ways in Cleveland was to be compartmentalized, the loss of the Detroit-built iron-hulled ship must have caused a few pangs of remorse among the Cleveland stockholders. Any faltering predilections that resulted from the bad publicity stemming from the *Brunswick*'s loss, however, were restored by April, 1882, when the new freighter, named the *Onoko*, left the yard in the Old River Bed.

The *Onoko* was the largest vessel on the Great Lakes. She measured 287 feet from stem to stern post, was thirty-eight feet wide, and measured 2,164 gross tons. She justified the confidence placed in her during that winter of 1881-82 by fighting the elements until she succumbed to Lake Superior in 1915.

12.   Samuel P. Orth, *A History of Cleveland, Ohio*, III, 956.
13.   J. B. Mansfield (ed.), *History of the Great Lakes*, I, 431.
14.   *Ibid.*, II, 7.

Not everyone was overjoyed by the apparent success of the Globe venture into iron shipbuilding. Henry Coffinberry's father wrote that he received news of a new contract with mixed feelings because "while it provided employment & more or less pecuniary profit," it also involved labor and responsibility which might sap his son's strength. He feared that Henry had "over done the 'brown bread, lean meat, & hard cider' diet."[15]

In spite of this fatherly concern, the Globe Ship Building Company turned out iron-hulled vessels until 1886. Three more bulk freighters, a sidewheel passenger steamer, a palatial steam yacht, and two tugs splashed into the Old River Bed. Globe's last vessel, the steamer *Spokane*, was designed for iron construction. But when the owner, Captain Thomas Wilson, found that the price differential between iron and steel was only $10,000, the *Spokane* became the first steel-hulled ore freighter on the lakes.[16] Because her design, scantlings, and dimensions were figured for iron, she was considered to be 20 per cent stronger than most steel-hulled vessels that were built in subsequent years.

In 1886, an internal disagreement between John Pankhurst and the other officers of the company resulted in an attempt to purchase Pankhurst's holdings in the company.[17] Failing in this, Coffinberry, Wallace, and Cowle sold their interests to Marcus A. and Howard M. Hanna, of Cleveland.

In July, 1886, the Globe Iron Works was reorganized with a capital of $500,000.[18] Howard M. Hanna was elected president; John Pankhurst, vice-president and general manager; and Luther Allen, secretary and treasurer. Allen formerly was secretary and treasurer of the Society for Savings in Cleveland. Howard M. Hanna, along with his brother Marcus, sold his oil interests to the Standard Oil Company in 1876, consolidated his lake shipping interests, and prospered accord-

---

15.   Letter from J. M. Coffinberry to Henry D. Coffinberry, March 22, 1885, Coffinberry Family Papers, Western Reserve Historical Society Library, Cleveland, Ohio. Hereafter cited as "Coffinberry Papers."
16.   *Marine Review*, V (February 18, 1892), 7.
17.   Samuel P. Orth, *A History of Cleveland, Ohio*, III, 956.
18.   J. B. Mansfield (ed.), *History of the Great Lakes*, I, 431.

ingly. This company hierarchy lasted until the American Ship Building Company was organized in 1899.

With the reorganization of the Globe Iron Works in 1886, the Globe Ship Building Company was absorbed, and George Presley sold Presley & Company to the new combine. The Globe Iron Works formed a subsidiary, the Cleveland Dry Dock Company, to operate the old Globe dry dock. Under this new firm name, the Cleveland Dry Dock Company launched three bulk freighters, a passenger steamer, and two ferries. All were of wooden construction. However, the yard was used primarily for repair work.

In March, 1888, a third dry dock company was formed which ultimately came under Globe control. Cleveland vessel operators formed the new company and appropriately called it The Ship Owners' Dry Dock Company. Thomas Wilson was president; M. A. Bradley, vice-president; Harvey D. Goulder, treasurer; and Gustave Cold, secretary. The board of directors included Henry Coffinberry, Robert Wallace, Valentine Fries, Philip Minch, and others who held large holdings in another newly-organized company, the Cleveland Ship Building Company. Quite naturally, the Ship Owners' Dry Dock Company worked in close cooperation with the new competitor of the Globe Iron Works.

William Radcliffe provided much of the motivation for the formation of the Ship Owners' Dry Dock Company. He, along with Stephen F. Langell, began building ships in Cleveland in 1872. Their yard was near the foot of Taylor Street on the Old River Bed. In 1878, Radcliffe & Langell took over Ira Lafrinier's yard. Radcliffe was associated with Lafrinier on a sub-contracting basis earlier. This yard was farther west, at the head of the Old River Bed.

Stephen Langell, who accompanied Radcliffe into the new dry dock firm, carried credentials comparable to those of George Presley. He served his apprenticeship, beginning in 1847, under George W. and Benjamin B. Jones in Cleveland. He was at various times associated with the early Cleveland shipbuilding firms of Roderick Caulkins, Quayle & Martin, Lafrinier & Stevenson, and Peck & Masters.[19]

19. *Ibid.*, II, 294.

The Ship Owners' Dry Dock Company began construction of a dry dock on the Radcliffe-Langell property in the spring of 1888, and it was completed at a cost of $100,000 in 1889.[20] William Radcliffe served as manager. Almost before the first dry dock was completed, business demanded the construction of another dry dock. Sample borings were taken in the ground adjacent to the newly-completed dry dock under the supervision of Captain George Stone, M. A. Bradley, and Radcliffe.[21] This resulted in an almost "his-and-hers" dry dock arrangement. The older, deeper dry dock was well suited for handling loaded vessels, while the newer dry dock was better adapted to vessels without cargo.[22] George E. Hartnell, a locally prominent civil engineer, designed both docks.[23] The older dock was lengthened and widened in 1895 to keep pace with the increase in the size of vessels.[24]

Under Radcliffe's supervision, the company built only two wooden steamers and a dredge. Radcliffe died in 1893, and George L. Quayle, who had been in the Cleveland shipbuilding business with his famous father, Thomas Quayle, replaced him. Under Quayle's supervision, the company continued to prosper. By the winter of 1896-97, as steel superseded wood in the construction of ships, and as the Cleveland Ship Building Company developed its own ship repair and dry dock facilities in Lorain, Ohio, Quayle and the other officers of the Ship Owners' Dry Dock Company deemed it advisable to enlarge the scope of their operations to include steel ship repairs. Accordingly, they modernized their plant with the addition of such heavy equipment as a punch, shears, rolls, forge, a counter-sinking machine, bolt cutter, and a vertical drill. Three dynamos provided the power.

Faced by competition both in Lorain and by the modernized Ship Owners' plant in Cleveland, the Globe Iron Works was forced to take

20.   *Ibid.*, I, 431-32.

21.   *Marine Review*, I (June 12, 1890), 8.

22.   *Ibid.*, II (August 7, 1890), 8. The older dry dock was 330 feet long, 48 feet wide, and had 17 feet of water over the sill. The newer dock was 300 feet long, 45 feet wide, and had 13 feet of water over the sill.

23.   *Ibid.*, XVII (March 10, 1898), 7.

24.   The new dimensions were 430 feet in length, 54 feet in width, and 17 feet of water over the sill.

action. Initially they planned a large—and expensive—steel floating dry dock. But before they began construction on it, the Ship Owners' Dry Dock Company facilities were declared expendable by the officers of the Cleveland Ship Building Company. In December, 1897, the principal stockholders of the Globe Iron Works purchased 2,256 shares from the total of 3,600 shares that comprised the capital stock of the Ship Owners' Dry Dock Company. The Globe people paid $441,000, or $122.50 per share, for the entire property. The retired stock realized a value of $245 for each $100 par value share. The value of the stock had doubled when the second dry dock was built in 1890.[25] All of the ship repair facilities on the Old River Bed were now indirectly under the control of the Globe Iron Works. But the Cleveland Dry Dock Company was still a separate corporate entity.

In 1895, thirty-six year old Captain W. W. Brown, fresh from the deck of the Pickands, Mather & Company ore freighter *Kearsarge*, replaced W. W. Watterson as superintendent of the Cleveland Dry Dock Company. The vigorous Brown immediately set to work modernizing the methods of the plant, and, in 1898, he succeeded in bringing about a merger of the Cleveland Dry Dock Company with the Ship Owners' Dry Dock Company.

Freight rates, suffering after the financial panic of 1893, began to climb in the spring of 1898. This gave promise to the possibility of extensive repairs to smaller wooden vessels, neglected during the lean years. Also, the lake underwriters began to make more stringent demands of vessel owners from the standpoint of repairs. Brown gained control of a small syndicate of stockholders and succeeded in holding the Cleveland Dry Dock Company stock at par, rather than selling at a lower figure as originally proposed.[26] The capital stock of the company, valued at $215,900, was sold outright to the Ship Owners' Dry Dock Company. The latter firm was then reorganized and its capital stock was increased from $360,000 to $750,000. The shareholders of both companies received stock in the new company on a pro rata plan based on earnings and inventories of the properties of the two

---

25. *Marine Review*, XVI (December 30, 1897), 10.
26. *Ibid.*, XXVII (February 19, 1903), 22.

firms. The new officers were H. A. Hawgood, president; Captain John Mitchell, vice-president; Robert L. Ireland, treasurer; and Captain Brown, secretary and general manager.[27]

The Globe Iron Works now directly controlled all three dry docks in Cleveland as well as a shipbuilding and repair yard that extended almost the entire length of the Old River Bed. Since the dry docks were under a single control, they simply received numbers. The larger of the two docks at the west end of the Old River Bed became Number One; the smaller adjacent dock, Number Two; and the Cleveland Dry Dock Company dock, at the east end of the Old River Bed, Number Three.

Before and during the period in which the dry dock mergers took place, the parent Globe Iron Works was far from idle. Between 1887 and 1900, no fewer than 108 new steel hulls splashed into the Cuyahoga River. Seventy of these were built by the Globe Works. John Pankhurst deserves much of the credit for such a record, but certainly John Smith, the Clyde-trained superintendent, merits a share. He supervised construction of the eight iron or steel hulls built prior to the reorganization of the company in 1886, and followed through with forty-one hulls after the reorganization. Unfortunately, the forty-seven year old Smith fell ill in July, 1893, and was confined to his bed until his death in October of that year.[28]

The most famous vessels constructed by Globe were the passenger steamers *North West* and *North Land*, which carried James J. Hill's Northern Steamship colors. The keel of the *North West* was laid on October 7, 1892. Two years later, on January 6, 1894, her gleaming white hull was launched into the dirty Cuyahoga. The number of people who witnessed the launch were estimated at from seven to fifteen thousand and included virtually every important shipping personality on the lakes. The launch was described as "simple." Two stands were constructed, one at the bow, the other about midships, some distance from the vessel's side. Electric bells from either end of the ship connected at the center stand. When all was ready, Howard M.

27. *Ibid.*, XVII (July 7, 1898), 8; XVIII (July 28, 1898), 7.
28. *Cleveland Plain Dealer*, October 22, 1893.

Hanna's daughter pressed a button from the center stand. When the bells rang, the ropes were cut and, at the same instant, Mrs. F. P. Gordon, wife of the assistant general manager of the Northern Steamship Company, swung an elaborately decorated bottle of champagne against the bow. The vessel slid sixty feet down the ways and dropped five feet into the water on a perfect launch.[29] The sister ship, the *North Land*, followed exactly one year later.

The vessels were designed by A. U. Sheldon, who was with the Thompsons on the Clyde before coming to Globe. They were built under the supervision of Walter G. Miller, who joined Globe after John Smith's death. Mr. Miers Coryell, as the American agent for the Belleville Company, worked with Miller on the installation of twenty-eight boilers and twin quadruple expansion engines that powered each vessel.

The interiors of the vessels were finished in true Victorian lavishness by Abner Crossman, of the interior decorating firm of Crossman & Lee, from Chicago. The interior was done completely on special order, right down to the door knobs. Most of the woodwork was in Cuban mahogany, supplemented by Michigan birch, white mahogany, and Pennsylvania cherry. Over 2,200 yards of carpets—Wiltons, velvets, and other costly makes—were manufactured on special order. The napery, with the name of the company and ship inwoven, came from Belfast, Ireland. The remainder of the vessels' needs and requirements were just as lavishly provided for. They were licensed to carry 800 persons, including 147 in the crew. Truly the Northern passenger boats were the most lavish ever to sail the Inland Seas!

The freight boats were not built for glamour, but in their own way they were just as graceful. Most of them were powered by triple expansion engines. The package freighters in particular were noted for their speed. The *Saranac* and *Tuscarora* were at various times said "to carry the broom," and the former carried the first steel mast on the lakes.[30] Many of the bulk freighters appeared sleek and streamlined with their fashionable turtleback bows.

29. *Marine Review*, IX (January 11, 1894), 7.
30. *Cleveland Plain Dealer*, February 9, 1890.

The launch of a freight boat was sure to attract a crowd. Those who were not fortunate enough to receive an invitation to view the launch from the shipyard would congregate either on the opposite side of the river, on Whiskey Island, or would crowd onto the gently sloping hills below Detroit Street. The vessel, bedecked in gaily colored flags, would slide down the greased ways and make a tremendous splash as she struck the water. With the cutting of the ropes, every factory, tug, and steamer in the neighborhood would greet her with shrill shrieks from their whistles. When the *Mariska* was launched, in February, 1890, over 1,000 persons witnessed the event and an additional 500 crowded into the shipyard.[31] The crowds were even greater in warmer weather. While John Smith was living, all launches at the Globe Works occurred promptly at three o'clock in the afternoon. Only after his death did the time vary.

An invitation to be the sponsor of a vessel and to christen her with the traditional bottle of champagne was (and is) an honor not to be taken lightly by a young lady. But the Globe Iron Works had what must be the all-time champion in Miss Carry Ashburne, of Cleveland. By 1890 she had christened fifteen vessels with a floating value of nearly $3,500,000, and she certainly must have christened a few more vessels after that date before her arm gave out. The *Marine Review* noted that she was considered "the priestess of the Globe Company," and that she had developed a certain dexterity which enabled her to "save the neck of the bottles each time and as a result the ghastly heads of more than a case of wine form a collection."[32]

After the Globe Iron Works was reorganized in 1886, the partners who left the concern were not the types to sit idly by and watch their old concern prosper. Of the three dissident voices, John B. Cowle turned his attentions to the Ship Owners' Dry Dock Company, in which he held an interest. The other two, Henry Coffinberry and Robert Wallace, rallied their shipping associates around them and immediately formed a rival steel shipbuilding plant, the Cleveland Ship Building Company. The firm was incorporated with a capital of

31. *Ibid.*, February 20, 1890.
32. *Marine Review*, II (July 24, 1890), 2.

$350,000, and had the financial backing of several prominent Cleve-landers, including J. H. Wade, Philip Minch, Mrs. Alva Bradley, and Robert R. Rhodes.[33] The new company officers consisted of Coffin-berry, president and financial manager; Wallace, vice-president and general superintendent; William M. Fitch, secretary; and Wallace's oldest son, James C. Wallace, designing engineer.[34] The company purchased the site and buildings of the old Cuyahoga Steam Furnace Company at the corner of Detroit and Center Streets. This firm had been manufacturing steam engines, including many marine engines, since 1834. With characteristic enthusiasm, the new management en-larged old buildings, purchased additional adjoining property, and constructed four building ways capable of handling steel-hulled ships. They also built new general offices on the Superior Street via-duct. Finally, Thomas W. Bristow, assistant superintendent of the Detroit Dry Dock Company plant at Wyandotte, Michigan, was hired as construction superintendent of the new yard in Cleveland.

Despite the professional preparations, one thing the new manage-ment could not control was the iron ore rates, which affected new vessel contracts. Evidently the old Cleveland shipbuilder and vessel-man, Elihu M. Peck, while visiting Coffinberry's somewhat skeptical father in Florida, knew what he was talking about when he predicted that "the coming season will be a very, very dull one on the Lakes. He [Peck] talks like an oracle but whether he knows more than the rest of the world I do not know."[35] The lakes experienced a reasonably profitable season in 1887, while the new yard was being constructed. But 1888 proved to be comparatively dull. The firmly-established Globe Iron Works launched six vessels and secured contracts for a few more, but the Cleveland Ship Building Company was able to launch only two ships. In 1889 business improved slightly and the new yard turned out three bulk freighters and a river railroad car ferry, but it was not until 1890 that they were able to fill their ways with construction.

33.   Samuel P. Orth, *History of Cleveland, Ohio,* III, 956; J. B. Mansfield (ed)., *History of the Great Lakes,* I, 432.

34.   J. B. Mansfield (ed.), *History of the Great Lakes,* II, 516.

35.   Letter from J. M. Coffinberry to Henry D. Coffinberry, Jacksonville, Florida, March 5, 1888, Coffinberry Papers.

In 1890, the Cleveland Ship Building Company launched four steel bulk freighters. Two of them, the *Western Reserve* and *W. H. Gilcher,* vied for ore carrying records. The following year proved to be another slow one, so the company turned to a diversification of hull types to take up the slack. They outbid the Globe Works and other lake shipbuilders by a scant $1,250 to build a government lighthouse tender.[36] They also launched the first steel-hulled fish tug on the Great Lakes, the *Ciscoe.*[37] As a tribute to workmanship and durability, she is still operating as the *Capama-S,* out of Bay City, Michigan. The company even rebuilt and launched the ninety-four-foot steam yacht *Straightaway.* David Bell, the venerable Buffalo, New York, iron shipbuilder, had built the hull several years earlier, but she was not completed until 1891.[38]

The pride of the yard in 1891 was J. H. Wade's large steam yacht *Wadena.* She had fine clipper-like lines and carried a figurehead of a gilt mermaid which, "in the matter of costume, would make Diana of the Tower blush with envy."[39] The *Wadena* had teakwood decks, several bathtubs, an ice machine, and many other luxuries. She even carried a grand piano with "delightful little cupids blowing their pipes" painted on it.

In the same year the Cleveland Ship Building Company secured a contract from the Lake Superior Iron Company to build two freighters that were a departure from the standard model. They resembled the McDougall whaleback with their peculiarly-shaped hulls and houses aft. Original plans called for a rounded turret forward to house deck windlasses, but the plans were altered and instead a slightly raised forecastle housed the winches. The aim of the "monitor," as the new design was called, was to cut the cost of construction and provide increased carrying capacity. Since only three were built, it is doubtful that they lived up to expectations. When Alexander McDougall was asked whether he thought lake shipbuilders would follow this design, he answered:

36. *Marine Review,* III (May 7, 1891), 10.
37. *Ibid.,* IV (September 3, 1891), 9.
38. *Ibid.,* III (June 18, 1891), 6.
39. *Ibid.,* V (January 28, 1892), 4.

We have patents covering a semi-cylindrical deck and
spoon-shaped bow as well as a great many other features in
the whaleback. We will allow these builders to go ahead and
turn out such boats but we will proceed against them after
the boats are built if there is the slightest indication of
infringement on our rights.[40]

The shipbuilding companies were not entirely dependent upon vessel construction and repair. They also contracted for other heavy
manufacturing jobs because they had the necessary equipment. Cleveland Ship Building Company built several marine engines for other
shipbuilding concerns along the lakes that had no engine and boiler
shops of their own. Non-maritime contracts were also secured. For
example, Henry Coffinberry returned from Washington in June, 1892,
with a contract from the Haskins Wood Vulcanizing Company for
four tanks, each of them 108 feet long and six and one-half feet wide,
plus other supplementary machinery. This contract alone was equal
to the construction of a large steamer.

In 1892, the Cleveland Ship Building Company performed the
pioneer operation of lengthening a steel-hulled ore carrier, the *Spokane*. The surgery was performed in the Ship Owners' Dry Dock
Number One. The vessel was lengthened sixty feet, which increased
her carrying capacity by 750 tons. All of the rivets were removed at a
point near midships. With nine-inch rope rove through blocks, attached to both sides of the vessel, and run to two capstans, the 700-
ton forward half of the steamer was inched apart on greased ways.
Two teams of horses provided motive power for the two capstans.
The new mid-section was then built and joined to the pulled-apart
halves of the steamer.

Henry Coffinberry retired from the presidency of the Cleveland
Ship Building firm in 1893, but not before he suffered a most mel-
ancholy experience. As was mentioned earlier, two Cleveland Ship
Building Company products, the steamers *Western Reserve* and
W. H. Gilcher, which were launched only four months apart, com-
peted for top ore carrying honors during the seasons of 1891 and 1892.
Within two months of each other, both vessels were lost.

40. *Ibid.*, IV (October 29, 1891), 3.

The steamer *R. J. Hackett*, the wooden forerunner of all Great Lakes ore carriers. *University of Detroit Marine Collection.*

The *Spokane*, first steel-hulled ore carrier, just prior to her launching by the Globe Iron Works in 1886. *Frank E. Hamilton.*

The prototype of the modern ore carrier, the iron-hulled *Onoko*, built by the Globe Ship Building Company for the Minch interests in 1882. *Author's Collection.*

The *Onoko* sinking on Lake Superior on September 14, 1915. This dramatic series of photographs was taken from a lifeboat before the crew was rescued. *Henry Steinbrenner.*

The *Choctaw* was a "monitor" designed vessel, a direct descendent of the whaleback. *Author's Collection.*

The "straightback," another innovation in ship design in the 1890's, is portrayed here by the package freighter *Mahoning. Author's Collection.*

The "turtleback" design was abandoned because it resulted in poor visibility and proved too expensive to build. The *German* is shown here about 1901. *Author's Collection.*

The ill-fated *Western Reserve*, lost in 1892, is shown here in a rare photograph. The insert shows the lone survivor of the disaster, Harry Stewart, in 1918, when he was master of the Kinsman Transit Company steamer *Matthew Andrews. Henry Steinbrenner.*

The barge *Bryn Mawr* under construction at the Chicago Ship Building Company in 1900. Notice stanchion type construction and pneumatic tools in foreground. *Author's Collection.*

Pneumatic tools changed the entire process of building steel ships. A deck riveter working on a tank top, and counter-sinking on the ship's side. A shell riveter working on a ship's bottom. All pictures were taken at the South Chicago plant about 1900. *Author's Collection.*

CLEVELAND SHIP BUILDERS. *Left to right, top row*: Robert Wallace, Globe Iron Works, Cleveland Ship Building Company, *Author's Collection*; Henry D. Coffinberry, Globe Iron Works, Cleveland Ship Building Company, *Author's Collection*. *Center*: John F. Pankhurst, Globe Iron Works, *Author's Collection*; W. W. Brown, Cleveland Dry Dock Company, *Author's Collection*; George L. Quayle, Ship Owner's Dry Dock Company, *W. F. Gerhauser*. *Bottom*: Alva Bradley, Isaac W. Nicholas, and Philip Minch. The last three were Vermilion, Ohio, shipbuilders and vessel owners who moved to Cleveland and invested heavily in the *Onoko* and other shipbuilding interests. *Great Lakes Historical Society Museum*.

The Cleveland Ship Building Company offices at 120 Viaduct, Cleveland, Ohio.
This building served as the general offices of the American Ship Building
Company for many years. *Western Reserve Historical Society.*

The steam yacht *Wadena* was built by the Cleveland Ship Building Company
for J. H. Wade in 1891. *Western Reserve Historical Society.*

The completed *Wadena.* Wade sailed her to Japan and back. She later returned
to the lakes and was scrapped in 1931. *Author's Collection.*

A painting of the *W. H. Gilcher* done by the noted lake marine artist Howard Sprague in 1892. The vessel was lost with all hands on Lake Michigan that same year. *Author's Collection.*

The new dry dock at the Cleveland Ship Building Company's plant at Lorain, Ohio, in use for the first time. The date was January 27, 1898, and the steamer, the *Sir William Fairbairn*. *University of Detroit Marine Collection.*

The first launching at the new Lorain shipbuilding facilities, the *Superior City,* on April 13, 1898. *Author's Collection.*

The *North Land* and her sister ship, the *North West*, built by the Globe Iron Works in 1895, were two of the most famous and elaborate passenger ships to sail the Great Lakes. *Frank E. Hamilton.*

The *Saranac* was typical of the package freighters built by the Globe Iron Works in Cleveland. *Author's Collection.*

Two views of Alexander McDougall's American Steel Barge Company at Superior, Wisconsin, 1892. *Dwight Boyer.*

(*Insert*) Alexander McDougall. *Author's Collection.*

The office staff of the American Steel Barge Company. McDougall is the third seated person from the left. Naval architect A. C. Diericx is to his left. *Wesley R. Harkins.*

The wooden steamer *Neshota* entered the new American Steel Barge Company dry dock for the first time on September 20, 1892. *Wesley R. Harkins.*

The launching of McDougall's first whaleback, the barge *101*, at Rice's Point
in Duluth, on June 23, 1888. *Kenneth E. Thro.*

The whaleback steamer *C. W. Wetmore* ran the Lachine Rapids, steamed across
the Atlantic Ocean, and later passed around Cape Horn on her way to the
Pacific coast of Washington. *University of Detroit Marine Collection.*

The whaleback passenger ship *Christopher Columbus*, shown here at the fit-out dock at Superior, was built for service at the Chicago World's Fair in 1893. *Kenneth E. Thro.*

The whaleback barges *115* and *118* at Conneaut, Ohio. The former snapped her towline and was lost on Lake Superior in 1898. Notice the Brown hoist unloading rigs on the dock. *Author's Collection.*

The *Western Reserve* was the first to go, on August 30, 1892. This disaster particularly shook the Cleveland shipping community because her owner, Captain Peter G. Minch, and his family, including three children, were lost with her. According to the sworn statement of the lone survivor, wheelsman Harry Stewart, the *Western Reserve* cleared Whitefish Point, just above the Sault, at four o'clock in the afternoon of that fateful Tuesday and Captain Albert Myers set his course across Lake Superior to clear the tip of Keweenaw Point. The wind was blowing from the west and the sea, running from the northwest, was increasing. Stewart went into his room about seven o'clock in the evening. For the next two hours the sea was heavy. The vessel labored and occasionally pounded, but she still made reasonably good time against the head wind and sea.

About nine o'clock, there was a violent jolting shock and jar, followed by the crash of a spar breaking and falling onto the deck. The aroused Stewart got up from his bunk and at that moment, Captain Myers opened the door and called to get out as the vessel was sinking. The partially-dressed Stewart ran aft, along the port side of the deck. He reported a break in the hull just forward of the mainmast, with the mainmast broken off near the middle and lying partially across the deck. The rest of the night was a nightmare. The crew was able to launch both lifeboats successfully, but the wind shifted and increased. According to Captain Myers' reckoning, the vessel sank about sixty miles above Whitefish Point. As the seas increased, one lifeboat capsized and the other lifeboat picked up the survivors, creating a terribly crowded condition. About seven o'clock the next morning, and a mile off the beach, the remaining lifeboat capsized in the surf and its occupants were thrown out. Only Harry Stewart was able to swim to shore and walk ten miles to the Deer Park Life Saving Station to report the disaster.[41] Thirty-one lives were lost in the *Western Reserve* disaster.

The *W. H. Gilcher* disappeared under more mysterious circumstances. A terrible gale swept across northern Lake Michigan on the

41. *Ibid.*, VI (September 15, 1892), 7; Dana Thomas Bowen, *Memories of the Lakes* (Daytona Beach: Dana Thomas Bowen, 1946), pp. 201-04.

night of October 28, 1892. By midnight, the wind was blowing between sixty and seventy miles per hour. The *Gilcher*, unlike her sister
ship, was loaded with 3,000 tons of coal. Since none of the eighteen
crew members survived the disaster, what actually happened that
wild Friday night will always remain unknown. However, as is the
case in a disaster of such magnitude, marine men have drawn upon
their own experiences to arrive at a possible hypothesis.

Captain Samuel Dodd, of the White Shoals Lightship, reported
what he believed to be the *Gilcher* passing his vessel about two
o'clock in the afternoon and taking the north passage around Beaver
Island from the Straits of Mackinac before turning south toward her
destination of Milwaukee. This being the case, she probably did not
break in two because, with a northwest wind, there was not enough
room for a good sea to make up.[42] Wreckage washed ashore on High
Island, northwest of Beaver Island, from both the *Gilcher* and the
schooner *Ostrich*, which also disappeared that night with the loss of
all hands. The stringbacks from the *Gilcher*, which held the canvas
covers to her lifeboats, were cut with an axe. The lifeboats were not
found among the wreckage and the supposition is that the two vessels collided at the height of the storm. Possibly the crew of the *Gilcher* did not have time to launch their lifeboats before their vessel
sank beneath them.[43] The more superstitious members of the maritime fraternity could merely nod their heads with an "I told you so"
attitude. After all, the *Gilcher* had been launched before she was assigned a name.[44]

The *Western Reserve* disaster had the more serious implications
from the standpoint of vessel construction, although both losses, coupled with several others, brought great concern to lake underwriters
and indirectly, to the shipbuilders.

One of the few persons to question publicly wheelsman Stewart's
account of the loss of the *Western Reserve* was Captain Thomas May-

42. Letter to the editor, E. A. Bouchard, Cheboygan, Michigan, December 26,
1892, *Marine Review*, VI (December 29, 1892), 8.
43. J. B. Mansfield (ed.), *History of the Great Lakes*, I, 763.
44. *Marine Review*, II (December 25, 1890), 4.

tham, of Buffalo. He doubted whether Stewart would have seen the crack in the hull in the darkness of the night and in the confusion. He further doubted that Stewart could have known the true conditions under which the vessel supposedly cracked as he was asleep in his room at the time. Maytham reasoned that if the crack was as much as three feet, as Stewart stated, the rudder chains would have snapped and the vessel would have rounded to in the trough of the sea. Also there was no mention of sagging at the ends of the vessel. If a break of the size described by Stewart had occurred amidships, there should have been a sag of as much as ten or twelve feet.[45]

The Cleveland Ship Building Company immediately made specifications of the vessel available. Experts looked them over and testimonies were forthcoming. Frank E. Kirby, of the Detroit Dry Dock Company, noted that the specifications provided "ample material, in fact superior to most ships." W. I. Babcock, of the Chicago Ship Building Company, wrote to the builders of the lost vessel, "that any blame attaches [sic.] to your company or the ship, . . . is absurd."[46]

But in the absence of other evidence, the statement of the lone survivor, that the vessel cracked in half at the forward hatch while being driven into a heavy head sea, with no water in her forward compartments, was generally accepted. The *Marine Review*, the sounding board of lake commerce, in an incriminating editorial, said that orders already had gone out from some of the vessel owners to stop forcing the high-powered vessels into all kinds of weather, with no cargo and little water ballast, in order to maintain a schedule of regularity "almost equal to that of railway trains."[47] In absolving the builders, the editorial also noted that a half dozen steamers had shown signs of breaking in the same way. In two or three cases, vessel owners even found it necessary to replace plates in order to strengthen their vessels.

After Coffinberry's retirement in 1893, Robert Wallace succeeded to the presidency and James C. Wallace advanced to the position of

45.   *Ibid.*, VI (September 29, 1892), 6.
46.   *Ibid.*, September 8, 1892, p. 10.
47.   *Ibid.*, p. 12.

vice-president. The company built only five vessels in the next three years as the financial panic that gripped the nation took hold. But in 1896, with iron ore rates on the rise, business picked up. Three huge ore carriers and a tug were built and were followed by two more giants in 1897. But company officials came more and more to the realization that if they were going to keep pace with demands for larger vessels, drastic steps would have to be taken. Their property on the Cuyahoga River simply was too limited.

Late in 1896, rumors were heard of a move to Lorain, Ohio. They were largely discounted because Lorain was not a principal port, and inaccessibility to the dry dock would cut the company out of repair jobs.[48] Then in February, 1897, following the annual meeting, James C. Wallace announced that the company's capital stock would be increased from $500,000 to $1,000,000, and that a wooden and steel shipbuilding plant and dry dock would be established at Lorain. The company had already purchased twenty acres of land on the east side of the Black River, about 200 feet south of the road bridge. Company officials were pleased with the site because vessels would have a straight shot into the dry dock under their own power, without using tugs. Two slips were to be cut into the property to provide five building berths for new construction, and dock room was planned for from thirty to forty ships to accommodate winter repairs.[49]

Construction was started almost immediately on the new dry dock, and on January 27, 1898, the big steamer *Sir William Fairbairn* was floated into the dry dock. The new and efficient shipyard represented $350,000 in actual investment. The emphasis was on electric and pneumatic tools, and it was estimated that the cost of new construction would be decreased by 10 per cent or more as compared with the old Cleveland yard.[50] The new dry dock was the largest on the lakes. A series of forty and fifty-eight foot span electric cranes connected the stock yard with the steel trestle work at each building berth.[51]

48. *Ibid.*, XIV (December 24, 1896), 7.
49. *Ibid.*, XV (February 4, 1897), 11.
50. *Ibid.*, XVII (January 27, 1898), 10.
51. *Ibid.* The dry dock was 560 feet long, 102 feet wide at the top, 60 feet wide at a point five feet from the bottom, and had 17 feet of water over the sill.

The first launching at the new yard, on April 13, 1898, was a gala occasion in Lorain. The *Lorain Times* printed a special souvenir edition. The Cleveland Society of Engineers chartered a special interurban car and the railroads did a land office business. Promptly at two-thirty in the afternoon, the steamer *Superior City* slid into the water to the cheers of the several thousand people lining both river banks. After the launch, several hundred guests retired to the mold loft for a luncheon. They also heard short addresses by mayors Coffinberry of Lorain and Leavengood of Elyria, as well as Zenith Transit Company representative James H. Hoyt.[52] The general impressions carried away by the Society of Engineers included the labor saving devices and the number of rivets saved by the ability of cranes to handle larger plates.[53]

At long last, the Cleveland Ship Building Company could compete on an equal basis with the Globe interests. The Cleveland plant was used strictly as a repair yard while the new Lorain plant was designated for both repair and new construction. That the new facilities placed the Cleveland Ship Building Company in a competitive position became evident early in 1898 when the Globe Iron Works was compelled to "make a price lower than has ever been accepted on such a vessel in this country" to beat out the Cleveland Ship Building Company in bidding for the Mitchell interests' new steamer *M. A. Bradley.*[54]

This was a situation which neither shipbuilding firm could long endure. It was a problem that was often solved during this period by consolidation.

52. *Lorain Times Souvenir*, April 13, 1898; *Marine Review*, XVII (April 14, 1898), 7. It is doubtful that the Lorain and Cleveland Coffinberrys were related.
53. *Marine Review*, XVII (April 14, 1898), 7.
54. *Ibid.*, February 3, 1898, p. 7.

3.

"The Cliff-men Had
a Little Barge ..."

Alexander McDougall was a sailorman. He came to Canada at the age of nine, in 1854. His family settled near Collingwood, on Georgian Bay, but within a year his father died. His mother, a strong and energetic woman, managed to keep the family together and healthy. But young Alex learned what it was to work, and, in the next six years, he learned a variety of skills and trades. At age sixteen, he left home to ship as a deckhand aboard the small passenger and freight steamer *Edith*. He stayed with the lakes until 1880, earning his way up through the ranks to captain. During those nineteen years he sailed on a variety of craft, learning the intricacies of lake navigation and pilotage. He landed passengers on the gravel beach at Minnesota Point before there was a Duluth, Minnesota. He sailed with Thomas Wilson aboard the *Meteor* and attended night school with him in Detroit.[1] He got to know every bend and pebble between Lake Superior and Buffalo.

1. Alexander McDougall, "The Autobiography of Captain Alexander McDougall," *Inland Seas*, XXIII (Summer, 1967), 102-03.

In 1870, McDougall received his first command, the steamer *Thomas A. Scott*, owned by the famous Anchor Line. During the following winter, he was introduced to the art of shipbuilding. The Anchor Line was constructing three iron passenger and freight steamers in Buffalo, the *India, China*, and *Japan*. Alex was given command of the *Japan*, and in that capacity, spent the winter in the Buffalo shipyard.[2]

McDougall received more insight into shipbuilding during the lean shipping years of 1875-76. He went into the commercial fishing business with Alexander Clark, of Collingwood. Over the winter, he built the wooden steam fish tug *Siskiwit* in the Gibson & Craig yard at Buffalo, hoping to capitalize on the great schools of trout found near Stannard Rock, Lake Superior.[3] Alex was forced to borrow the necessary money for building the fifty-eight foot tug from his close personal friend, E. T. Evans, manager of the Anchor Line.[4] The venture was a huge success measured by the size of their catch, but unfortunately the bottom dropped out of the fish market and he lost his entire investment.

During the winter of 1879-80, McDougall again joined forces with Thomas Wilson. Wilson asked him to supervise construction of the steamer *Hiawatha* and schooner-barge *Minnehaha*, which were being built for him at the Linn & Craig shipyard at Gibraltar, Michigan. Alex assumed command of the *Hiawatha* when she was finished.

While sailing the *Hiawatha*, with the *Minnehaha* in tow, Alex thought out a plan to build an iron boat designed to carry the greatest cargo on the least amount of water. In its design he incorporated the years of practical lake experience he had accumulated, plus insights gained in his shipyard experiences. He developed some models that illustrated his ideas. They had a rounded top to allow water to run off, a spoon-shaped bow to follow the line of strain with the least use of the rudder, and with turrets on deck to allow passage into the inte-

---

2. *Ibid.*, Fall, 1967, p. 202.

3. Buffalo, New York, Permanent Enrollment No. 69, May 18, 1876, National Archives, Record Group No. 41.

4. McDougall, *Inland Seas*, XXIII (Fall, 1967), 210.

rior of the hull. He may have conceived the idea of a cylindrical hull on a visit to England in 1873, where he had an opportunity to examine such a hull designed to carry the Egyptian obelisk from Alexandria to London.[5]

Alex tried to interest lake people in his highly imaginative design, but he was met only with skepticism and open abuse. But such remarks as "you call that damn thing a boat,—why it looks more like a pig," and "she will roll over, having no masts to hold her up," did not dampen his enthusiasm.[6]

In 1887, McDougall signed a contract with the Pusey & Jones Shipbuilding Company, of Wilmington, Delaware, for the construction of a conoidal-shaped bow and stern. He deemed this necessary because of a lack of skilled shipfitters in Duluth.[7] At the same time, he began construction of the mid-body of a barge of his design, using chiefly stevedores as a labor force.[8] The bow and stern were built at Wilmington, disassembled and shipped to Duluth, then reassembled and joined to the mid-body. On June 23, 1888, the first "whaleback" barge, named simply *101*, splashed into the water from the Robert Clark shipyard at Fifteenth Avenue West and Railroad Avenue, in Duluth.[9] The *101* was small, 191 feet long, with only a twenty-one foot beam, and measured 428 gross tons, but she carried 1,200 tons of iron ore. She was built at McDougall's expense, and as she struck the water, his wife, Emmeline, remarked to her sister-in-law, "there goes our last dollar!"[10]

Alex now turned his attentions to a considerably larger model of his prototype. In 1889, he thought that with iron ore rates running high and with more of a demand for steel hulls, he could interest lake ves-

5. *Marine Review*, XV (May 27, 1897), 12.

6. McDougall, *Inland Seas*, XXIII (Winter, 1967), 282.

7. George Carrington Mason, "McDougall's Dream: The Whaleback," *Inland Seas*, IX (Spring, 1953), 4.

8. McDougall, *Inland Seas*, XXIII (Winter, 1967), 282.

9. Wesley R. Harkins, "Head of the Lakes Shipbuilding Industry; Steel Vessels Built," unpublished manuscript, Superior, Wisconsin, 1963 (Mimeographed.); Mason, *Inland Seas*, IX (Spring, 1953), 4.

10. McDougall, *Inland Seas*, XXIII (Winter, 1967), 283, n. 4.

sel owners in his design. Again they listened, more politely this time, but they still turned him down. So Alex went to New York where he interested Colgate Hoyt, a close associate of John D. Rockefeller, in his whaleback concept.

Hoyt got in touch with other New York capitalists and almost immediately a new company, the American Steel Barge Company, was formed. The original board of directors included Colgate Hoyt, Charles L. and James L. Colby, Charles L. Wetmore, Edward B. Bartlett, George W. Weiffenbach, Robert D. Murray, and Pinckney F. Green, all of New York, and Alexander McDougall.[11] Alex agreed to sell all of his patents to the new company for $25,000. This sum was to be taken out in stock in the new company, with the company setting aside an additional 20 per cent of the stock and carrying it in McDougall's name until he could pay for it.[12]

With the necessary finances behind him, Alex returned to Duluth to begin operations in a grand manner. He launched two 253-foot barges in 1889 and followed them with two 276-footers in 1890. Much of McDougall's success during those first two years resulted from the ease with which his barges secured contracts. Undoubtedly Thomas Wilson was responsible for this. He had a large financial interest in the American Steel Barge Company, and his steamers towed the first McDougall barges.[13]

In 1890, the Duluth shipyard launched the first whaleback steamer, appropriately named *Colgate Hoyt*. She was the same size as the last two barges that were built, but her hull below the load line took on the same lines as the conventional Wilson-owned steamer *Spokane*. The purpose of this was to provide more "fullness" forward for resistance in steering.[14] The *Hoyt* cost $120,000 to build, compared to $66,000, the cost of her sister barges, but she soon justified her expense.[15] A Superior, Wisconsin, newspaper, quoting the *Buffalo Courier*, bragged:

11. *Ibid.*, p. 283.
12. *Ibid.*
13. *Marine Review*, II (July 24, 1890), 1.
14. *Ibid.*, I (June 12, 1890), 4.
15. Alexander McDougall, Expense Account Book, hand-written notebook in possession of McDougall's grandson, Alexander McDougall, of Cleveland, Ohio.

The steam pig is in port. . . . It has been claimed that this
"pig" can run close to 16 miles an hour, and that only the *Oswego*
[*Owego*] and *Chemung* have any business with her. The "pig"
family is growing rapidly, and by and by the Lakes will be
bristling with hogbacks—maybe. If the "pig" tribe comes up to
expectations there will be grunting by some owners
of lake ships.[16]

Even before the *Hoyt* was launched, Alex McDougall was looking
for bigger quarters for the American Steel Barge Company. He originally wanted to enlarge the Duluth yard, but the owners set too high a
price tag on it because the shipyard was "too noisy for the heart of the
great city" that boom-times were expected to make of it.[17] He was offered a site and $200,000 of stock in the company if he would locate
the yard in West Duluth.[18]

However Superior, Wisconsin, the "twin-city" of Duluth, was just
beginning to develop in 1889. They offered McDougall 10 per cent of
the payroll of the American Steel Barge Company, land, and dry
dock costs, all of which amounted to $200,000, so Alex decided to
move his operations across the bay. Mr. R. J. Wemyss, general manager of the Land & River Improvement Company, had much to do
with offering the barge works such a great inducement, and it was on
his company's land that the plant was erected.[19]

There was a great rivalry between the two cities, and up to that
point Superior did not have much to boast about. The maneuver was
considered quite a coup, and the Superior newspapers delighted in
rubbing salt into the "cliff-men's" wounds. One such barb was penned
by "P.D.Q. Fizzymagig":

McDougall's Little Lamb

  The cliff-men had a little barge—
   McDougall ran the crew;

16. *Superior Daily Call*, October 3, 1890.
17. McDougall, *Inland Seas*, XXIII (Winter, 1967), 284.
18. *Ibid.*
19. Warranty deed from American Steel Barge Company to The Superior Shipbuilding Company, April 14, 1899, land deed in possession of the Fraser Shipyards, Inc., Superior, Wisconsin.

> And everywhere McDougall went,
> The barge-works got there, too.
>
> They followed Mac to make a deal
> With Wemyss, across the bay;
> And cliff-men, how the poor things squeal,
> To see things come this way.[20]

The new shipyard was built at the head and south side of Howard's Bay, a small needle of water that separated Connors Point from the mainland. The once desolate swamp area hummed with activity in the spring of 1890. Large gangs of men wheelbarrowed earth from the head of the slips to the interior of the punch shop to level the floor even as masons, bricklayers, and carpenters erected the building. More sand was brought in from Northern Pacific Junction until the once-swampy area became a "glistening level of sand with great buildings dotting the grounds and a row of docks extending 350 feet from shore. . . ."[21]

Four slips were dredged to a depth of eight feet on each side and sloped to thirteen feet in the center to accommodate the launching ways. Washington fir for the launching skeds, measuring eighteen by eighteen inches and from fifty to sixty feet long, was shipped from the Pacific coast.

Colgate Hoyt paid the new barge works a visit in May, 1890. He arrived on a special train of the Wisconsin Central, and his comments only added to Superior's enthusiasm. He indicated that his business interests would "use the barges extensively in transporting ore from the Gogebic country to Lake Erie ports."[22]

As a concession to severe northern winters, McDougall built huge barn-like structures over some of the building ways so that time would not be lost in vessel construction. The roofs were supported by cantilever tresses so that the launch ways would be clear of supporting posts, and the sides of the buildings were made movable.

20. *Superior Evening Telegram*, May 15, 1890.
21. *Ibid.*, June 27, 1890.
22. *Ibid.*, May 14, 1890.

The first barge launched in Superior was the *107*, on August 16, 1890. She was a duplicate of the last two barges launched in the Duluth yard. In November, the first steamer was launched at the new yard. She was named after a director of the American Steel Barge Company, Joseph L. Colby, and a gala day was planned by the city fathers. The LaBelle Wagon Works closed their doors for the day, and the West Superior Iron & Steel Company began work at four o'clock in the morning so their workers would be out by noon. The spirits were somewhat dampened by news of the death of H. D. Minot, a locally prominent citizen, and the Superior Military Band, dressed in their resplendent uniforms, helmets, and plumes, wore black crepe armbands as they marched down Third Street. The shipyard workers appeared "more than elated" as the launching hour approached.[23] As one old-timer recalled, "launchings were quite an occasion in those days. The boys really got drunk. . . . Used to have big parties on the day of launching."[24] When the *Joseph L. Colby* dropped into the water, at three o'clock, she succeeded in thoroughly wetting a few hundred spectators. She was followed into her natural element just thirty-three minutes later by the barge *109*.

In 1891, the barge works launched ten hulls, three steamers and six barges of the whaleback design, and one conventional oil barge. Launchings became so commonplace that the people of Superior barely took notice. In 1892, the shipyard produced six freighters, a passenger steamer, three barges, all of the whaleback design, and a yard tug.

During the winter of 1890-91, the American Steel Barge Company increased its capital stock from $2,000,000 to $5,000,000.[25] In 1892, the company had a capitalization double that of the next largest business in Superior, the West Superior Iron & Steel Company, from whom they bought much of their ship steel. They employed 400 skilled

23. *Superior Daily Call*, November 15, 1890.
24. Tape-recorded interview with Mr. Louis Dahlgren, Superior, Wisconsin, May 10, 1960, by Wesley R. Harkins and Barney B. Barstow. (Typed transcription.)
25. *Marine Review*, II (July 24, 1890), 1.

workmen and 810 laborers, and contributed $925,000 in annual wages to the prosperity of the town.[26]

Alex McDougall had come a long way from the small log cabin near Collingwood, and he had plans for going a long way further. In 1892 he closed a contract with the Merritt Brothers to carry all of their Mesabi iron ore for a period of fifteen years. This enabled him to control the ore docks. In this connection, he also was directly involved with developing the Duluth, Mesabi & Iron Range Railway, to haul ore from the mines to the docks. Through several connections, the Merritts, Charles L. Wetmore, and John D. Rockefeller came together. McDougall's connection was Colgate Hoyt. By this syndicated arrangement, Rockefeller invested heavily in iron ore properties and the barge works.

Wetmore and Charles L. Colby also had extensive holdings in the Pacific Northwest, and McDougall soon saw advantages there. He envisioned whaleback steamers and barges trading on salt water. One possibility was hauling ore from Rockefeller mines in Cuba. Another was the coastal trade on the Pacific coast until completion of the proposed Nicaragua Canal opened the wheat, ore, and timber trade of the booming northwest to the east coast. As early as 1890, McDougall and his eastern associates formed the Pacific Steel Barge Company. Alex made several trips to the Pacific Northwest to select a site and decided that a spot on the Snohomish Peninsula, in the state of Washington, was ideally suited for vessel construction. Soon a boom-town, Everett, Washington, sprang up. It was tailored to meet every whim of the predominantly male population, including stores, more than enough saloons, and a sprinkling of bawdy houses. By June, 1892, a 75-acre, $600,000 shipyard, that even included a three-story boarding house for the men, began construction on a McDougall whaleback.[27]

McDougall's practical imagination, coupled with eastern money, continued to expand. With complete faith in the future of Lake Supe-

26. Frank A. Flower (ed.), *The Eye of the Northwest: Report of the City Statistician for the Year 1892* (Superior: By authority of the city statistician, 1892), p. 117.
27. Alfred L. Lomax, "Whalebacks Promised a Shining Future for Early-Day Everett," *Seattle Times*, November 11, 1962.

rior iron ore and steel-hulled carriers, Alex realized the value of a dry dock at the northernmost terminal point of lake shipping.

In 1890, R. J. Wemyss, of the Land & River Improvement Company, reported that certain Chicago and Milwaukee shipbuilders were interested in building a dry dock at the Lakehead.[28] The deal failed to materialize and on Christmas Day, 1891, the American Steel Barge Company began construction on a dry dock on property adjoining its shipyard at Superior. George E. Hartnell, who designed the dry dock for the Ship Owners' Dry Dock Company, in Cleveland, was hired to superintend construction.[29] It cost less than $900,000, including machinery, dock face, and a well drilled for drinking water.[30] On September 20, 1892, the dock entertained its first patient, the wooden freighter *Neshota*.[31] Superior now had the largest dry dock on the Great Lakes.

The dock was dug entirely by hand with horses pulling drags. The "water-end" of the dock was left intact as a natural cofferdam. The interior of the dry dock was completed, a wooden floating gate constructed and fitted, then the dirt and clay end was dug out and water permitted to enter. Louis Dahlgren, a ten-year old "water boy" at the time, recalled that "it was awfully mucky ground to work in but we didn't pay much attention to that in those days, . . . Mud or anything like that didn't mean anything to us—the mothers washed the clothes you know."[32]

Alexander McDougall was on the verge of creating an empire, with a Rockefeller as king and a McDougall as prince of the northern provinces of the realm. Then the Panic of 1893 struck and the walls came tumbling down. Alexander McDougall relied completely on the business mind and influence of Colgate Hoyt to guide him. Unfortunately, in the fall of 1892 Hoyt developed typhoid and went to Europe to recuperate.

28.   *Superior Evening Telegram*, May 23, 1890.

29.   *Marine Review*, XVII (March 10, 1898), 7.

30.   McDougall, *Inland Seas*, XXIII (Winter, 1967), 284-85.

31.   Dated photograph in possession of Wesley R. Harkins, Superior Wisconsin. The dry dock was 537 feet long, 52 feet wide at the bottom, and had 18 feet of water over the sill.

32.   Tape-recorded interview with Louis Dahlgren.

Rockefeller sent out Frederick T. Gates, his right-hand man and troubleshooter, to replace Hoyt. At this time McDougall was on a trip to Everett, Washington. When McDougall returned to Superior, he found that Gates had cancelled the fifteen-year ore carrying contract with the Merritts. Gates also ousted the Merritts from control of the Lake Superior Consolidated Iron Mines Company, which owned the mines and the railroad.[33] Alex was offered the opportunity to manage the company, but he refused on the grounds that he was a vessel man and shipbuilder, not a miner and railroader.[34] Then Gates tried to involve McDougall in a personal dispute between himself and Colgate Hoyt, who had returned from Europe. McDougall showed his true colors and refused to turn his back on Hoyt because he "was my principal and had always been square with me," knowing that it could well mean his financial ruin.[35]

The Pacific Steel Barge Company suffered the blow of foreclosure first. The unfinished whaleback and shipyard property were deeded to the American Steel Barge Company, and both firms were mortgaged to a New York trust company for $4,000,000. The mortgage included McDougall's whaleback patents.[36] Then Alex discovered that a protective clause in his original contract with the American Steel Barge Company, in which the company carried $150,000 of company stock in his account, was not valid. He had leased his shipyard and services to the company in 1890 for one dollar a year. Much to his sorrow he found that the lease superseded his original contract, and he was asked to repay the $150,000. He was forced to let his stock, which had been worth double par, go for fifty cents on the dollar, thanks to Gates' "blundering."[37]

Alex still retained the title of general manager of the American Steel Barge Company, although the blow took its toll. Gone were aspirations for grandiose plans with the barge works as a focal point. In

<hr>

33. An excellent popular account of the legendary Merritts is Paul DeKruif's *Seven Iron Men*, published in 1929.
34. McDougall, *Inland Seas*, XXIII (Winter, 1967), 298.
35. *Ibid.*
36. Lomax, *Seattle Times*, November 11, 1962.
37. McDougall, *Inland Seas*, XXIII (Winter, 1967), 299.

1894, he returned to Everett and completed his whaleback steamer, the *City of Everett*. This trip must have been enjoyable as he was united with members of the Colby family and with Colgate Hoyt. There still must have been some challenge inasmuch as he attempted to negotiate contracts for whalebacks for the Alaska trade. Certainly his influence in Duluth-Superior was undiminished, as was evidenced by his being prevailed upon, as president of the Joint Duluth-Superior River and Harbor Commission, to recommend a twenty-foot channel for that harbor.[38]

In 1894, the board of directors of the American Steel Barge Company consisted of McDougall, Colgate Hoyt, A. D. Thompson, Samuel Mather, James and Joseph Colby, Thomas Wilson, James B. Colgate, and Frank Rockefeller. Hoyt was president and treasurer; Colgate, vice-president; and Russell C. Wetmore, secretary. The shipbuilding aspects of the company still fell under McDougall's scrutiny, but his very able superintendent, Joseph Kidd, actually supervised construction. Kidd started with McDougall in 1889.[39] James Clark served as chief draftsman and was probably responsible, along with McDougall, for refining the hull lines of the vessels that followed the *101*. He left the barge company's employ in 1893 in an unsuccessful attempt to become a competitor.[40] Clark was replaced by A. C. Diericx, whose experience came largely from English employment.[41] Thus there were still many familiar faces around the shipyard office in 1894; but still, it just wasn't the same.

The addition of Samuel Mather to the board of directors had some direct results. In 1892, the barge works built the steamer *Pathfinder*

<hr>

38. Letter from Alexander McDougall to General Orlando M. Poe, Everett, Washington, September 20, 1894, quoted in Ralph S. Knowlton, "A Short History of the Improvements of Duluth-Superior Harbor," address given before the St. Louis County Historical Society, Duluth, Minnesota, March 24, 1959. (Mimeographed.)

39. F. A. Miller, "The Superior Shipbuilding Company; from the Whaleback to the Modern Freighter," *Live Wire*, I (May, 1915), 2.

40. Newspaper notation dated January 23, 1893, Wesley R. Harkins, "Notes on Duluth-Superior Shipbuilding History: American Steel Barge Company," unpublished manuscript, Superior, Wisconsin.

41. *Marine Review*, XVII (August 18, 1898), 8.

and consort *Sagamore* for Mather's Huron Barge Company. In 1895, the Pickands Mather Company took over management of the American Steel Barge Company fleet, removing one more responsibility from McDougall.[42]

Shipbuilding all over the lakes suffered following the panic of 1893. The American Steel Barge Company was no exception. In 1893, they launched six barges, but the last three were launched on the same day, June 17th. They built nothing in 1894 and three vessels in 1895. Only one of those three, the steamer *John B. Trevor*, was a whaleback. The other two were conventional oil barges for the Standard Oil Company. The year 1896 was only slightly better. Three vessels were launched, but two of them were steamers. The last of these, the barge *Alexander Holley*, was the last hull constructed with a "pure" whaleback design. One more steamer was built with whaleback lines, but she had a conventional lake freighter bow. It was only fitting that she carried her builder's name, *Alexander McDougall*. She was the largest of this type of vessel built, being 413 feet long, 50 feet wide, and 3,672 gross tons.

By the turn of the century, the whalebacks were eclipsed in size by more modern freighters. More serious defects were the rounded deck and the fore-and-aft stringers under the outer edges of the small hatch covers. They were not large enough to accommodate the huge clamshell buckets that came into common use on the lakes. By their simplicity of design, the whalebacks were cheap and easy to build. But even their economy features were lost as modern technology invaded the shipyards. The 2,721-ton *Alexander Holley* cost $130,639.74 to build in 1896, and the conventional-hulled 3,231-ton barge *Constitution*, built by the same company the following year, cost $114,485.81.[43] Figures such as these were hard to dispute.

The period from 1895 to 1899 could hardly match the first five years of the yard's existence in new vessel construction. But the presence of the only major dry dock on Lake Superior kept the company well sup-

42.   Walter Havighurst, *Vein of Iron, the Pickands Mather Story* (Cleveland: World Publishing Co., 1958), p. 92.

43.   McDougall, Expense Account Book.

plied with repair and winter work. One of the more interesting jobs in this line was the lengthening of the whaleback steamer *Joseph L. Colby* and the whaleback barges *201* and *202* during the winter of 1896-97. The barges were built on the east coast in 1892 and came to the lakes during the summer of 1896. At the barge works, they were hauled out lengthwise on a slip to a height of four feet, permitting necessary bottom work, and lengthened 61 feet 4 inches, without tying up the dry dock.[44]

The office force at the American Steel Barge Company was considered for many years to be one of the most harmonious on the lakes. Even through the dark days of 1893-94, there were no major changes. Considering the turnovers that normally occurred in most large shipbuilding concerns, this loyalty was a rarity that had to be attributed to the personality of McDougall. The fact that there was relative harmony between shipyard workers and management can be credited to the amiable, respected yard superintendent, Joseph Kidd. In May, 1897, when the balding, mustached Kidd decided to leave the barge works to go into business for himself as a consulting marine engineer, an assembly composed of office workers and yard workers presented him with the traditional gold watch, chain, and fob, but supplemented them with a complete set of office furniture. Such was the show of appreciation for the eight years he had devoted to making the company a success. Much of the time the entire operation of the yard had fallen on his shoulders while McDougall traveled from coast to coast.

Daniel E. Ford, who had supervised construction of Rockefeller vessels at Cleveland, Bay City, and Buffalo, replaced Kidd. It was expected, however, that the former Chicago tug boatman in his new position would represent interests more closely allied to Colgate Hoyt and other eastern capitalists, rather than Rockefeller.[45]

The most pressing job that Dan Ford had to tackle was modernizing the shipyard. Repair business was increasing and the company was forced to bring its yard operation into a more competitive position

44. *Marine Review*, XV (February 18, 1897), 9.
45. *Ibid.*, May 20, 1897, p. 11.

with the other lake shipyards. Over the winter of 1897-98, the appearance of the yard was substantially changed by the addition of a large machine shop and a cantilever gantry crane. The yard was also equipped with an electric lighting plant and a complete system of pneumatic tools. Work on a second dry dock was also begun, but it was not completed under the old management.

The American Steel Barge Company never had its own engine plant. Nine of the whalebacks were powered by engines manufactured by the S. F. Hodge Engine Works, of Detroit, Michigan. The first three steamers carried compound engines. But in 1897, McDougall decided to experiment with a triple expansion steam plant. The Northeastern Engine Works, of Sunderland, England, supplied the engine for the *E. B. Bartlett*, and the Hodge Company, for the *A. D. Thompson*. The English engine had closely connected cylinders, while the Hodge engine was not very closely connected and supposedly distributed the work more evenly.[46] On her first trip, the *Thompson*'s boilers failed because the half-inch steel plate was too soft and huge blisters appeared.[47] But her engine's performance was judged superior, and no other Northeastern engines were used.

The barge company officials were pleased with the performance of the triple expansion engine, and the remainder of their steamers, with one exception, were powered by them. The engines for the *Samuel Mather*, *Pathfinder*, and *City of Everett* came from the Frontier Iron Works, of Detroit. The Marinette Iron Works, of Duluth, supplied the plant for the *James B. Colgate*; the Cleveland Ship Building Company, for the *Frank Rockefeller* and *John Ericsson*. The latter company also built the quadruple expansion engine for that lone exception to the "triples," the *Alexander McDougall*.

The most famous ship built by the barge works, and possibly the most famous ever to sail the Great Lakes, was beyond question, the lone whaleback passenger steamer, the *Christopher Columbus*. McDougall had discussed the possibility of such a vessel for the Chicago World's Fair with some of his close associates. He made models and

46. *Superior Daily Call*, April 20, 1891.
47. *Ibid.*, July 25, 1891.

plans and presented them to his eastern associates at the Seawanhaka Club, at Oyster Bay, New York, on August 26, 1892. He proposed that if they would sign a contract on that same day, he would build and launch the boat, and have her machinery set in place in three months. He further guaranteed that she would run twenty miles per hour and load 5,000 people in five minutes.[48] The *Columbus* was launched on December 3, 1892, at a cost of $361,670.73, including a neat profit of $35,270.73.[49]

Although the *Columbus* appeared awkward with seven turrets supporting her passenger deck and pilothouse, this very appearance made her one of the most popular attractions at the Fair.[50] During the season of 1893, her trip was only six miles long, from the downtown docks at Randolph Street to Jackson Park, but she carried an estimated 2,000,000 passengers without loss of life.[51] When the Fair ended, she was sold to the Hurson Line, which soon ran into financial difficulties. After this, she was operated by the Columbian Whaleback Steamship Company, of which Alexander McDougall was general manager. During this period, she ran from Chicago to Milwaukee. The Goodrich Transit Company placed its crack liner, the *Virginia*, in opposition to the *Christopher Columbus*. In 1894, the two steamers had several unofficial races, and, strangely enough, the *Columbus* usually won in calm weather and the *Virginia* in heavy weather.[52] The *Columbus* was purchased by the Goodrich Line in 1898 and sailed for many years in the Lake Michigan passenger trade. She was scrapped at Manitowoc, Wisconsin in 1937.

Most of the whaleback barges and some of the steamers ultimately saw service on the ocean. One of them, the steamer *Charles W. Wetmore*, steamed to Kingston, Ontario, in the spring of 1891, where her

48.   McDougall, *Inland Seas*, *XXIII* (Winter, 1967), 285.
49.   McDougall, Expense Account Book.
50.   A second passenger deck was later added.
51.   Dana Thomas Bowen, *Lore of the Lakes* (Daytona Beach: by the author, 1940), p. 77.
52.   James L. Elliott, *Red Stacks Over the Horizon: The Story of the Goodrich Steamboat Line* (Grand Rapids: William B. Eerdmans Publishing Co., 1967), p. 155.

cargo of grain was lightered for transshipment. Then McDougall piloted her down the Lachine Rapids to Montreal, where she was reloaded with wheat. The whaleback was fifteen days from Montreal to Liverpool, but only eleven from Sidney, Nova Scotia, where she coaled. Alex McDougall took great pride in an article in the *Pall Mall Budget* about the *Wetmore*'s arrival at Liverpool:

> As evidence of her steadiness at sea, when the hatchings
> were taken off the foot prints and shovel marks of the grain
> trimmers were plainly visible in the cargo. The wheat had not
> shifted at all in the voyage, so steadily did the whaleback run.[53]

After an uneventful trip across the Atlantic to New York, the *Wetmore* sailed to Philadelphia, where she loaded 2,000 tons of machinery and other necessities for the new shipyard at Everett, Washington. She departed from Philadelphia on September 19, 1891, rounded Cape Horn, and arrived at Coronel, Chili, on November 5th. On her run up the Pacific Coast she weathered one of the worst gales of many years in that area. In the process, she lost her rudder plates and arrived at the mouth of the Columbia River on December 8, 1891, rather ignominiously at the end of a tow rope attached to the British freighter *Zambesi*.[54] After repairs at Astoria, Oregon, she proceeded on to Everett and arrived safely. All in all, the perilous gamble was considered a success. If the Panic of 1893 had not struck, more whalebacks would have followed, and certainly more would have been built by the Pacific Steel Barge Company.

The Panic of 1893 brought about many changes in the American Steel Barge Company, as has already been seen. The carefree days were gone, days when George N. Beauchamp, walking back to Superior from Duluth each Saturday, would set down his leather bag containing $2,000 in cash, the barge works payroll, while he went swimming.[55] A street car ran out to the end of Connors Point to provide

53. *Superior Daily Call*, August 14, 1891.
54. *Inland Ocean* (Superior), December 27, 1891.
55. Letter from George A. Beauchamp, Grosse Pointe Shores, Michigan, to Wesley R. Harkins, Superior, Wisconsin, August 18, 1964.

transportation for the four hundred families that lived there, including many shipyard workers. Old Tom Scott was still splicing cable and caring for the yard mule, Blenda.[56] However the Lamborn Avenue bridge swung open more often now, and more freighters spent winters in the "Pocket." The barge works had grown a great deal in a decade. The strings that controlled its destiny stretched from coast to coast, and possibly even farther.

Reflecting on Alex McDougall's life, one writer felt that he typified the entire development of lake transportation, from forecastle to bridge, from a belief and gamble on a radical ship design to success with the lions of Wall Street.[57] But all of this wasn't quite enough. If the American Steel Barge Company was to continue garnering the lucrative lake trade, it would have to fall in line with the overpowering business patterns of the day, patterns that became most pronounced after 1893.

56. Tape-recorded interview with Louis Dahlgren.
57. Grace Lee Nute, *Lake Superior* (Indianapolis: Bobbs-Merrill Co., 1944), p. 129.

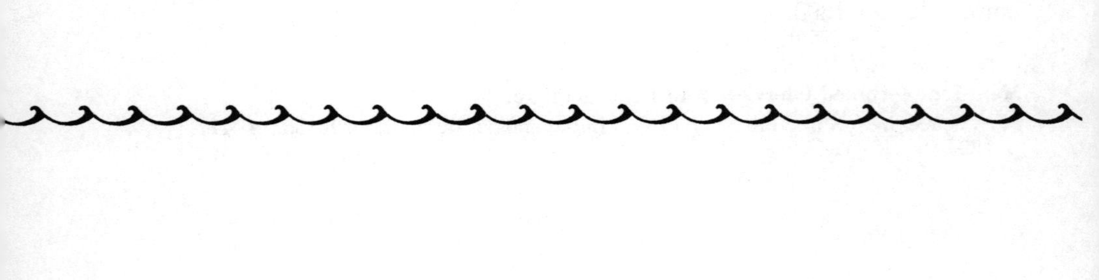

4.

From the Kinnickinnic to the Calumet

At the turn of the twentieth century, Lake Michigan could boast of two predecessor companies to the American Ship Building Company. The Chicago Ship Building Company was the last major steel ship-building yard to develop on the Great Lakes prior to 1900. Milwaukee never built steel vessels on a large scale, and none prior to 1918. In fact, Milwaukee seldom built even wooden ships for anyone other than Milwaukeeans!

The most prominent of the early shipbuilders in Milwaukee were the Jones boys, Benjamin Buel and James Madison, of the illustrious Ohio Jones shipbuilding family. Benjamin came to Milwaukee shortly after his father's death in 1841 and began a modest shipbuilding establishment just west of Reed Street, on the South Menominee River. In the early 1850's, he was joined by his brother and they moved their operations to the island that still bears their name in the Kinnickinnic Basin. The financial depression of 1857 hit them hard, and a bad storm two years later practically finished them. James left for Detroit,

Michigan, where he continued building ships until he was caught by the depression in 1873. Benjamin stayed in Milwaukee, where he continued to build ships until his death in 1870.

One of Benjamin Jones's foremen was a young man who emigrated from Germany in 1849, William H. Wolf. In the early 1850's, Wolf served as foreman for a short time with a little-known shipbuilder, E. Eunice, who had a shipyard near the Oneida Street bridge on the Milwaukee River. Then he joined the Joneses in the Kinnickinnic Basin. In 1858, the enterprising Wolf formed a partnership with Theodore Lawrence, and they started a shipyard on the Burnham Canal in Milwaukee.[1] The only vessel of record built by Wolf & Lawrence was the schooner *Dick Somers*, so business must have been difficult. In 1863, T. C. Dousman, of Green Bay, Wisconsin, was able to lure Wolf to Green Bay to start a shipyard. Wolf was referred to at that time as "an accomplished and successful contractor" whose reputation was "widespread among vessel owners."[2] Wolf, no stranger to Green Bay, took forty or fifty unemployed ship carpenters with him, and in the next five years built over a dozen vessels there.[3]

When the partnership of Wolf & Lawrence ended, they sold their holdings to Ellsworth & Davidson. Lemuel Ellsworth was the son-in-law of Benjamin Jones. Thomas Davidson emigrated from Scotland in 1854 and found employment with shipbuilder Eunice in building the schooner *C. Harrison* at Eunice's Oneida Street yard. Following this, Davidson worked in the Jones shipyard. Here he undoubtedly became acquainted with Lem Ellsworth. From their yard, located at the foot of Greenbush Avenue, Ellsworth & Davidson turned out at least seven sailing vessels.[4]

Lem Ellsworth retired from shipbuilding in 1868 to go into the wrecking business. William Wolf now saw more opportunity for himself in Milwaukee than in Green Bay and "came home" to form the partnership of Wolf & Davidson. Soon they moved their shipyard site

1. Frank E. Hamilton, "Notes . . . on Shipbuilding . . . ."
2. *Milwaukee Sentinel*, March 3, 1863.
3. In 1852, Wolf built the sidewheel steamer *Morgan L. Martin* at Green Bay.
4. Vessel Enrollments, 1862-67, Milwaukee Customs District, National Archives, Record Group No. 41.

GENEALOGY OF THE MILWAUKEE DRY DOCK COMPANY

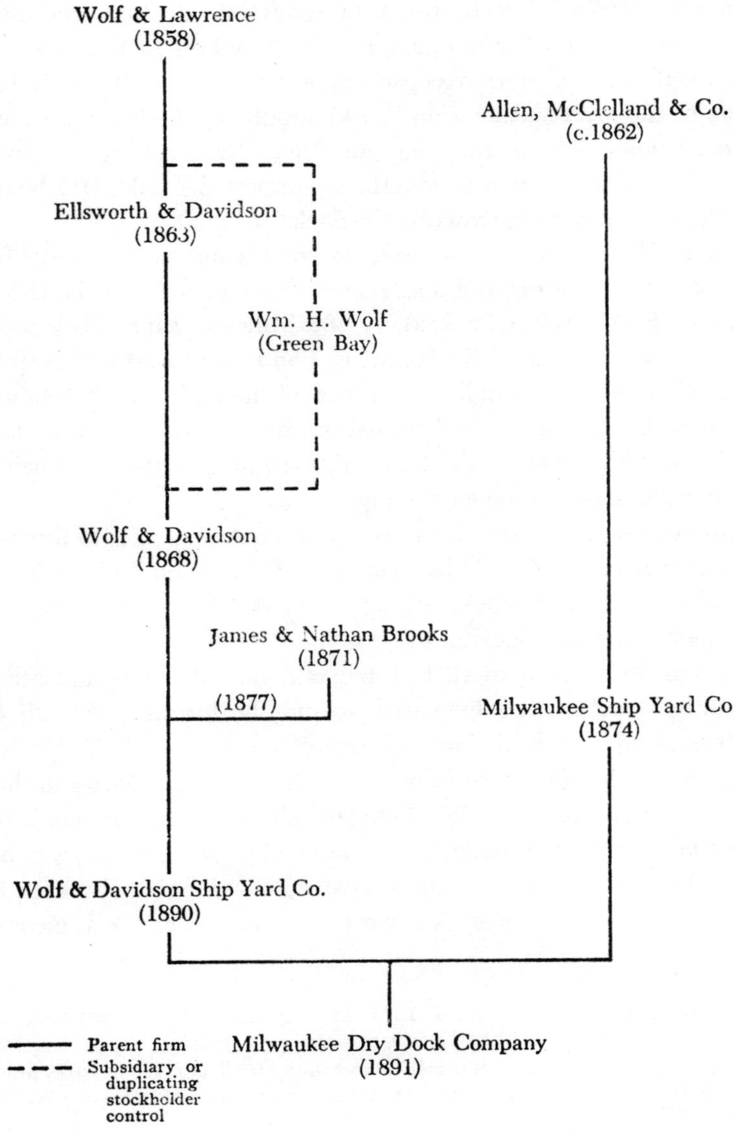

from the Kneeland Canal to the undeveloped marshland area in the Kinnickinnic Basin. They located on the waterfront between Washington and Mineral Streets, opposite Jones Island. New contracts were not immediately forthcoming, but the vessel repair business was good. In 1871, they started construction on a dry dock, with Jim Sheriffs of the local Vulcan Iron Works supplying the iron.[5] Because of the swampy terrain, they had to drive 3,500 oak spiles, from twenty to twenty-five feet in length, to support the 2,000,000 board feet of lumber used in constructing the dock.[6]

In 1871, Wolf & Davidson secured contracts from local interests for the construction of a tug and a schooner. The launching of the latter, the *Angus Smith*, was witnessed by 500 Milwaukeeans. They were serenaded by the South Side Harmony Band, after which they partook of refreshments through the courtesy of the builders.[7] It is singular to note that the new vessel settled on the water as "graceful as a swan," as did all of the locally-built ships—so long as the same newspaper reporter covered the launchings.

Excitement of a different nature occurred on August 28, 1871, when the tug *American Eagle* collided with one of the sections of the Wolf & Davidson floating dry dock, tearing out the end of it. The tug lost her smokestack and a great deal of dignity.[8]

As the grain interests of R. P. Fitzgerald, Joseph Page, and other Milwaukee vessel owners increased, so did the fortunes of Wolf & Davidson. They launched three schooners and a tug in 1872. One of the schooners, the *Joseph Page*, was the largest vessel built up to that time on the west coast of Lake Michigan. The next year proved to be the best year of the firm, judging by the number of vessels they built. Wolf & Davidson built one tug, one steamer, and six schooners in 1873. They employed over 200 workmen, and their total income

5. *Milwaukee Sentinel*, February 4, 1871. The dry dock was 333 feet long, 50 feet wide at the bottom, and had 17 feet of water over the sill.
6. Charles B. Harger (ed.), *Milwaukee Illustrated: Its Trade, Commerce, Manufacturing Interests, and Advantages as A Residence City* (Milwaukee: W. W. Coleman, 1877), p. 87.
7. *Milwaukee Sentinel*, August 7, 1871.
8. *Ibid.*, August 28, 1871.

amounted to $224,805.56, which was divided between vessel repairs ($130,771.31) and new construction ($94,034.25). They also placed eight vessels in dry dock at an average rate of over $1,000 per vessel.[9]

As an example of how new vessels were contracted for in the heyday of sailing vessels when the grain rates increased, the Wolf & Davidson manipulations are of interest. R. P. and John Fitzgerald, and Joseph Page contracted with them for a new schooner to be built along the lines of two other vessels that the shipbuilding partners had already constructed. The contract price was $37,000, including the bark *Parana*, valued at $25,000.[10] The shipbuilders then sold the bark to other parties for a price unknown, but undoubtedly beneficial to themselves. This type of business transaction involving "trade-in tonnage," very similar to trade-in allowances in the modern automobile market, was quite common in the days of independently owned wooden ships.

Wolf & Davidson had such a prosperous year in 1873 that, in spite of the financial depression and the consequent dwindling lake trade, they launched a canal schooner, the *Lem Ellsworth*, on builders' account.[11]

For the next six years, the shipyard existed on its repair business. The yard was well equipped to handle wooden repairs. It had a nine-section floating dry dock, the permanent dry dock, a steam-operated joiner shop and saws, a Daniels steam planing mill, a steam derrick for hoisting spars, along with other miscellaneous tools. The firm averaged two new vessels per year, but several were tugs. They built the popular sidewheeler *Flora* in 1875, as well as an Al Capp-like creation called a "swill boat" for the Menominee Distilling Company.[12]

In 1877, Wolf & Davidson purchased the small boatbuilding business of Nathan Brooks, including shop, materials, tools, and boats on

9.   Charles B. Harger (ed.), *Milwaukee Illustrated:* . . . , p. 88.

10.   *Milwaukee Sentinel*, August 24, 1872.

11.   *Ibid.*, November 13, 1872 and August 5, 1874. A canal schooner had a square stern and straight stem; the bowsprit was mounted on a swivel so it could be swung inboard. This afforded a "snug fit" for vessels engaged in the Welland Canal trade.

12.   *Ibid.*, April 13, 1875.

hand.[13] Brooks and his father, James N. Brooks, built a number of small steam craft, including several tugs, in Milwaukee between 1871 and 1877. In August, 1876, one of their craft, the small steam yacht *Silva*, capsized and drowned the elder Brooks. The accident also killed Nathan's desire to carry on the business.

William Wolf was interested in promoting new businesses in Milwaukee. He realized that new businesses and an increasing population meant more carrying trade for the city. In 1878, as an alderman, he was known as "the Falstaff of the Common Council." He showed his sardonic humor when, in asking for an appropriation of $2,000 to be split between the local English and German newspaper writing the best editorial on why businessmen should locate in Milwaukee, he stipulated one condition—no lying. To illustrate the idea he suggested how to get rich with only $1,000 capital: "spend $999 in advertising, and invest the other dollar in flour and make pills."[14] On another occasion, when the ship carpenters and caulkers were demanding an eight-hour, $2.50 day, Wolf showed his humor when he replied, "If you had waited just one week, boys, I would have gone a strike with you."[15]

Although Wolf & Davidson did not invest in flour and pills during the decade of the 1880's, they did build several ships. Some, such as the *Minnesota, Progress, Jim Sheriffs,* and *W. J. Carter,* were typical of the small wooden bulk freighters that crowded the lakes during that period. They were relatively inexpensive to build and, with minor adjustments, carried coal, ore, grain, or lumber. During the late eighties, the firm began building some of the largest wooden bulk freighters constructed on the lakes. They were designed principally for the iron ore trade, and many came out with twin smokestacks set athwartships. The *Roswell P. Flower, William H. Wolf,* and *Thomas Davidson* were of this type.

The partners launched the *Fred Pabst* in 1890. Her launching festivities were almost too much even for William Wolf's sardonic humor.

13. *Ibid.,* July 24, 1877.
14. *Ibid.,* July 23, 1878.
15. *Marine Review,* III (May 28, 1891), 5.

She really wasn't a bad looking vessel; in fact, she was typical of wooden vessels of her era. She was large for a wooden freighter— 2,430 gross tons and 287 feet long. After she was fitted out, she was sprightly with her light upper works and dark hull, especially when the brightly-striped awning was set over her forecastle deck. But that launching! Just about the whole town turned out on April 5, 1890, to see her unladylike splash into the Kinnickinnic Basin. The brewery entrepreneur, after whom she was named, sent a carload of beer to honor the occasion, and there was no mention that any was left over. Young society ladies drank with ship carpenters and "Bad Boy" Peck took a "schooner" with Mayor Brown, whom he had just defeated for re-election.[16] William Wolf's few comments were that she was strong, could carry big loads, and as an ore lugger should be a success. It was indeed fitting that she carried beer-keg masthead ornaments and barrels on her deck-houses, "thus increasing the suggestiveness of a floating brewery."[17]

Shortly after the launch of the *Pabst*, Thomas Davidson sold his interest in the partnership to William Wolf. Then he gave the money back to Wolf as partial payment for a new vessel that Wolf was to build for him.

"Commodore" Wolf incorporated a new company, the Wolf & Davidson Ship Yard Company, with a capital of $250,000. The capital stock was divided into 10,000 shares with a value of $25 per share. Many of the old employees became stockholders. The concern employed about 200 men.[18] Although Davidson may have maintained a financial interest in the new company, his name was undoubtedly retained for purposes of business and local tradition.

In 1891 William W. Bates, the Commissioner of Navigation, sent out a circular informing all Collectors of Customs that Section 4178 of the revised Statutes of the United States, relating to the markings of vessels' names, had been amended, effective July 1, 1892. After that date it was mandatory to display the vessel's name on the bow and

16. *Ibid.*, I (April 10, 1890), 2.
17. *Ibid.*, (May 8, 1890), p. 7, quoted from the *Milwaukee Evening Wisconsin.*
18. *Ibid.*, (June 5, 1890), p. 8.

stern, as well as on the pilothouse, in letters no smaller than four inches in size.[19] Ordinarily this statute would not cause consternation to a shipbuilder, but to the Wolf & Davidson Ship Yard Company in 1891, it must have caused a little measuring. The only major addition to the lake fleet that the reorganized company built proved to be one of the longest wooden freighters constructed on the lake. But more than that, she carried one of the longest names, *Ferdinand Schlesinger*! She measured 2,607 gross tons, was 305 feet long and, fortunately, forty-three feet wide. When she was launched, in March, 1891, her namesake graciously supplied the flags and bunting, sparing Commodore Wolf that extra expense. The *Schlesinger* was no thing of beauty, but she was a good carrier. Other than her size and the length of her name, the only unique thing that she could boast of was her water bottom. She was only the second wooden bulk freighter to be built with a compartmentalized double bottom into which water could be pumped for ballast. The first such wooden freighter was the *Fred Pabst*.[20] Steel-hulled ships were the ones normally accorded that luxury.

During the period in which Wolf & Davidson enjoyed their greatest prosperity, the company had one solid competitor in Milwaukee. This was the Milwaukee Ship Yard Company. After Ellsworth & Davidson purchased the tools and equipment of Wolf & Lawrence in 1863, and relocated at the foot of Greenbush Avenue, another shipbuilding company started on the Kneeland Canal. Allen, McClelland & Company's yard was located on the south side of the Kneeland Canal, just west of and adjacent to Holton's Slip, roughly between Sixth and Eighth Streets. Robert Allen was another former employee of Benjamin Jones.

The company started in an inauspicious manner by launching the forty-five foot sloop *Trial* in 1863. They apparently built no more new vessels until 1866. The man who spearheaded new construction in that year was Lewis Pahlow. He served as master carpenter, timber scout, and in other capacities. In 1866 Allen, McClelland & Com-

19. *Ibid.*, III (March 12, 1891), 3.
20. *Ibid.*, (January 1), 1891, p. 7.

pany launched the tug *William Goodnow* and the sailing scow *Flora*. In the next two years, four more hulls, including the tug *B. W. Aldrich* and the schooner *Rouse Simmons*, were built. Most of their business stemmed from vessel repairs, and they had a floating dry dock that would accommodate at least a 300-ton schooner.

By 1873, their launching ways paralleled the west side of Holton's Slip. The vessels they built were mostly for Milwaukee parties, as were also those of Wolf & Davidson. Prominent among vessel owners ordering ships from the firm were the Fitzgeralds and James and William Porter. One schooner, the *Porter*, built for her namesake and the Fitzgeralds, made such a large wave when she was launched that she succeeded in drenching many people who were watching the launch from the west side of the slip. The force of the wave was great enough to sweep a wagon back several feet.[21]

In 1874 Allen, McClelland & Company sold its holdings to the newly-formed Milwaukee Ship Yard Company. The new company was formed with a working capital of $51,000.[22] John Fitzgerald was president; Andrew M. Joys, secretary and treasurer; and Robert Allen and Lewis Pahlow were in charge of yard operations.[23] The company immediately embarked on a program of expansion and improvement. From E. D. Holton, they purchased a large piece of property adjoining the yard on the west. This purchase extended their river frontage to 340 feet, not including leased land. Changing the course of their slip to run from northeast to southwest eased the access into the slip and made it possible for them to handle larger vessels.[24] Construction was started on a permanent dry dock.[25] Some old sections of the Allen, McClelland & Company floating dry dock were also raised and reconditioned.[26]

When the program was completed, the company's 200 feet of new steam-powered floating dry docks could handle the largest

21. *Milwaukee Sentinel*, March 23, 1874.
22. J. B. Mansfield (ed.), *History of the Great Lakes*, I, 345.
23. *Milwaukee Sentinel*, June 12, 1875.
24. *Ibid.*, August 5, 1874.
25. *Ibid.*, August 13, and 24; September 25, 1874; March 24, April 13, 1874.
26. *Ibid.*, July 11, August 24, 1874.

freighters on the lakes. A ninety-foot reconditioned floating dry dock could take smaller vessels, and a permanent dry dock vessels for major repairs.[27] Company officials experienced some anxiety when the engine house of the new sectional dry dock caught fire during the rebuilding of the schooner *Arab*. Through the exertions of a bucket brigade and the timely arrival of a steam pumper, the flames were quickly brought under control with a minimum of damage.[28] But the incident illustrates one of the great hazards in the early wooden shipbuilding yards.

William L. Kellogg sold his fifth interest in the Milwaukee Ship Yard Company to H. H. and George C. Markham in 1875.[29] Markham, a young lawyer, later played a prominent role in the affairs of the company.

During the late 1870's, the Milwaukee Ship Yard Company's operations were relegated strictly to the vessel repair business. The company began to be secure new vessel contracts again in 1880, and throughout that decade built several small wooden lumber steamers, such as the *C. H. Starke*, *Marshall F. Butters*, and *George C. Markham*. In the late 1880's, the firm built several large wooden freighters for the "Green" fleet, owned by the shipyard's officers and stockholders, John B. Merrill, the Fitzgeralds, and Frank Smith.[30] Among them were the *Omaha*, *Topeka*, *Denver*, and *Pueblo*.

One of the bulwarks of the company, Lewis Pahlow, had a misunderstanding with John Fitzgerald in 1890, and quit without a word of warning.[31] The disagreement did not noticeably alter the operations of the yard, but only one year passed before the two gentlemen were together in a new business venture.

On October 31, 1891, the Milwaukee Dry Dock Company was incorporated by John Fitzgerald, Thomas Davidson, and Frederick C.

---

27.   The new dry dock was 311 feet long, 70 feet wide at the bottom, and had 15 feet of water over the sill.

28.   *Milwaukee Sentinel*, June 23, 1875.

29.   *Ibid.*, August 14 and 26, 1875.

30.   Rev. Edward J. Dowling, "Milwaukee's Freighter Fleets," *Inland Seas*, XV (Summer, 1959), 117-18.

31.   *Marine Review*, II (October 2, 1890), 3.

Starke, all of Milwaukee. The corporation had a capital stock of $413,000, divided into 413 shares valued at $1,000 per share.[32] Thirty-six year old Fred Starke was personally responsible for the merger of the Wolf & Davidson and Milwaukee Ship Yard Companies into this new organization. He purchased the former company the week before for $250,000.[33] Starke was well acquainted with Milwaukee marine affairs as he had captained tugs for his father's Starke Dredge & Dock Company and had managed the Milwaukee Tug Boat Line from 1880 to 1891.[34] He held twice as much stock as anyone else in the new company. The Starke Family, which included Fred, C.H., and William A., held 129 shares. Other prominent Milwaukeeans holding sizable amounts of stock were John Fitzgerald and his son, William E., Thomas Davidson, Andrew M. Joys, Lewis Pahlow, and George C. Markham.[35] The board of directors consisted of Fred and C. H. Starke, John Fitzgerald, Thomas Davidson, Andrew Joys, John B. Merrill, and George Markham. John Fitzgerald was president; Fred Starke, vice-president; and W. E. Fitzgerald, secretary and treasurer.

It is interesting that Commodore William H. Wolf retired from the shipbuilding business and Thomas Davidson came out of retirement. Actually, ever since "Honest Tom" had retired, he had spent almost every day, rain or shine, visiting his old stamping ground. His life was bound up by the shipbuilding business and it was only there that he could find happiness. He died in Milwaukee on February 2, 1895.

Fred Starke managed the old Wolf & Davidson yard, designated the South Yard. The Milwaukee Ship Yard plant, called the West Yard, was managed by William E. Fitzgerald. Starke disposed of his property in the Milwaukee Tug Boat Line, involving six tugs and the steamers *Veronica* and *Helena*, in order to devote full time to shipyard affairs.[36]

---

32.   Minutes of the Milwaukee Dry Dock Company, October 31, 1891, in possession of Edmund Fitzgerald, Milwaukee, Wisconsin, on loan to the Marine & Local History Room, Milwaukee Public Library.

33.   *Marine Review*, IV (November 5, 1891), 5.

34.   J. B. Mansfield (ed.), *History of the Great Lakes*, II, 98.

35.   Minutes . . . Milwaukee Dry Dock Company, November 3, 1891.

36.   *Marine Review*, V (December 31, 1891), 4.

In 1892 and 1893, the newly formed company built its last vessels, the tugs *Golden, Calumet*, and *Henry Gust*, and the small sand steamer *Ellen*. A combination of the financial panic in 1893 and an unwillingness on the part of vessel owners to invest in wooden ships resulted in the Milwaukee yards becoming strictly repair yards. But by its conservative approach to business, the company was able to weather the financial storm in 1893 when firms of comparable size failed.

Early in 1893 the board of directors approved the purchase and lease of land in an expansion and improvement program.[37] The South Yard received a new saw mill, steam hammer, and bolt cutter. Plans were made to extend the dry dock in the West Yard, but this was not accomplished for another four years.[38] A summary of twenty months' business, as of July 1, 1893, showed a net gain of $35,432.47, which justified the improvements.[39]

In 1894, the company was in a relatively good position. It was not caught by a huge expansion expenditure, and its overhead was held to a minimum. The officers were able to negotiate the sale of two sets of "boxes," or sections of floating dry dock, from the South Yard with J. B. Bates, who ran a small repair yard in Chicago.[40] They also purchased the old package freight steamer *Nebraska* to protect an old repair claim they had against her. After cutting the vessel down to a bulk freighter, they sold her to Underwood & Hebard, agents for the Soo Line. The Soo Line chartered her from May 1st to November 3rd for $10,000, with an option to buy the vessel for $26,000, including a $5,000 fit-out bill and rental charges to the date of purchase.[41] The company gained $31,158.30 through the sale of the *Nebraska*.[42] By dealings of this nature, the stockholders received a 4 per cent dividend in 1894.

37.   Board of Directors Meeting, February 15 and March 8, 1893, Minutes . . . Milwaukee Dry Dock Company.

38.   *Ibid.*, July 8, 1893.

39.   *Ibid.*

40.   *Ibid.*, July 12, 1893.

41.   *Ibid.*, Special Board of Directors Meeting, January 2 and 16, February 23, 1894.

42.   *Ibid.*, Board of Directors Meeting, July 12, 1894.

The company did even better in 1895. The season looked more promising to vessel owners, and they were more willing to carry out neglected repairs. This was particularly important to a wooden repair yard because they thrived on the older, smaller wooden vessels. The company declared a dividend of 7 per cent in June, 1895, and still showed a profit of $42,792.95.[43]

The patriarch of the company, Captain John Fitzgerald, died on August 22, 1896. The offices and yards were closed on the day of his funeral, and the workers sent home with a half day's wages. Captain John was spared the humiliation of the "loss" of the *Muskegon* the following month.

On September 22, 1896, the Goodrich Transit Company steamer was placed in dry dock at the West Yard to have a few holding-down bolts on the engine bed tightened. She was an old style sidewheeler with side arches, an octagonal pilothouse, and a beam engine. But she was considered sturdy and in good condition. After the water was pumped from the dry dock, the vessel suddenly slipped off the keel blocks, laid over to starboard, and plunged forward a bit. Those keel blocks that she didn't trip pierced her bottom. Her keel broke in three or four places forward and one aft; both side arches broke clean through; and the cabin forward was broken to pieces and twisted out of shape. After much hard work, she was cleared from the dock, towed to Manitowoc, Wisconsin, and dismantled. One observer said that the accident was caused by the Milwaukee Dry Dock Company's practice of not using horizontal side shores to brace the vessel and by the poor fit of the few bilge blocks that were used.[44] George Markham, the company's legal counsel, searched for some possibility to sue Goodrich for a small amount to save face and to shift some of the burden from the dry dock company.[45] This move was to no avail, and, after extended litigation, the dry dock company lost the suit to the Goodrich Line.[46] Thus the *Muskeg*on had the ignoble distinction

43.   *Ibid.*, June 8, 1895; Annual Meeting of Stockholders, July 15, 1895.

44.   *Marine Review*, XIV (October 1, 1896), 12.

45.   Board of Directors Meeting, September 22, 1896, Minutes . . . Milwaukee Dry Dock Company.

46.   James L. Elliott, *Red Stacks Over the Horizon . . .* , p. 73.

of being ship-wrecked and lost while out of her intended element, and it fell to the lot of the Milwaukee Dry Dock Company to perpetrate the accident.

Prior to the *Muskegon* incident, the stockholders of the company learned that they would be the beneficiaries of a 10 per cent dividend, split into two payments.[47] For the year ending June 30, 1896, the Milwaukee Dry Dock Company showed a net gain of $53,919.71, and a total surplus of $61,680.54.[48] In other actions, the board of directors elected William E. Fitzgerald to replace his deceased father as president of the firm. Andrew M. Joys assumed the position of secretary and treasurer.

Through the stimulus and leadership of William E. Fitzgerald, the conservative Milwaukeeans finally faced reality in 1897. If they were going to compete with other lake shipyards, they would have to make some accommodations to repair steel-hulled vessels. Accordingly, the board of directors appointed a committee composed of the company officers and W. A. Starke to look further into the matter. They reported that the south dry dock could be enlarged for an estimated $30,000. The officers were authorized to erect some overhead trolley work in a new shop that was to house the equipment necessary for steel repair.[49] By the winter of 1897-98, the new tools were installed, and the enlarged dry dock was ready to received its first customer, the steel-hulled steamer *L. C. Waldo.*[50]

The rather grudging accommodations made by the Milwaukee Dry Dock Company to steel-hulled vessels showed immediate results. Fitzgerald read a statement to the board of directors in June, 1898, that showed company earnings for an eleven month period were $251,675.26, compared to $154,208.00 for the same eleven month

47.   Board of Directors Meeting, July 13, 1896, Minutes . . . Milwaukee Dry Dock Company.

48.   *Ibid.,* "Annual Statement of the Milwaukee Dry Dock Company for the Year Ended June 30, 1896," Annual Meeting of Stockholders, July 15, 1896.

49.   *Ibid.,* Board of Directors Meeting, December 24, 1896 and September 25, 1897.

50.   *Marine Review,* XVI (December 16, 1897), 14. The dry dock was extended to 450 feet on the blocks.

period of the previous year.[51] By October, he announced that the amount of business for 1898 was running about $20,000 better than the previous year.[52]

The operations of the Milwaukee Dry Dock Company were small compared to the total steel shipbuilding picture on the Great Lakes. But because of their location and potential, they had to be seriously considered from the competitive standpoint by 1898. Some people felt that Milwaukee could at one time have become a great center for steel shipbuilding. They blamed both Commodore Wolf and the Milwaukee Ship Yard Company for their conservative actions in not seeking outside contracts for fear of "strikes and other adverse influences." They also blamed Wolf for having a "marked determination to enforce his own peculiar ideas upon those who wished to have vessels built."[53]

More than once, the Globe Iron Works, of Cleveland, Ohio, wished that they had started a branch shipyard on Jones Island, rather than on a site in South Chicago.[54]

The site they selected in South Chicago had an interesting history. On October 27, 1832, Commissioners Jonathan Jennings, John W. Davis, and Marks Crume, representing the Government of the United States at the signing of an Indian treaty on the Tippecanoe River in Indiana, deeded two sections of land in the state of Illinois to the Pottawatomie chief Ashkum. The land title filtered down through his daughter, Pa-zhgo, and grandson, Ain-wahw-sa, to relatives of a Belgian missionary who died in Niles, Michigan. Since the missionary's relatives were still in Ghent, Belgium, the land meant little to them, so it passed through several more parties and eventually fell into the hands of the South Chicago Brewing Company.[55] Thus the historic cycle from Indian to firewater was completed.

51. Board of Directors Meeting, June 13, 1898, Minutes . . . Milwaukee Dry Dock Company.

52. *Ibid.*, October 12, 1898.

53. *Marine Review*, IV (December 3, 1891), 6.

54. *Ibid.*

55. Examination to Lots 31 and 32 in Block 16 and All of Block 19 in James H. Bowen's Addn to South Chicago, for D. S. Taylor, Dated December 23, 1881; Abstract of Title to Part of Lot 19 in James H. Bowen's Add. to South Chicago

At a meeting on January 6, 1890, the board of directors of the brewery decided to sell the land to the Chicago Ship Building Company for $4,500.[56] The parcel of land was on the east bank of the Calumet River at 101st Street, about a mile from Lake Michigan. The president of the new shipbuilding company was John F. Pankhurst, who was also the vice-president of the Globe Iron Works, in Cleveland, Ohio. Luther Allen, secretary and treasurer of the Globe Works, was vice-president of the Chicago Ship Building Company.

The new shipyard was a result of the tremendous surge in steel shipbuilding that swept the lakes during 1890-91. In 1890, the Globe Iron Works had contracts for fourteen vessels. They simply did not have enough building ways and, expecting the building boom to continue, they decided to expand. Two of the fourteen contracts were placed with the Chicago branch firm before they even had a shipbuilding plant on the Calumet River.[57]

The yard occupied about twenty-three acres and had a river frontage of 1400 feet. Because of the narrowness of the river, three slips were dredged to accommodate six building berths. The plant layout was unique in that it was designed as a steel shipbuilding yard planned with an eye to the future, though it began with the barest of necessities. Company officials hoped that through a process of gradual additions, they would end up with one of the most modern and efficient shipyards in the country. On the two tongues of land that projected out between the launching slips, they built high trestles on which ran a Brown steam cantilever crane with a center-line capacity of ten tons. They also had a travelling crane at the rear of the punch shop that extended over railroad tracks, making it possible to unload steel plate directly from the cars to the storage area.[58]

Washington Irving Babcock, a graduate of Brooklyn Polytechnic

---

and Part of Block "B" in South Chicago Dock Co.'s Add. to S. Chicago, for Walter F. Cobb, Dated March 11, 1899, abstracts of title in Chicago Ship Building Company Papers, in possession of author.

56. *Ibid.*, Abstract of Title . . . Walter F. Cobb . . . .

57. *Marine Review*, I (April 3, 1890), 4.

58. *Chicago Ship Building Company, Ship Builders and Engineers* (Philadelphia: Armstrong & Fears, 1899), published catalog.

Institute and Rensselaer, became general manager of the new plant. He was thirty-one years old and came directly from the Union Dry Dock Company in Buffalo, where he had been superintendent. Prior to that, he worked for the Morgan Iron Works, John Roach & Sons Shipyard, and the Providence & Stonington Steamship Company.[59] W. I. Babcock proved to be one of the most talented marine engineers to emerge from the lake region. His bold concepts in yard management and naval architecture revolutionized the cost and design of bulk freighters on the lakes.

On July 1, 1890, at 1:40 P.M., the first piece of keel was laid down at the Chicago Ship Building Company. Manager Babcock telegraphed Vice-President Allen that "the event was the occasion of considerable cheering."[60] The vessel was built for the Minnesota Steamship Company, and Robert C. Campbell, as yard superintendent, was directly responsible for her construction. All was in readiness for her launching on March 14, 1891. Streamers of bunting were broken out for the vessels lying in winter quarters in the vicinity. A brass band escorted the many notables to the launching stand from the seven-coach train that brought them from the Pittsburg, Fort Wayne & Chicago Railway depot to the shipyard.[61] A contingent from Chicago Lodge No. 3 of the Excelsior Marine Benevolent Association were easily identified by badges pinned on their lapels. Stocky old Peter White, with his brilliantly white overflowing beard, came down from Marquette, Michigan. Chicago's Mayor Cregier, and Fire Marshal Swenie were there, as were Globe Iron Works' John Pankhurst, Luther Allen, and John Smith. Mrs. W. I. Babcock swung the bottle of champagne, and the *Marina*, the first steel-hulled ship built on Lake Michigan, slid down the ways. The cheers of the 350 shipyard workers and the shrieking of whistles drowned out the sighs of relief from the yard's department "bosses," draftsman J. A. Ubsdell, loftsman Frank Pahlow, patternmaker Frank Brown, joiner A. M. Thompson, machinist

<hr>

59. *Transactions of the Society of Naval Architects and Marine Engineers,* XXV (1917), ff. 340.
60. *Marine Review,* II (July 10, 1890), 7.
61. *Ibid.,* III (March 19, 1891), 5; *Chicago Herald,* March 2, 1891.

George Beers, blacksmith Fred Hull, painter Charles Louis, riveter James Thompson, and yard superintendent Campbell.

The launching of the *Masaba*, the second Minnesota Steamship Company boat, followed three weeks later. Her launching was as successful as the first, except that she suffered a six-inch crack in one plate caused by a timber smashing into it. The company built the steam yacht *Whileaway*, then was forced to shut down for a lack of contracts. A small skeleton crew was retained to care for plant maintenance and small repair jobs. The Globe Company was apparently going to use the yard only when a surplus of contracts demanded it. Before the yard was reopened, an opportunity arose to dispose of it.

In the summer of 1892 the company was reorganized. On July 5, 1892, J. H. Chandler, acting as trustee, purchased 3,500 shares of $100 par value stock from the Globe interests. Two days later, he sold 3,063 shares to twenty-five individuals. The largest single subscriber was Marshall Field with 250 shares. Other large investors included Jay C. Morse, H. H. Porter, A. J. Forbes-Leith, A. A. Sprague, Harvey H. Brown, W. I. Babcock, Samuel Mather, and Orin W. Potter.[62] The Illinois Steel Company was well represented by Porter, Forbes-Leith, and Potter. Emmons Blaine, eldest son of statesman James G. Blaine, was elected president and treasurer; Norman Williams, vice-president; and O. R. Sinclair, secretary and assistant treasurer. They soon contracted for another Minnesota Steamship Company vessel and one for the Cleveland-Cliffs Iron Company.

In June, 1892, the company suffered a shock when their thirty-five year old president, Emmons Blaine, died. He was succeeded by William L. Brown, of Chicago.

By the time the reorganized company's first vessel, the *Maritana*, was launched, they had three more freighters under contract. The *Maritana* was not a credit to the skill of her builders when she first came out of the shipyard because she vibrated so badly. Her engineer, George Waterbury, recalled the return half of her maiden voyage, which was made at half speed because of her condition. When they reached the South Chicago ore docks, Captain Frank D. Root spied

62. Stock Certificate Book, Chicago Ship Building Company Records.

W. I. Babcock walking along the dock to meet them. The slip was long, and there were no other boats in it. Root rang up full speed ahead, then full speed astern, then full ahead again. Waterbury never saw a ship spring as did the *Maritana* on that occasion. Babcock, livid with rage, threatened to have Root and Waterbury removed from the ship for trying to break her in half. George replied that "it would be better to break in the slip than in a gale of wind and then drown everybody." Captain Root's vocabulary was also equal to the occasion. On the *Maritana*'s next trip, she had several experts on board to try to find the cause of the vibration. After a series of throttle maneuvers, Frank E. Kirby, the famous Detroit naval architect, asked Waterbury what he thought the trouble was. Waterbury replied:

> Mr. Kirby, my opinion is, the poor work in the construction, design and weakness in the thickness of steel. The work is not riveted tight, and the engine is too large for a boat such as the *Maritana*, and the construction of the ship is a disgrace to Mr. Babcock the builder.[63]

The cause of the vibrations must have eventually been detected and repaired, because the vessel lived a long life, finally feeling the shipbreakers' torches in 1947.

The next few years saw many changes in and around the shipyard. Late in 1893, Walter F. Cobb became vice-president and treasurer. In 1894, the company built a large dry dock. It was designed by C. V. Powell, of Chicago, and placed in operation on November 1, 1894.[64] James Mowatt, formerly with the South Branch Shipyards Company, of Chicago, was the dry dock superintendent. The southernmost launching slip was used for the dry dock, which reduced the number of building berths by one, but the repair advantages more than justified the move. The Chicago Ship Building Company now had the only dry dock on Lake Michigan equipped to handle major steel vessel repairs.

63. George Waterbury, "Memories of the Steamer *Maritana*, 1892-3-4-5," *Inland Seas*, VI (Spring, 1950), 54-5.
64. Special Notice, *Marine Review*, X (October 18, 1894), ff. 10. The dry dock was 425 feet long, 80 feet wide at the bottom, and had 17 feet of water over the sill.

Shipyards are intriguing places, but during the winter of 1894-95 the Chicago yard was particularly so. Indeed, it took on the appearance of a page from a Jules Verne novel. The whaleback passenger steamer *Christopher Columbus* and another whaleback steamer wintered there. The Spanish caravels, hold-overs from the World's Fair, several steam and sailing yachts, and the new passenger steamer *Manitou* added more flavor. Two big steel barges were receiving their finishing touches, and two steamers and another barge were under construction. A wrecked steamer, the remnant of late season sailing, was being repaired in the dry dock. To complete the apparition, George C. Baker's egg-shaped "submarine boat" was tied up across the slip from the cigar-shaped *Columbus*.[65] That winter was surely unique in the annals of winter lay-up fleets on the lakes!

The Chicago-built steamer *Kearsarge* has already been noted for pioneering the use of channel construction on the lakes in 1894. She also carried a new system of eight electric push buttons on the bridge which, when pushed, raised cards in the engine room with orders such as "Stop," "Back," and "Go Ahead" inscribed on them. A bell rang to notify the engineer as each order was changed and as another card popped up. A button box was also installed in the engine room so that the engineer could acknowledge the orders. A printing mechanism was attached to the system that recorded each order and the exact time it was given.[66] This was in contrast to the old speaking tubes, bell-pulls, and chadburnes then in use. The "pop-up" card system, though novel, was not as enduring as was the channel construction, which is still in common use today.

The Chicago Ship Building Company never fell victim to the "heresies" that afflicted other lake shipbuilders when it came to vessel design. W. I. Babcock continued to build ships along established lines. However, he did have a few ideas that were incorporated into vessel design. The *Victory* and *Zenith City*, built in 1895, had their crews' quarters below deck. There was no after deckhouse and the smoke stacks literally projected up through the deck. Babcock's idea was to

<hr>

65. *Chicago Sunday Tribune*, March 24, 1895, p. 41.
66. *Marine Record*, XVII (June 7, 1894), 5.

keep the deck completely clear of obstructions that might impede or foul the unloading machinery then coming into common use.

Babcock also felt that sails on barges were worse than useless. Should a barge break away from her towing steamer during a storm, he felt that generally the barge could end in worse trouble with sails than without them. If the barge captain had no sails to hoist, he could drift until he could drop his anchors. In Babcock's opinion, the advantage of power gained by the use of sails was more than offset by the cost of upkeep and the great weights involved in masts, rigging, and sails.[67] These ideas resulted in the construction of several large steel-hulled barges by the Chicago Ship Building Company, designed specifically for the iron ore trade.

Most financial cost figures for early steel ship construction on the lakes have long since been lost. But they do exist for three such barges built by the Chicago company in 1895-96, the *Manda*, *Martha*, and *George E. Hartnell*. The contract price for each of the three ships was $135,500, or a total of $406,500. Some of the costs for the total of all three ships were as follows:

Hull: Material	$139,178.05
Labor	88,720.00
Launching	2,215.86
Painting, etc.	6,422.50
Carpentry Work	5,777.77
Joiner Work	7,020.86
Boilers	4,679.01
Outfit	47,463.97

The Chicago Ship Building Company made a total profit on the three vessels of $54,138.71.[68]

During the last half of the decade, the company expanded at a great rate. They enlarged their dry dock in 1897 to stay ahead of the trends in vessel construction on the Great Lakes.[69] In 1896, they hired

67. *Chicago Sunday Tribune*, March 24, 1895, p. 41.
68. Cost Book, Hull Nos. 17-18 and 19, Chicago Ship Building Company Records.
69. The enlarged dry dock was 525 feet long, 80 feet wide at the bottom, and had 18 feet of water over the sill.

Henry Penton, a well-known practical marine engineer. Using the meager machine shop facilities in the yard, he developed one of the first quadruple expansion steam engines on the lakes.[70] Over the winter of 1896-97, Babcock supervised the installation of a complete pneumatic tool system.

Because of the efficient yard operations, the company finished the barge *Carrington* twelve days ahead of schedule, the steamer *Minneapolis* ten days ahead, and the steamer *St. Paul* twenty-three days ahead, and earned a premium of $100 per day per vessel.[71] The last two vessels were launched the same day, one hour apart.

As a result of the frantic building pace conducted by the yard in 1896-97, during which seven big steel-hulled barges and five steamers were launched, the company showed a surplus of about $225,000— after payment of an annual 6 per cent dividend. The surplus was equal to half of the capital stock of the company, which was $450,000. Under the leadership of William L. Brown and W. I. Babcock, the company annually paid a 6 per cent dividend. By 1897 the only debts or obligations carried by the firm were in current accounts. The output of the company in 1896 for new construction valuation was around $1,000,000. By February, 1897, the valuation for that year was already around $900,000.[72]

Company operations were so financially rewarding that during the winter of 1897-98 they again went on an expansion program. The crane facilities were remodelled and increased so that each building berth was serviced by two electric travelling cranes with a five-ton capacity each. Centilever trusses were extended every forty feet along the trestle work between the building slips to further increase the reach and efficiency of the cranes. A new machine shop, constructed entirely of steel and glass, housed heavy machinery for building steam engines, another new operation on the part of the company.

The greatest tribute paid to the Chicago firm came in a telegram from stockholder A. J. Forbes-Leith, of the Illinois Steel Company, to William L. Brown:

70. *Marine Review*, XVI (October 7, 1897), 11.
71. *Ibid.*, XV (April 22, 1897), 11.
72. *Ibid.*, (February 18, 1897), p. 11.

I am told Mr. Yarrow, the English ship builder, had been
all over this country and reported the best equipped ship
building concern, with the best tools which he desired to copy,
was the Chicago Ship Building Co. I think you and Babcock
will be glad to hear this.[73]

One of the things that prompted this compliment from the cradle
of international iron and steel shipbuilding was Babcock's perfecting
of the mould system of construction. This system was made possible
by the high degree of efficiency brought about through the integration
of pneumatic tools, travelling cranes, and placement of shop buildings
in the operation of the yard.

In practice, the system hinged on the modern technique of fabrication in shipbuilding. To develop the mould system of construction,
the keel, center keelson, and all of the angles were erected in position
and riveted on the building way, and the bottom plates were put up
and shored. While this was being done, the floors (i.e., bottom framing), brackets, and stiffening angles were assembled and riveted in
another section of the yard. The assembled floors were then carried to
the travelling overhead cranes by a locomotive crane and lowered into
position across the bottom plating, already in position on the building
way. By this method, the entire bottom of the ship was completed before the sides and their framing were commenced, a broad, firm platform from which to work was provided, and truer fitting of the side
frames resulted. Construction was also quicker and more economical.

By 1899, the Chicago Ship Building Company was the most progressive and productive shipyard on the Great Lakes. From the standpoint of valuation, it was second only to the Cleveland Ship Building
Company, which had two shipbuilding plants. Its meteoric rise was
due to the originality and daring practicality displayed by W. I. Babcock, its general manager and to the progressive forethought displayed by the board of directors under the able leadership of William
L. Brown. Should a consolidation movement take place in lake shipbuilding, the Chicago Ship Building Company could not be disre-
garded.

73.   *Ibid.,* XVII (February 24, 1898), 12, quoting the *Marine Journal,* New York.

5.

The Ends of the Lake

In 1825, the Erie Canal opened the Great Lakes region to the eastern seaboard by way of an all-water route. As commerce developed, it was natural that the two cities at either end of Lake Erie should develop and grow with the shipping trade, as both Buffalo and Detroit did.

A harbor committee met in 1847 to discuss improvements to Buffalo's harbor facilities. In flowery rhetoric it reported:

> Our city, so long as the Erie Canal is in existence, will be, not the only, but the chief and favorite center of intercommunication of the trade of the Lakes and the trade of the seaboard. . . . Our position is secure—established beyond a preadventure. Buffalo must advance with the development of the resources of the exhaustless West. She can pine only when trade declines, and perish only with the utter extinction of the commerce of the Lakes.[1]

1. *Report of the Harbor Committee in Relation to an Increase of Harbor Facilities at the City of Buffalo* (Buffalo: Jewett, Thomas & Co., Printers, 1847), p. 8.

No one on the committee was more aware of this than was Jacob W. Banta of the shipbuilding firm of Bidwell & Banta.

From the outset Benjamin Bidwell was a part of Buffalo shipbuilding. He served an apprenticeship under his brother-in-law, Asa Stanard, who had a shipyard on the North River in New York. In 1808, Stanard came to Lewiston, New York, at the Lake Ontario end of the Niagara River, to build a schooner for Porter, Barton & Company, pioneer merchants from Black Rock, New York. Because of severe ice conditions, Stanard and Bidwell were unable to complete the vessel until the following spring. Porter, Barton & Company then contracted with Stanard to repair their vessels lying at Black Rock, on the Lake Erie side of Niagara Falls. This led Stanard to establish his own shipyard in Black Rock. Benjamin Bidwell stayed with him.[2]

During the War of 1812, Bidwell helped to build Perry's fleet at Erie, Pennsylvania. He also worked on American warships at Scajaquada Creek, near Black Rock, and at Sacketts Harbor, on Lake Ontario. During his absence, he suffered the loss of his house when the British burned the towns of Black Rock and Buffalo in December, 1813. His wife, carrying their sixteen-month old son on her back, escaped by walking through mud and over rough roads to Williamsville, where she spent the remainder of the war.[3]

Sill, Thompson & Company started a shipyard at Black Rock in 1816 and placed Stanard and Bidwell in charge. There they built the schooners *Erie* and *Michigan*. In 1817 and 1818 Bidwell helped the New York shipbuilders Adam and Noah Brown, friends from the war years, to build the first steamboat on the upper lakes, the *Walk-in-the-Water*.

Stanard & Bidwell later joined with James Carrick and continued building ships in the yard on Scajaquada Creek, near Black Rock. After Stanard's death, Bidwell continued the association with James Carrick. This yard turned out many of the early steamboats that plied Lake Erie, such as the *Henry Clay, Daniel Webster,* and *General Porter.* But it was obvious that Black Rock was losing its place of

<hr>

2. *Buffalo Morning Express,* January 1, 1863.
3. *Buffalo Sunday Times,* June 9, 1901.

GENEALOGY OF THE UNION DRY DOCK COMPANY

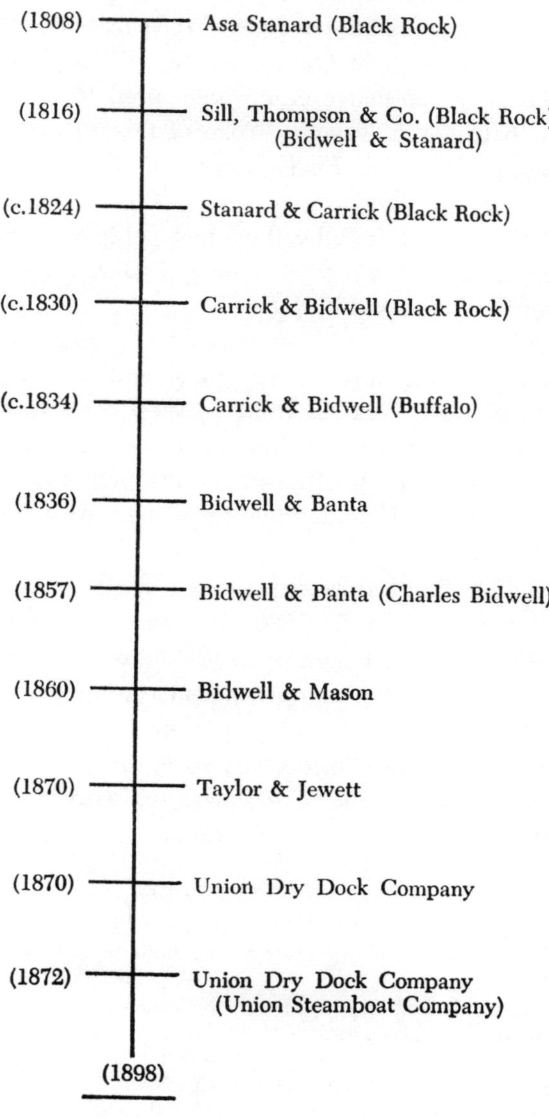

prominence after Buffalo was selected as the terminus to the Erie Canal. The last steamboat built by Carrick & Bidwell at Black Rock was the *New England,* in 1837. One of the difficulties with Black Rock was that the low pressure engines of the early steamboats did not have enough power to fight the current of the Niagara River. Oxen, referred to as a "horned breeze," were used to tow the steamers upstream to the lake. Twenty "Yoke of Ox-(s)team power" were required to pull the *New England* upstream to Buffalo after her launching.[4]

By 1834, Carrick & Bidwell opened a shipyard on Buffalo Creek at Ohio Street, near the foot of Michigan. Here they built the steamers *Victory, Mazeppa,* and *Buffalo.*

In 1836, Benjamin Bidwell formed a partnership with Jacob W. Banta. Banta was apprenticed young and was educated by Henry Eckford of New York. Eckford & Westervelt was one of the best known naval architectural firms in the country at that time.[5] Henry Eckford was in charge of naval construction at Sacketts Harbor during the War of 1812 and, while there, became acquainted with Benjamin Bidwell.

Bidwell & Banta operated a small marine railway powered by a horse-turned capstan. In 1836, they also opened a shipyard on the other side of Buffalo Creek, opposite the foot of Chicago Street. There they constructed a steam-operated marine railway. Two years later, they built the first stationary dry dock on the Great Lakes in their yard opposite Chicago Street.[6] By 1866, this first dry dock, which was perpendicular to Buffalo Creek, was replaced by a larger dock running at a forty-five degree angle from the creek. Also by 1866, the ma-

---

4.   Samuel M. Welch, *Home History, Recollections of Buffalo During the Decade from 1830 to 1840, or Fifty Years Since* (Buffalo: Peter Paul & Brother, 1891), p. 18.

5.   Augustus Walker, "Early Days on the Lakes, with an Account of the Cholera Visitation of 1832," *Publications of the Buffalo Historical Society,* V (1902), 292.

6.   *Marine Review,* XIII (April 23, 1896), 9. The dry dock had 8 feet of water over the sill. Its other dimensions are not known, but it was lengthened in 1844 and again in 1848. For a good coverage of the Buffalo waterfront see Henry A. Baxter and Erik Heyl, *Maps Buffalo Harbor, 1804-1964* (Buffalo: Lower Lakes Marine Chapter of Buffalo & Erie County Historical Society, 1965), pp. 15-17.

rine railway had been replaced by a second dry dock running perpendicular to the creek.[7]

From 1840 to 1860, Bidwell & Banta was the most acclaimed shipyard on the Great Lakes. They competed with the Cleveland shipbuilders for top honors in turning out the lavish "palace steamers" of that era. A typical representative of those classic steamers was the *Baltic*, built in 1847 by the Buffalo firm. She measured 825 tons, was 230 feet long and 53 feet wide. Her 200-foot salon cabin was divided into sixty staterooms, and sixteen of the staterooms were connected by folding doors.[8] "Buckeye" described her "princely" accommodations to Cleveland readers as follows:

> To describe a table loaded with the richest viands would
> require the pen of a "Stephens or Mrs. Childs." The best hotels
> are outdone. Let every body and his wife, in their peregrinations,
> take a trip up the lakes on the *Baltic*, and if they don't
> pronounce it the most delightful journey they ever performed
> you may appoint me Major brevet of the regiment of liars,
> and I will wear "that white hat." The popularity of the boat is
> evinced in the large number of highly respectable
> passengers she carries.[9]

About 1850, Bidwell & Banta centralized all of their shipbuilding and repair business in the yard opposite Chicago Street. With better facilities, the yard produced some of the largest and most famous passenger steamers of the period. Among them were the *Lady Elgin, Northern Indiana, Southern Michigan, Plymouth Rock, Western Metropolis,* and *Western World*. With his more formal training, Jacob Banta served as naval architect. Benjamin Bidwell, with his practical knowledge gained through long experience, served as superintendent. Bidwell's sons also worked in the yard. Charles and Vincent Bidwell, along with F. J. Reynolds, were foremen. John Bidwell was a ship joiner.

7. "Maps of Buffalo Waterfront, 1866," Henry A. Baxter and Erik Heyl, *Maps Buffalo Harbor, . . . ,* p. 19.

8. *Cleveland Weekly Herald,* May 12, 1847.

9. *Ibid.,* June 9, 1847.

In 1857, Benjamin Bidwell retired from the firm and Charles Bidwell took his father's position.[10] This combination lasted only a short time. Jacob Banta left the firm in 1860 to start a shipyard in Chicago. His interests were purchased by Andrew S. Mason, and the firm of Bidwell & Mason continued to turn out vessels. But the grand days of the fifties were gone. They built several tugs and a few freighters, but competition with yards farther west was keen. Ship timber was more expensive and had to be shipped to Buffalo. In 1869 and 1870, they built the steamers *Jay Gould* and *James Fisk, Jr.* Then, after suffering some severe reverses, Charles Bidwell retired.[11]

The yard was taken over temporarily by Taylor & Jewett until a new firm, the Union Dry Dock Company, was organized on September 9, 1870, to take over its operation.[12] This company built the freight steamer *William H. Tweed* in 1871 for the Union Steamboat Company. In 1872, the Union Steamboat Company, which was affiliated with the Erie Railroad, purchased one-fourth of the Union Dry Dock Company's stock. They ultimately acquired complete ownership of the shipbuilding firm.[13]

Captain Marcus M. Drake was appointed superintendent of the dry dock firm in 1871. He was an experienced lake steamboat captain, having come up "through the hawse pipe." In 1861, he enlisted as a private in the 72d New York Volunteers and at the war's end he was a first lieutenant.[14] Drake remained with the Union Dry Dock Company for sixteen years. During that time, the yard launched forty-four hulls of all descriptions. Most of the freighters were built for the parent Union Steamboat Company.

Between 1872 and 1880, the company averaged only one freighter a year, although they did build several tugs. Most of their business came from repairs. The winter of 1872-73 was particularly note-

10. *Buffalo Morning Express*, July 8, 1878.

11. *Buffalo Commercial Advertiser & Journal*, July 8, 1878.

12. J. B. Mansfield (ed.), *History of the Great Lakes*, I, 427; letter, Department of State, State of New York, Albany, to the author, March 27, 1968.

13. J. B. Mansfield (ed.), *History of the Great Lakes*, I, 454.

14. *Marine Review*, XXXVI (October 3, 1907), 62.

worthy. They rebuilt the steamer *Dean Richmond*, which had burned in Mud Lake, below the Sault, in the fall of 1871. The steamers *Elmira* and *Toledo* received new arches, frames, and decks. The schooner *Dan Marble* had her keelsons and keel-box rebuilt and other bottom work done. The biggest job was that of lengthening the *Merchant*, the first iron-hulled freighter built on the Great Lakes.[15] This pioneer iron ship was launched into Evans Ship Canal, only a short distance from the Union Dry Dock site, by David Bell on July 12, 1862. The launching took place at 5 o'clock in the morning to avoid any crowd. The opposite bank of the canal was lined with baled straw to prevent damages in case the vessel got out of control. Fortunately for the future of iron shipbuilding on the lakes, everything went according to plan. When the Union Dry Dock Company lengthened her in 1872-73, they cut her in half, built a new thirty-foot section, then joined the vessel again. They also removed most of her passenger and deck cabins so that she was thereafter exclusively a freight boat.[16]

The iron work done by the Union Dry Dock Company on the *Merchant* was a rarity. The only reason that the company was honored with the job was that it was the closest dry dock to the Buffalo firm of Gibson & Craig, which built most of the iron boats in the early 1870's. The Union Dry Dock Company was still basically a wood shipbuilding yard. In 1874, they launched the steamer *Waverly* with a "cold water" ceremony.[17] She was followed in successive years by the steamers *Starrucca*, *Portage*, *Wissahickon*, and *Avon*. The *Wissahickon* was built in 1876, at a cost of $95,000, to replace the *Merchant* which was lost the year before. She was described as a "beautiful craft in everything but name."[18]

It is to the credit of the Union Steamboat Line that they could keep their shipyard occupied with even one ship per year during this pe-

15. *Buffalo Morning Express*, March 3, 1873.

16. Erik Heyl, *Early American Steamers* (5 vols.; Buffalo: Erik Heyl, 1964), III, 227-28.

17. *Buffalo Morning Express*, May 29, 1874. No bottle-breaking or other ceremony was observed in her launching; thus it was described as a "cold water affair."

18. *Ibid.*, July 3, 1876.

riod. The general stagnation that struck lake shipping and shipbuilding after the financial depression of 1873 showed definite signs of lifting by the spring of 1876. Ship carpenters and caulkers received a daily wage of from $1.75 to $2.00 per day. The *Buffalo Morning Express* reported that if the "managers of our shipyards [are] as niggardly as some would have us believe, . . . the yards could be filled at $1.50 per day."[19] The Union Dry Dock was working about ninety men and expected to double that force within a few weeks. They were building a freighter and a tug and had contracts for another freighter and tug to follow those already on the stocks.

One of the major repair jobs in the spring of 1876 was installing four-inch rock-elm planking on the bottom of the iron-hulled passenger and freight steamer *Japan*, from the keel to the turn of the bilge. It was fastened with iron bolts and nuts having rubber washers. The reason for this was an A-1 insurance rating which indicated that although iron vessels were accepted on the lakes, they had not yet gained the full confidence of the lake underwriters.[20]

The Union Dry Dock Company began to equip their yard for iron work in 1880. The first iron hull designed and built by Marcus Drake was the package freighter *H. J. Jewett*, in 1882. But the Union Steamboat Company and the subsidiary dry dock company were slow to turn to iron, except for repair. The dry dock company built a few iron-hulled tugs in the eighties. They were also the successful bidders on four iron revenue cutters and a steam launch for the Treasury Department. But compared to the other major lake shipbuilding firms, iron shipbuilding plans were relatively quiet in the Union Dry Dock Company yard.

In 1886, Drake built his last iron boat at the Buffalo yard, the *Susquehanna*. His interests had begun to stray from the dry dock's operations in the late 1870's. In 1882, he was appointed interim mayor after Grover Cleveland resigned that position to become governor of New

19. *Ibid.*, February 5, 1876.

20. E. P. Dorr (ed.), *Rules for the Construction, Inspection and Characterization of Sail and Steam Vessels* (Buffalo: International Board of Lake Underwriters, 1876), p. 78.

York. Drake acquired a wide circle of political and business friends and, in 1887, he resigned his position with the Union Dry Dock Company to accept that of superintendent of the Lackawanna Transportation Company. The new job would allow him more freedom to follow his pursuits, whereas running a shipyard kept him tied down.

Drake was succeeded by Washington I. Babcock, who has already been described through his connection with the Chicago Ship Building Company. Babcock stayed with the Buffalo firm for only two years. But in that time he built four freighters and four tugs. Two of the steamers, the *Owego* and *Chemung*, were the fastest freight vessels on the lakes for almost a decade. The 325-foot *Owego* was built in 1888, and her sister ship followed the next year. The former cost over $328,000 and the latter almost $319,000 to build. Oddly enough, the labor costs for the *Chemung* were $8,500 more than on the *Owego*. Steel costs for the hull of the *Owego* were $106,395, compared with the *Chemung*'s $91,408.[21] The great difference in the costs of the two almost identical vessels can be explained by Babcock's ability to negotiate favorable contracts with the steel suppliers.

The negotiation of sub-contracts was critical to the Union Dry Dock Company because the firm had few machines for shaping and fabricating steel. It was a "shipbuilding company" in the strictest sense of the word. The company relied heavily on Carnegie, Phipps & Company, of Pittsburgh, Pennsylvania, for steel plates, and upon the Cleveland Forge Company, of Cleveland, Ohio, and the Delaney Forge Company, of Buffalo, for large castings such as stem and stern posts.[22] The U. F. Palmer, Jr. Company, of New York, furnished the engines for the *Owego* and *Chemung*, but later engines were manufactured by the King Iron Works in Buffalo. Others came from Cleveland and Detroit. Most of the earlier engines were built by H. G. Trout & Company of Buffalo, although the Shepard Iron Works, in the same city, built the *William H. Tweed*'s engine and the Cuyahoga Steam

21.   Abstract of Expenditures, Hull 43 and Hull 44, Buffalo Dry Dock Company Papers, in possession of Christian J. Stellrecht, Orchard Park, New York; microfilm copy in possession of the author.

22.   Godrey L. Carden, "Ship-Building on the Great Lakes," *Harpers' Weekly*, XXXVI (July 23, 1893), 707.

Furnace Company, in Cleveland, built the steam plant for the *Waverly*.[23] Most boilers came from the Lake Erie Engineering Works in Buffalo. In September, 1889, W. I. Babcock left Buffalo to take charge of the new shipbuilding plant in South Chicago. Edward F. W. Gaskin became the new superintendent. Gaskin grew up with iron shipbuilding in Buffalo. His father, John F. Gaskin, worked for the early iron shipbuilding firm of Gibson & Craig, in the Evans Canal in Buffalo. When Ed turned sixteen, he began to learn the machinist's trade from another "iron pioneer," David Bell. He was apprenticed to the Union Dry Dock Company in 1873 and learned the shipbuilding trade under several foremen, including John Lennon, Bill Reed, and Frank Williams. In 1885, he was appointed assistant superintendent of both wood and steel construction. When he became superintendent he was only thirty-four years old.[24]

The yard followed the same basic building pattern under Gaskin as it had done under his predecessors. He built a few package freighters, including the *Brazil, S. C. Reynolds, Codorus,* and *George J. Gould,* but most new construction centered around the building of tugs. The yard continued to prosper from winter repair work gained as the result of Buffalo's being the principal grain-receiving port on the lakes. Its two dry docks were usually filled from fall lay-up to spring fit-out.[25]

During the winter of 1892-93, the plant facilities were reorganized. The dry dock company purchased land adjacent to their yard facing on Buffalo Creek and transferred their steel building equipment to that side of the property.[26] Prior to that time, the steel building yard faced the City Ship Canal. In the winter of 1897-98, the company began to enlarge one of its dry docks. The only notable feature about the dry dock was that a five-foot working space was left between the dry

<hr>

23.   Statement showing Class, Cost, Dimension &c., of Sundry Steamers of the Union Steamboat Company's Fleet, Buffalo Dry Dock Company Papers.

24.   J. B. Mansfield (ed.), *History of the Great Lakes,* II, 504-07.

25.   By this time, the upper dry dock was 343 feet long, 48 feet wide, and had 10½ feet of water over the sill. The lower dry dock was 343 feet long, 44 feet wide, and had 15½ feet of water over the sill.

26.   *Marine Review,* VII (February 2, 1893), 12.

dock floor and the bottoms of the ships, thus permitting more space for the workmen. During that winter, 700 men were employed in the yard.[27] The enlarged dry dock was not completed until February, 1898, when the steamer *S. S. Curry* was floated in for repairs.[28]

The Union Dry Dock Company could now accommodate a 400-foot ship. In 1898, it also added an electric travelling crane that serviced only one building berth, but could be used throughout the yard. These improvements were necessary to keep up with lake shipbuilding trends and to cut labor costs, but they were not designed to place Buffalo in a competitive position with other lake cities for new construction contracts. Even Ed Gaskin spoke in the past tense when he talked about the shipbuilding future of Buffalo:

> Our location was good; but all the timber for building the
> old wooden ships was transported to us from the West, and the
> business went nearer to the source of supply. When the day
> of metal ships dawned, the western builders were in good shape,
> with experienced workmen, established plants and money
> to control the industry.[29]

In other words, Buffalo was left behind by the more energetic western lake shipbuilders. But as long as the grain fleet laid up in Buffalo each year, her shipyards would be important to the vessel owners because of the repair facilities they offered. Buffalo would not be critical to a consolidation movement among the shipbuilders, but nonetheless it would be important.

Whenever a wooden shipbuilding yard located in a town, there was a practical reason for it. Usually it was proximity to timber, with a stream that had suitable depth and a riverbank that was high enough —but not too high—to launch a boat. Sometimes, the town was a terminal point of a particular trade. Such towns were Buffalo, Cleveland, Milwaukee, Chicago, and Duluth. But Detroit was different. It had all the advantages of these towns plus a few more.

27. *Ibid.*, XV (February 11, 1897), 11.

28. *Ibid.*, XVII (February 24, 1898), 7. The enlarged dry dock was 440 feet long on the blocks, 60 feet wide at the gate, and had 16 feet of water over the sill.

29. J. N. Larned, *A History of Buffalo Delineating the Evolution of the City* (2 vols.; New York: The Progress of the Empire State Co., 1911), I, 121.

It was reasonably close to timber resources. It was the junction of several railroads. More than that, it was situated on the main water artery between the Erie Canal and the West. Vessels could stop for repairs with a minimum loss of time and travel. Because vessel traffic was so heavy on the shallow, constricted Detroit-St. Clair River system, there were many accidents that brought added business into the Detroit shipyards.

In 1852, these incentives prompted Canadian-born John Owen, a prominent Detroit citizen, to give up a highly successful drug business and enter the risky shipbuilding business. He was only forty-one years old but he already had been deeply involved with the volunteer fire department, the state temperance society, and the local board of education. He also had been an alderman-at-large, a director on the board of regents for the University of Michigan, and a national presidential elector.[30]

In the fall of 1852, Owen and Gordon Campbell, his partner in the venture, built a dry dock at the foot of Orleans Street, fronting on the Detroit River.[31] They hired Charles C. Keeler as master carpenter and went into the vessel repair business. Keeler was well qualified to run a shipyard, having built the sailing vessels *Robert Hollister* and *St. Marys* at Perrysburg, Ohio, in the late 1840's.

In 1861, Campbell & Owen built their first vessel, the 384-ton bark *Superior*. That summer, they employed eighty men.[32] In the next three years, they built four more sailing vessels and a tug. By 1865 the timber supply was diminished in the Lake Ontario region, and Campbell & Owen hired the well known Clayton, New York, shipbuilder John Oades to superintend their Detroit yard.[33] Oades remained with the firm for two years. In that time, he superintended construction of

30.   Clarence M. Burton (ed.), *The City of Detroit, Michigan, 1701-1922* (5 vols.; Detroit: S. J. Clarke Publishing Co., 1922), IV, 125; Francis Duncan, "The Story of the D & C," *Inland Seas*, VIII (Spring, 1952), 53.

31.   Clarence M. Burton (ed.), *The City of Detroit, . . . ,* (I), 544. The dimensions of the dry dock were 240 feet in length, 54 feet in width, and it had 8½ feet of water over the sill.

32.   *Detroit Tribune*, November 14, 1861.

33.   J. M. Mansfield (ed.), *History of the Great Lakes*, II, 278.

a second dry dock and built the passenger steamer *R. N. Rice.*[34] The *Rice* was built for a stock company in which John Owen owned 20 per cent of the shares.[35]

Between 1867 and 1872, a steady procession of vessels left the ways of the Orleans Street yard. They included eight schooners, five steamers, three tugs, and a small sidewheel ferry. The big Detroit River tug *Champion*, immortalized with its eight-schooner tow by lithographer S. R. Whipple, was by far the best remembered of the early vessels built by Campbell & Owen.

Stephen R. Kirby joined the company in 1869 and assumed charge of the mechanical details of the firm. Kirby learned the shipbuilding trade in the Peck & Masters yard in Cleveland during the 1850's. In 1857, Jesse Hoyt, owner of a large portion of the town of East Saginaw, Michigan, employed him there as a general mechanical engineer. In this capacity, Kirby built the big wrecking tug *Magnet* and the steamer *Reindeer*, several other vessels, and some buildings and mills. By 1865, he was back in Cleveland where he joined Elihu M. Peck to build two revenue cutters for the government. He went to Montana in 1866 to build a stamp gold quartz mill for Hoyt and, in 1867-68, he built a copper mill in the Lake Superior region.[36] Kirby's many talents guided construction in the Orleans Street shipyard for three prosperous years before he left to set up a business in New York.

In 1872, Eldridge G. Merrick, Henry Esselstyne, and John Flower, all of whom owned the Clayton, New York, shipyard, formerly operated by John Oades, joined forces with Gordon Campbell and John Owen.[37] They formed a new company, the Detroit Dry Dock Company, and continued to build ships at the Orleans Street site.

In the same year, the genesis of iron and steel shipbuilding in the Detroit area occurred. Part of it began several years before in East Saginaw, Michigan, when Jesse Hoyt noticed charcoal sketches on the bottoms of feed boxes in the Saginaw lumber mills. Upon inquiry,

34. The second dry dock was 365 feet long, 65 feet wide at the bottom, and had 13½ feet of water over the sill.
35. Francis Duncan, *Inland Seas*, VIII (Spring, 1952), 50.
36. *Marine Review*, XXXIII (February 15, 1906), 21.
37. Frank E. Hamilton, "Notes on . . . Shipbuilding . . ."

Frank E. Kirby, the younger of Stephen Kirby's two sons, was discovered to be the artist. The wealthy Hoyt decided that Frank should have more formal training, perhaps even study under Hoyt's cartoonist friend, Tom Nast.[38] So Frank Kirby went to a Poughkeepsie, New York, school to study, then went to see Nast. But because of a talent for figures that he inherited from his engineer father, Frank ended up studying naval architecture at the Cooper Institute Night School in New York.[39] His first practical experience was gained with the Delamater Iron Works of New York.

On a train during a trip home in 1870, twenty-one year old Frank Kirby was introduced to Captain Eber B. Ward, the other man who brought about the beginning of iron and steel shipbuilding in the Detroit area. By this time, Ward was one of the leading industrialists in the Midwest. In 1864, he and William Kelly introduced the Bessemer process of steel production to the United States at the Eureka Iron & Steel Company, Wyandotte, Michigan. His family also controlled a large line of lake steamers. It was natural that the two interests should be combined. Ward had the rare quality of recognizing talent in individuals, and Frank Kirby created a good impression. Ward thought more about his ideas and in 1871 brought Frank and his older brother, Fitz Albert, commonly called "Joe," to Wyandotte to build an iron-hulled ship.

Frank and Joe Kirby supervised construction of a machine shop and dock at the foot of Plum Street in Wyandotte. In the early spring, 1872, they laid the keel to a large iron tug. The 136-foot *E. B. Ward, Jr.* was launched in August, 1872.[40] The engine was built by the Samuel F. Hodge Company, and the boiler by J. & T. McGregor, both of Detroit. Frank Kirby designed them both.[41] Fifty pounds

38.   John Hubert Greusel, "Frank E. Kirby, Designer of Vessels," *Detroit Free Press,* January 7, 1906.

39.   Gordon P. Bugbee, *The Lake Erie Sidewheel Steamers of Frank E. Kirby* (Detroit: Great Lakes Model Shipbuilders' Guild, 1955), p. 6.

40.   Newspaper clipping, n.d., "Local History, Industrial/Shipbuilding" folder, Pamphlet & Miscellaneous file, Wyandotte Public Library, Wyandotte, Michigan.

41.   Newspaper clipping, n.d., quoting *Wyandotte Herald,* Frank E. Kirby Scrapbook, Vol. I., Burton Historical Collection, Detroit Public Library, Detroit, Michigan.

of steam, making 100 to 125 revolutions, propelled the tug at a speed of twenty miles an hour. She made the trip from Detroit to Cleveland, a distance of 120 miles, in seven hours and thirty minutes, causing the comment that the Kirby's "first boat . . . has turned out to be such a success, . . . It will certainly bring them orders for more of the same class."[42]

Also in 1872, the Kirbys built the neat little sidewheel passenger steamer *Queen of the Lakes* for Dexter & Noble of Elk Rapids, Michigan. The hull lines of later Kirby-designed steamers were already apparent in this vessel, designed for river and inland lake navigation. She cost about $24,000 to build.[43]

In the fall of 1872, Frank went with his mother and father to Europe where he had a chance to observe English iron shipbuilding methods. This trip was to be repeated many times in his life. Although the saloon passenger list of the Cunard liner *Baltic* included Senator Charles Sumner, it is not known whether or not the Kirbys made his acquaintance.[44] Joe Kirby stayed home to begin construction of another tug.

In 1873 the Kirby Brothers launched the iron tug *Sport*. Frank later recalled that "there was a pile of ingots in the mill yard which I had rolled into plates from which I got more than enough good stuff to build the boat. I sold the surplus to the Detroit Safe Company."[45] The small iron shipbuilding company also built the boilers for the steamer *Amazon*, then building downriver at Trenton, Michigan.

The maiden trip of the *Sport* almost proved to be the death of Eber Ward. In the spring of 1873, the tug went to New Jerusalem, Ohio, about thirteen miles east of Toledo, to pick up a new barge built there for the Ward interests. During the night, a gale grounded the

---

42. *Ibid.*

43. Walter C. Cowles, "Queen of the Lakes," *Inland Seas*, XX (Spring, 1964), 54.

44. Salon Passenger List, *S.S. Baltic*, November 14, 1872, from Liverpool to New York, Frank E. Kirby Scrapbook, Vol. I.

45. "Dedication of Carnegie Library, Girardin Notes, no date," type-written copy, Shipbuilding Notes, Notebook II, Wyandotte Public Library, Wyandotte, Michigan.

barge in two feet of mud at the entrance to Ward's Canal. Ward was standing at the stern of the tug while she was straining to pull the barge off. A seven inch line snapped, and one end flew back and struck him a glancing blow on the head, knocking his hat into the water. Had it struck him three inches lower, he would have been killed.

The steam yacht *Myrtle*, built in 1875, was the next Kirby creation. She was seventy feet long, only eight feet wide, and fast. The *Detroit Free Press* described her as "the only boat on the Lakes that could make a hole in the water, and then get out of it quick enough to see it."[46] Shortly after she was built, the "cigar-shaped" craft was loaded onto a platform car, hauled to Cairo, Illinois, and launched into the Mississippi River. She was towed down the river to New Orleans, taking time out on the way down to defeat the river tug *DeSoto* in a race at Memphis, and was placed in service carrying the United States Mail from the Crescent City to Eads's Jetties.[47]

Eber Ward died in 1875, but not before he purchased more land near the foot of Plum Street from the Wyandotte Silver Smelting & Refining Company and the Eureka Iron & Steel Company.[48] Ward's last will and testament suffered through lengthy litigation, but in 1877, a reorganized Detroit Dry Dock Company, composed of the old company stockholders and the Kirby Brothers, purchased the Wyandotte shipyard. They merged it with the Orleans Street yard in Detroit. The new officers were John Owen, president; E. G. Merrick, treasurer; Alexander McVittie, a Canadian-born Scotchman who joined the company as a bookkeeper in 1872, as secretary; and Frank Kirby, as consulting engineer of the "iron shipbuilding department." The board of directors consisted of Owen, Merrick, R. P. Toms, Stephen R. Kirby, and Henry Esselstyne.[49] The planning of a new

---

46. Newspaper clipping, Toledo, Ohio, c. June 8, 1875, Frank E. Kirby Scrapbook, Vol. I.

47. *Vicksburg Daily Herald*, n.d., *Ibid.*

48. Assignment of Properties from Detroit Ship Building Company to Biddle Avenue Realty Corporation, June 18, 1930, Property Deed, Detroit Ship Building Company Papers, in possession of author.

49. Advertisement, J. W. Hall (comp.), *Hall's Record of Lake Marine Embracing: The Marine Casualties of 1877, Rules of Navigation—Collisions—Insurance—*

passenger steamer by the Detroit & Cleveland Steam Navigation Company was the reason for this reorganization.

The D & C Company considered building a "composite" ship. Composite hulls were built of closely-spaced iron frames upon which oak planking was longitudinally fastened. Iron plates covered the wood planking from the waterline to the main deck.[50] The opportunity presented itself in 1875 when the D & C steamer *Northwest* suffered several engine breakdowns. These led the owners to consider replacing her. A new wooden hull would cost about $49,000. A hull diagonally strapped with iron would cost an estimated $55,000, while the cost of a composite hull was estimated at $67,860.[51] In August, 1875, the "Wyandotte Iron Ship Building Company" offered to build an iron hull to the dimensions of another D & C steamer, the *R. N. Rice*, for $80,000.[52] But as business conditions worsened, the steamer line decided instead to install the second-hand engine from the old steamer *Detroit* in the suffering *Northwest*.[53] The old engine was lying on the wharf of the Detroit Dry Dock Company yard at Orleans Street, and the D & C Company paid $12,000 for it.[54]

The D & C steamer *R. N. Rice* burned in 1877 and presented the company with a second opportunity to build a new ship. They entered into a contract with the Detroit Dry Dock Company to build a composite hull for the *Rice*'s machinery. The directors of the D & C company levied an assessment on the stockholders to raise the necessary capital, estimated at $95,000.[55] When some of the stockholders re-

---

Courses and Distances—Steamboats and Propellers; also, the Names of Deceased Captains, Etc., Etc. (Detroit: William Grahams Steam Presses, 1878), p. 126.

50. William A. McDonald, "Composite Steamers Built by the Detroit Drydock Company," *Inland Seas*, XV (Summer, 1959), 114.

51. Francis Duncan, *Inland Seas*, VIII (Fall, 1952), 170-71.

52. *Ibid.*, p. 171, n. 7.

53. "Great Lakes Vessels with Second-Hand Engines," notebook compiled by the author.

54. Francis Duncan, *Inland Seas*, VIII (Fall, 1952), 170-71.

55. *Ibid.*, (Winter, 1952), p. 270, quoting Directors' Meeting, July 17, 1877, *Record of the Board of Directors' Meetings, (1868-1897)*, p. 124, *Detroit & Cleveland Steam Navigation Company, D & C Papers*, in possession of Fred Kolowich, of the Detroit & Cleveland Navigation Company; hereafter cited as *D & C Papers*.

fused to pay the levy, Secretary David Carter was forced to arrange for the sale of the delinquent shares. In this way 4,622 shares changed hands. The greatest numbers were purchased by three men: John Owen, who remained the single largest stockholder in the D & C company, James McMillan, and John S. Newberry.[56] Both of the newcomers were prominent Detroit industrialists who grew wealthy through the establishment of the Michigan Car Company, manufacturers of railroad cars.

The new sidewheeler was named the *City of Detroit*. She was followed two years later by a sister ship, the *City of Cleveland*, built at a cost of $154,673.07.[57] The latter vessel represented an advance in paddle-steamer design in that she carried the first "feathering" wheels used on the Great Lakes.[58] The old style paddle-wheels had rigid blades that "slapped" the water as they struck. They not only made considerable noise, but they wasted power. On the feathering wheels, the blades rotated just enough to permit them to enter the water at a more perpendicular angle and stay in that position longer. This reduced the noise and gave greater power. Between the two "City" boats, the Detroit Dry Dock Company also launched the small iron passenger steamer *Grace McMillan*, named after James McMillan's daughter. She was built for other McMillan interests.

The shipbuilding tempo picked up in the early 1880's. The Orleans Street yard was used for wooden construction. The building ways were at a right angle to the river, and the ships were launched stern-first. All iron construction was done at the Wyandotte yard, then towed to Oreleans Street for fitting out and the receiving of machinery. Most attention was focused on the Wyandotte yard where Joe Kirby was superintendent, and Frank Kirby naval architect.

When times were good, experienced labor was at a premium. By the late fall of 1880, Joe Kirby was already experiencing difficulty with the riveters, who were "addicted to drinking, and therefore

56. *Ibid.*, p. 271.
57. *Ibid.*, p. 272, quoting loose-leaf notebook entitled *General Manager, Detroit & Cleveland Navigation Company, D & C Papers.*
58. *Detroit News*, May 14, 1880.

rather irregular at their work."[59] Joe tried to solve this problem by converting ship carpenters to riveters and was at least temporarily successful. But labor was only one of the problems confronting the rapidly expanding Wyandotte yard.

In December, 1880, Joe went on a tour of eastern tool manufacturers but was able to purchase only $10,000 worth of iron shipbuilding tools. The factories were sold out as much as a year in advance. The solution to Kirby was simple—use one of the new company buildings to construct their own tools. The company purchased 100 feet of land from the Eureka Iron Works and erected another building. It also enlarged the building slip to handle more new construction.[60]

Still another problem was obtaining enough iron. The Eureka Iron & Steel Company ws producing ten to twelve tons of iron plate per day. By working day and night, the iron company was achieving the best rate of production in their history, but it still was not enough. They were forced to give up one contract with the shipbuilding firm and permit them to go elsewhere for iron.[61]

The need for experienced workmen finally became so acute that the Detroit Dry Dock Company recruited contract labor from Scotland. On February 19, 1881, a force of 114 Clyde shipbuilders, who presented "the appearance of sober, hardworking, intelligent men . . . ," arrived in Wyandotte. They agreed to come for six months at a stipulated wage in exchange for their travel expenses. At the end of that time, they would have their expenses paid back to Scotland or, should they choose, receive the equivalent in money.[62] The night of their arrival, the town held a party for them at Maple Hall. The stage was decorated with greenery that spelled out "Welcome to Wyandotte." Food abounded, cigars were passed out, the usual speeches were made, and everyone joined in song and entertainment. The warm feelings of welcome manifested by the local populace dissipated rapidly.

59. *Wyandotte Herald*, December 17, 1880.
60. *Ibid.*, December 24, 1880.
61. *Ibid.*
62. *Ibid.*, February 25, 1881.

Joe Kirby soon discovered that by paying his new arrivals $2.00 per day, he was not getting even a half day's worth of work from them. On March 12th, he tried to cut their wages and the Scotsmen promptly threatened to demolish the shipyard. Although they received their full wages, their Scottish feelings were ruffled and they began drinking. Then they went on a rampage and broke windows in some of the boarding houses, insulted "decent" women on the street, and finally fell asleep in fence corners and on snow drifts. Some chased a shipyard employee, but they soon tired of this sport after five of them were " 'laid out' by the brawny arm of the 'wild Irishman'. . . ."[63] In April, more of the Scots went on a Sunday drunk and drove a horse and buggy up and down Wyandotte's streets until the horse became heated. So they drove it into a ditch to cool it off, "showing the natural intelligence of the Scotch mind when full of liquor."[64] It was obvious that though the Scotsmen were getting their bellies full of liquor, the local citizens were getting their bellyful of Scotch.

The Scotsmen soon learned that though they received a higher daily wage in Wyandotte than on the Clyde, they actually realized less because of time lost by bad weather and because of the higher cost of living. Their Scottish temperaments were not soothed when they learned they were paid considerably less than resident workmen, and that some old hands were laid off when they arrived in Wyandotte.[65] When their contracts expired, most of the Clyde shipbuilders returned to their homeland, "satisfied that in the trade they were full as well off there as here," much to the relief of Wyandotte.[66]

During the interim of Scottish "influence," the Detroit Dry Dock Company experienced their greatest output of ships in the decade of the eighties. In 1881, they launched ten vessels, half of which were built of iron. In 1883-84, another ten vessels were built. With their yards full of new construction, and with an eye toward the repair business, the Detroit Dry Dock Company leased the John P. Clark shipyard in Detroit.

63.   *Ibid.*, March 18, 1881.
64.   *Ibid.*, April 15, 1881.
65.   *Ibid.*, April 22, 1881.
66.   *Ibid.*, October 28, 1881.

GENEALOGY OF THE DETROIT DRY DOCK COMPANY

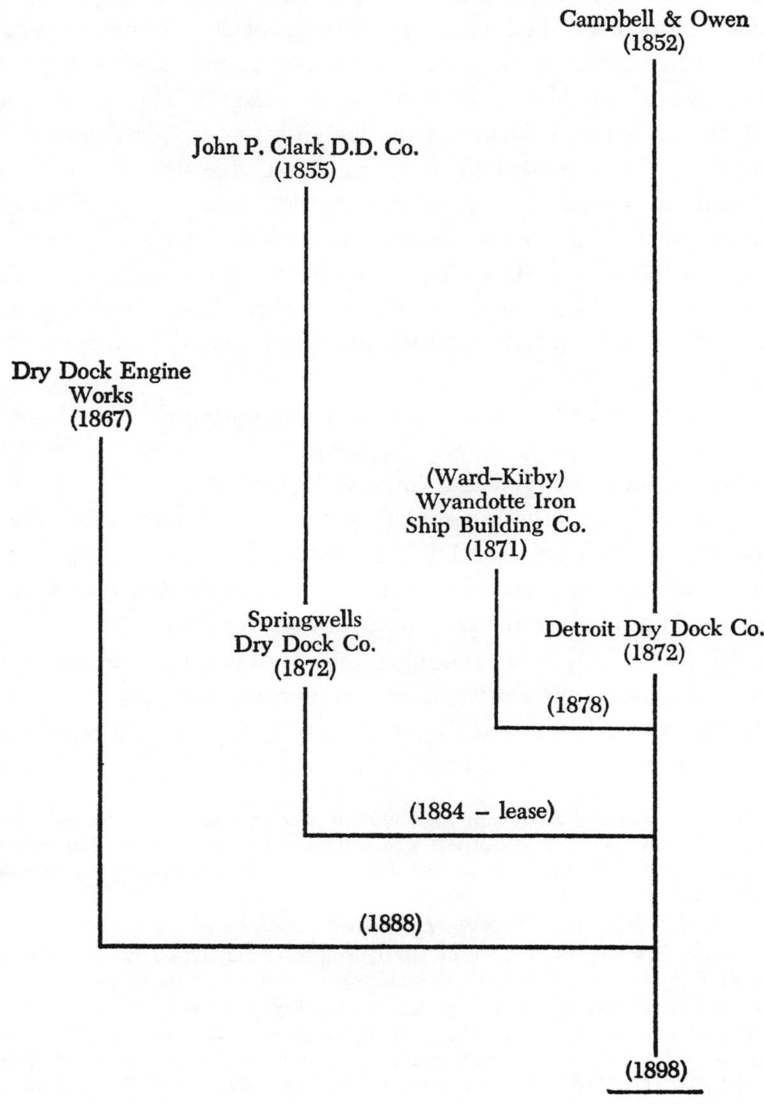

The Clark shipyard, usually referred to as the Springwells yard, was started in 1855 when Clark built a dry dock at the foot of Clark Street, about three miles below Woodward Avenue.[67] John P. Clark was anything but a shipbuilder. He made considerable money in the commercial fishing business on Lake Michigan and also engaged in some towing and vessel interests on the lakes.[68] The Springwells yard was primarily a repair yard although a few wooden ships were built there. Clark depended on hiring good superintendents to run his dry dock. Two of the early superintendents were George Irwin and John Stupinsky. Stupinsky later ran his own yard between Hastings and Rivard Streets in Detroit.[69] Some of the steamers built in this yard, such as the *Jay Cooke* and *Gazelle*, were familiar sights on the river and around the Lake Erie islands. Clark retained a financial interest in many of them.

In 1866, Clark added another dry dock and purchased more land to give him wider access to the slip just below the dry docks.[70] The additions very much enlarged and improved his winter repair capacity. By 1872 Clark, apparently decided to withdraw his personal attentions from the shipbuilding business and he leased the yard to the well known Cleveland shipbuilder Elihu M. Peck.[71] Clark maintained this type of business arrangement until his death in 1888.

In 1874, Elihu M. Peck brought in John Drackett to build the large wooden freighter *John Pridgeon, Jr.* Drackett worked as foreman and master carpenter for several shipbuilders from Cleveland to Saginaw.

67. *Marine Review*, XIII (April 23, 1896), 9. The dry dock was 220 feet long, 60 feet wide, and had 12½ feet of water over the sill. Lewis, John, and Hiram Ives built a dry dock at the foot of Swain Avenue in 1851. There is a possibility that the two dry docks were one and the same.

68. J. B. Mansfield (ed.), *History of the Great Lakes*, II, 66.

69. *Detroit Tribune*, November 14, 1861. Stupinsky purchased the shipyard of John McDermott, which was the oldest shipyard along the Detroit River.

70. Land Sale Agreement between Detroit Ship Building Company and William McBain, of Toronto, Canada, January 6, 1913, Detroit Ship Building Company Papers. The dry dock was 368 feet long, 66 feet wide, and had 11½ feet of water over the sill. The *Marine Review* (see note 67) says this dry dock was built in 1857, but this is doubtful.

71. Frank E. Hamilton, "Notes on . . . Shipbuilding . . . ," quoting an advertisement from 1872.

He was superintendent of the Peck & Masters yard in Cleveland in the early 1860's, which prompted his reunion with Peck in Detroit.[72] Under Drackett's supervision the yard built the *Pridgeon, Jr.,* the passenger sidewheeler *Pearl,* and converted the revenue cutter *John Sherman* to a passenger steamer. Drackett left Detroit in 1876. It is not known who succeeded him. In 1878, the sidewheeler *Alaska* was the last vessel built at the Springwells yard.

The Springwells Dry Dock Company was operating the yard by 1882. Edward T. Peck was overseeing its operations, although Elihu M. Peck was still involved with the yard.[73] It is very possible that the Detroit Dry Dock Company had an interest in the Springwells Company by this time.[74] J. C. Parker was yard superintendent.

In June, 1884, John Owen and Alexander McVittie signed a two-year lease with John P. Clark for the use of the Springwells yard at an annual rental of $1,318.58.[75] The lease was extended for a year in 1886, with Clark retaining the right to use the slip on the east side of the yard for wintering vessels "at the same rate as E. M. Peck."[76] In 1887, the lease was again extended for a year. The same terms were agreed upon, except for a rental increase of $500—to $10,500—and that the "lessees shall saw in their Mill, at cost, any Timbers that may be required for the repair of Dry Dock."[77] Finally, in 1888, the Detroit Dry Dock Company obtained a five-year lease at $8,000 rental per year, with the same basic docking privileges.[78] John P. Clark died in

72. J. B. Mansfield (ed.), *History of the Great Lakes,* II, 686.

73. Receipts, Springwells Dry Dock Company, May 3, 1882, to the order of Detroit Dry Dock Company, in names of E. T. Peck and E. M. Peck, Detroit Ship Building Company Papers. The receipts are for dividends on stock to be paid to the Detroit Dry Dock Company by the treasurer of the Springwells Dry Dock Company. The relationship between E. M. and Edward T. Peck is unknown. E. M. Peck had two children, both of whom died while still young.

74. *Ibid.,* July 10, 1884. Receipts made on this date are in names of both Pecks, Alexander McVittie, Frank E. Kirby, and T. J. Darling. The latter married Kirby's sister.

75. Lease between Detroit Dry Dock Company and John P. Clark, June 27, 1884, Detroit Ship Building Company Papers.

76. *Ibid.,* May 3, 1886.

77. *Ibid.,* June 11, 1887.

78. *Ibid.,* June 20, 1888, pencilled notation on cover of envelope marked "Clark Dry Dock Co. Leases."

September of that year. Clark's heirs continued to hold the yard until 1899.

By 1884, the Detroit Dry Dock Company controlled four dry docks, two wooden shipbuilding and repair yards, and one iron shipbuilding plant along the Detroit River. During the decade of the eighties, they built sixty-six hulls, including twenty-one iron and seven composite ships. A great variety of crafts slid down the ways: schooners, bulk and package freighters, railroad car ferries, and sidewheel passenger boats.

With John Owen as president of both the D & C Navigation Company and the dry dock company, the shipbuilding firm built three sidewheelers for the steamer company in the eighties. All were designed by Frank E. Kirby, and all followed the tradition of their owners by being named after cities into which they traded: *City of Mackinac*, a second *City of Cleveland*, and a second *City of Detroit*.[79] When the contract for the last of the trio was signed in 1887, the delivery date was set for May 1, 1889, "unless hindered by strikes, lockouts, accidents or other causes" beyond the control of the dry dock company.[80]

The lake shipping business was booming in 1887. The dry dock company had four boats valued at $1,000,000 on the ways. With boom times, shipyard labor was difficult to find. Joe Kirby again turned to imported labor, but he did not go so far this time. On February 3, 1887, twenty-five Maine ship carpenters arrived at the Wyandotte yard, with the likelihood that another fifty might be required. They were described as "old fashioned in their manners, but quiet and industrious—a welcome contrast to the Scotsmen who were imported several years ago."[81] Shortly before the arrival of the Pine Staters, James McMillan, who had "plenty of money" and was "a business hustler from way back," purchased the controlling interest in the De-

---

79. The first *City of Cleveland* was renamed *City of Alpena* and the first *City of Detroit* later became *City of the Straits*.

80. Francis Duncan, *Inland Seas*, IX (Spring, 1953), 31, quoting Directors' Meeting, September 7, 1887, *Record of the Board of Directors' Meetings (1868-1897)*, p. 165, *D & C Papers*.

81. *Wyandotte Herald*, February 11, 1887.

troit Dry Dock Company.[82] This "business hustler" became the junior senator from Michigan two years later. In the same year, 1889, he became president of the Detroit Dry Dock Company. John Owen went into retirement.

The last three years of the decade were relatively uneventful. Ship launchings had long since lost their novelty. With the shipbuilding company enjoying the prosperity of the lake trade, the people connected with the dry dock company had few problems. The only group that appeared to be out of step were the riveters at the Wyandotte yard. In April, 1887, the dry dock company granted a 10 per cent wage increase to all employees. This raised carpenters' wages to $2.75 per day. On July 11, 1887, the following notice was posted on the gate at the shipyard:

> To all workmen, including riveters:
> The habit of losing time, especially on Monday, will not be permitted hereafter.
> The timekeeper is instructed to report any one not here on regular working hours.
> Any workman employed in this yard who cannot work steadily each whole working day need not work at all.
> F. A. Kirby, Supt.[83]

The men remained at work all that week, but the following week, about ninety men, mostly shipfitters and riveters, stayed away. This meant that others were laid off for lack of work. Joe Kirby refused to talk with the men as a group. Instead he walked about the yard and promised to raise wages on an individual basis. By July 25, the strike was broken, and the local newspaper reported that "everything is lovely and the goose hangs high. . . ."[84]

Twenty joiners went on strike in 1888 when the company refused to fire a non-union joiner who had reneged on his promise to join the union. The strike was not officially approved, caused no great inconvenience to the operations of the yard, and was not expected to be a

82. *Ibid.*, January 28, 1887.
83. *Ibid.*, July 22, 1887.
84. *Ibid.*, July 29, 1888.

"gilt edged success."[85] The strikes were minor diversions during a period of prosperity—incidents in the normal course of events in any good-sized business.

An event of a more serious nature occurred on September 1, 1888. Shortly after midnight, a watchman discovered smoke in the blacksmith shop at the north end of the iron shipbuilding plant. He awoke Alexander McVittie, who was sleeping in the office. McVittie got steam up in the boiler so the fire hoses could be used, but the blacksmith shop was totally destroyed. Eight forges and a furnace for heating angle iron were in the building. The loss was set at from $6,000 to $7,000, only half of which was covered by insurance.

In 1890, the capital stock of the Detroit Dry Dock Company was increased from $400,000 to $600,000. The stockholders included James McMillan, William C. McMillan, Emory Wendall, Edmund J. Owen, Frank E. Kirby, and Alexander McVittie.[86]

The experience of the company during the decade of the nineties was similar to that of the other steel shipbuilding yards on the lakes. Steel gradually replaced wood as construction material. The Orleans Street yard was still used for repair work and for installing machinery in the steel hulls. The reason for this was the subsidiary engine company owned by the dry dock company, the Dry Dock Engine Works. The engine works started as a separate company in 1867, with William Cowie, Edward D. Jones, and Robert Donaldson as incorporators.[87] Their plant was located at Dequindre and Atwater Streets, across the street from the Orleans Street shipyard.

William Cowie was one of the founders of Cowie, Hodge & Company in 1863, a Detroit engine manufacturing company that later became famous as Samuel F. Hodge & Company. Cowie retired from that company in 1865 and two years later joined forces with Jones and Donaldson. Robert Donaldson worked for William Barclay, another of the founders of the Hodge company. Two years after leaving Barclay's employ, he joined with Jones and Cowie in the new engine

85.　*Ibid.*, May 18, 1888.
86.　*Ibid.*, January 31 and May 2, 1890.
87.　*Detroit Tribune*, February 1, 1867.

company venture. With Donaldson acting as superintendent, the company gradually gained fame and success, much of it coming from the construction of marine engines. The company continued in business independently until they sold out to the Detroit Dry Dock Company on November 3, 1888.[88] By this time, the firm employed over 300 men.

The only property that the engine company did not own on Atwater, between Orleans and Dequindre Streets, was the two-story brick Dry Dock Hotel which, in 1888, was leased to Robert and Mathilde Horne for a boarding house and saloon.[89] Because of its proximity, this must have been a source of satisfaction to foundrymen and shipbuilders alike. Unfortunately, this too came into the possession of the engine works in 1892, giving them possession of the entire block.[90]

After the hotel property was acquired, the interior of the Dry Dock Engine Works was entirely rebuilt. Electric travelling cranes were installed, and several large steel-shaping machines added. The boiler shop, on the opposite corner of Dequindre and Atwater Streets, was also improved, and a railroad siding was brought in from the Detroit, Grand Haven & Milwaukee Railroad. This siding ran straight down Dequindre Street to the shipyard. The company was limited, however, to the movement of cars "not propelled by steam power except between the hours of 6 P.M. and 7 A.M."[91] Despite this poorly worded stipulation, the improvements placed the Detroit Dry Dock Company in a competitive position by 1893, just in time for the financial panic of that year.

A new slip was completed in 1892 at Wyandotte which doubled that yard's facilities. The dry dock company had under contract for delivery in 1893 four steel and one wooden steamers and a tug, totalling $1,365,000.[92] This, plus the McMillan Family resources, per-

---

88.   J. B. Mansfield (ed.), *History of the Great Lakes*, II, 288.

89.   Lease between Anna Maria Klintwort and Robert and Mathilde Horne, Detroit, Michigan, July 1, 1888, Detroit Ship Building Company Papers.

90.   *Ibid.*, Discharge of Mortgage, Anna Maria Klintwort to Dry Dock Engine Works, May 27, 1892.

91.   Railroad ordinance approved by Detroit City Council, May 14, 1889, filed and accepted by Detroit Dry Dock Company, July 15, 1892, *Ibid.*

92.   *Marine Review*, VI (November 3, 1892), 13.

mitted the company to weather the financial storms of the next two years.

In 1895, the Detroit Dry Dock Company showed a paid in capital of $600,000, and the Dry Dock Engine Works, $400,000. The principal stockholders were James McMillan, Gilbert N. McMillan, Hugh McMillan, William C. McMillan, Frank E. Kirby, and Alexander McVittie.[93] In that year, another important figure, Charles B. Calder, was hired as superintendent of the Dry Dock Engine Works. Calder spent three years as fleet engineer for M. A. Hanna & Company, of Cleveland, before joining the firm.[94]

Calder kept a daily journal of shop happenings and the entries give interesting—and sometimes humorous—insight into the daily routine of the engine plant. On March 13, 1895, James C. Wallace, of the Cleveland Ship Building Company, tried to get Calder to finish some boilers for him. Calder commented that "their men struck on. Could not take them as our men would strike."[95] A few weeks later, vesselman John Shaw came in "cussing us for what we *did not* do."[96] But one of the most depressing decisions that Calder faced was effected in November, 1895, when he "decided to let the Girls go in the Drawing office."[97] Unfortunately, he gave no hints as to the cause of his decision, nor did he comment upon the effect of his decision on office morale.

During the last four years of the century the company launched eight steel steamers. One of them, the passenger steamer *City of Erie*, was the first steamer built for the Cleveland & Buffalo Transit Company, and the last steamer on the Great Lakes to carry a famous Fletcher beam engine. The C & B Line encountered some difficulty in raising funds to build the vessel. The proposed steamer was to cost $375,000, with the C & B Transit Company paying $10,000 in cash and providing notes for the balance. Senator McMillan did not think that

<hr>

93. Newspaper clipping in back page of journal, n.d., [Charles B. Calder], Daily Journal, 1895, Toledo Ship Building Company Papers, in possession of author.
94. *Toledo Blade*, November 27, 1905.
95. Journal entry, March 13, 1895, [Charles B. Calder], Daily Journal.
96. *Ibid.*, March 27, 1895.
97. *Ibid.*, November 15, 1895.

the shipbuilding company should assume such a burden because the risks of disaster and competition on the part of the C & B company were too great.[98] When it was suggested that the Dry Dock Engine Works could invest in the new steamer, McMillan was afraid to "load the concern with securities that may be difficult to dispose of."[99] He was particularly upset with the eastern engine builders because

> the Fletcher people who have had our business for so many
> years should not be willing to take their share of the securities.
> If it is possible to build engines ourselves or get some one else
> to do so, I should certainly favor such a course, unless those
> people did the proper thing. Of course we cannot take risks
> when building such boats but it is disgusting when you meet
> people who are not willing to accommodate their customers.[100]

The Senator was trying to get the Fletcher Engine Company to assume $100,000 in notes.[101] He evidently succeeded, because Mr. Fletcher arrived at the Dry Dock Engine Works on June 1, 1898, when the *City of Erie*'s engines were worked for the first time.[102]

Senator McMillan's influence in Washington was very useful in selling steamer bonds for new construction. But the influence and prestige earned by Frank E. Kirby in the field of naval architecture and marine engineering went far beyond Washington.

Kirby-designed sidewheeler passenger vessels are still remembered as the most graceful hulls to float on inland waters. One of these, the *City of Mackinac*, is still in service today as a humble floating platform for the Columbia Yacht Club in Chicago. The symmetry and curves of her hull rival those of the submarine *Silversides*, moored on the opposite side of the Naval Armory, and they completely eclipse the angular modern clubhouse perched on top of the old hull.

98.   Letter, James McMillan to William C. McMillan, Washington, D.C., March 6, 1897, James McMillan Correspondence, Burton Historical Collection, Detroit Public Library, Detroit, Michigan.

99.   *Ibid.*, March 22, 1897.

100.   *Ibid.*

101.   *Ibid.*, March 9, 1897.

102.   Journal entry, June 1, 1898, [Charles B. Calder], Daily Journal.

Kirby devised the plan of putting a propeller on the bow of ice breakers on the lakes. When he noticed that the car ferries on Lake Michigan often made better progress when going astern in ice, he designed the car ferry steamer *St. Ignace* in 1888 with a bow propeller. In action, the car ferry kept her bow against the pack ice by using her main engines. By working her bow propeller in reverse, a stream of water was sent onto the ice, breaking the grip of separate blocks. When the motion of the bow propeller was reversed, the lumps of ice were carried aft by the streams of water thus created.[103]

The Russian Government became interested in Kirby's ice breaker designs and sent representatives to Detroit during the winter of 1894-95. They asked Kirby to come to St. Petersburg to discuss the possibilities of such a vessel for use on Lake Baikal, in connection with the Trans-Siberian Railroad. Kirby drew up plans and, arriving in St. Petersburg, deposited his plans with the Russian officials. Afterward, he was so shunned by the Russians that he gave up in disgust and departed. The czarist regime literally stole the plans and later gave a contract for the ice breaker to Armstrong, Whitworth & Company, of Newcastle, England, to be built from Kirby's designs.[104]

At the beginning of the Spanish-American War, the United States found themselves with virtually no troop transports. The Secretary of War contacted Kirby and asked him to serve as consulting engineer. On Kirby's recommendation, the War Department purchased fourteen ships, totalling $6,000,000. Then Kirby took charge of their remodelling, and by commuting at night between New York and Newport News, he had them ready in record time.[105] Frank traveled much of the time at his own expense, and when he rendered a bill to the government for a reported $50,000, vesselmen agreed that the bill was a reasonable one and that he earned every penny of it.[106]

103.   Robert Runeberg, *Steamers for Winter Navigation and Ice-Breaking* ("Excerpt Minutes of Proceedings of The Institution of Civil Engineers," Vol. CXL, Session 1899-1900, Part ii; London: The Institution of Civil Engineers, 1900), p. 9; *Marine Review*, XII (October 10, 1895), 6.
104.   Robert Runeberg, *Steamers for Winter Navigation . . .* , p. 10.
105.   John Hubert Greusel, *Detroit Free Press*, January 7, 1906.
106.   *Wyandotte Herald*, December 16, 1898.

Frank's mind went in many directions. He was intensely interested in steam yacht design, and in 1890 was elected president of the Detroit Boat Works.[107] He made many trips to Europe, and his scrapbooks are filled with technical literature and marine engineering catalogs from European sources. The same was true of his personal library.[108] Nothing was too trivial for inquiry. His scrapbooks contain many examples of artwork, scrolls, and interior decorating schemes that later appeared in modified forms in the interior of his passenger ships. He was interested in improving a self-righting lifeboat. He designed marine hardware, from door knobs to hurricane lamps, all of which carry his name. He even invented an improved steam whistle.

Yet, despite his inventive genius, should someone stop by and interrupt him, Frank would drop everything to sit and "yarn." If someone needed something, Frank would stop what he was doing and take care of it, even if it required travelling. His brother, Joe Kirby, had many of these qualities, though he was not so imaginative as Frank. Their talents complemented rather than competed with each other.

When the Navy needed riveters to aid in raising two Spanish cruisers sunk at Santiago, Frank and Joe Kirby saw to it that the Detroit Dry Dock Company sent twenty men to handle the job.[109] The company would never have attained the high reputation with lake vessel owners that it enjoyed without Frank and Joe Kirby. When it was apparent that steel shipbuilding techniques were giving other yards a slight advantage over the Wyandotte yard, Joe invented machines that helped to narrow the competitive gap. He devised a machine for cold plate flanging and for opening and closing angles.[110] As early as 1896, the company tested a portable riveter with satisfactory results.[111] They later turned almost completely to pneumatic tools.

107. *Marine Review*, II (July 3, 1890), 2.

108. Charles E. Gardiner, Rare Book List No. 320, Bayside, New York, 1968, lists several examples from Kirby's library.

109. *Wyandotte Herald*, August 5, 1898.

110. *Marine Review*, XVII (June 9, 1898), 13.

111. Journal entry, April 30, 1896, [Charles B. Calder], Daily Journal.

With the financial mind and influences of James McMillan, the sharp eye for overall shipyard operations of Alexander McVittie, and the inventive and imaginative minds of the Kirby Brothers, the Detroit Dry Dock Company was in a good position in 1899 to consider any consolidation movement among lake shipbuilders. They had at their command an engine manufacturing plant, a steel shipbuilding plant, and four dry docks along the heavily-travelled Detroit River that could not be ignored. Although their firm had a long continuous history, they were not wedded to that tradition. They were not leaders in accepting innovations in shipyard techniques, but once the techniques proved successful, the Detroit company would accept and install them. It would not take them long to catch up with leaders such as were found in Chicago or Cleveland.

The *Pueblo* was typical of the large wooden freighters built by the Milwaukee
Ship Yard Company in the 1880's. Picture is at Oswego, New York.
Author's Collection.

When Milwaukee's Wolf & Davidson Ship Yard Company launched the
Ferdinand Schlesinger in 1891, her name matched her length. She was one of the
longest wooden freighters on the Great Lakes. *Author's Collection.*

The Wolf & Davidson-built *Fred Pabst* was said to have carried the suggestiveness of a floating brewry because of her ornamental beer kegs. One can be seen alongside the mid-ship deckhouse. *Marine Historical Society of Detroit.*

A cartoon in *Marine Review* shows Samuel Mather's agent, Henry G. Dalton, playing John D. Rockefeller's game of accepting bids for new ships in 1895. *Left to right*: James Wallace, Cleveland Ship Building Company; Frank Kirby, Detroit Dry Dock Company; Frank Wheeler, Wheeler & Company; John Pankhurst, Globe Iron Works; Alexander McDougall, American Steel Barge Company; and Washington I. Babcock, Chicago Ship Building Company.

Left to right: William E. Fitzgerald, Milwaukee Dry Dock Company. *Author's Collection*. Washington I. Babcock, Chicago Ship Building Company. *Author's Collection*. and William L. Brown, Chicago Ship Building Company. *Author's Collection*.

The barge *George E. Hartnell* ready for launching at the Chicago Ship Building Company in March 1896. *Author's Collection.*

The *Hartnell* is a good example of the large steel barges built for the iron ore trade. She received engines in 1923 and was scrapped in 1937 as the Canadian steamer *Portsmouth*. *University of Detroit Marine Collection.*

The steamer *Cadillac* being launched on May 24, 1892, at the Chicago Ship Building Company. Notice latticework alongside unfinished steamer *Thomas Maytham* in background. *Cleveland-Cliffs Iron Company.*

The *Maritana* was a disappointment to her Chicago builders because she vibrated so badly on her maiden voyage in 1892. *Author's Collection.*

Washington I. Babcock pioneered the use of channel construction in lake steamers with the building of the *Kearsarge* in 1894. *University of Detroit Marine Collection.*

In 1895 Babcock did away with the after cabins of the *Victory* (*above*) and the *Zenith City* to keep the deck clear of obstructions which might foul unloading machinery. *Author's Collection.*

A rare photograph showing the "big splash" of the barge *Aurania* at Chicago in 1895. The ore-carrying barges carried small steam engines for steering purposes. *Author's Collection.*

Left, Edward F. W. Gaskin, Union Dry Dock Company, Buffalo, New York. *Author's Collection. Right*, Frank E. Kirby, Detroit Dry Dock Company. *Author's Collection.*

Check from the Detroit Dry Dock Company to the Spring Wells Dry Dock Company in 1884, signed by Frank E. Kirby. *Author's Collection.*

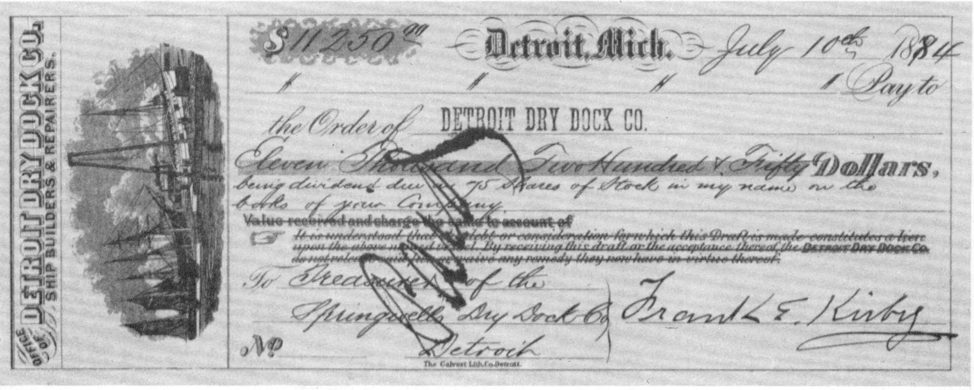

Bidwell & Banta built several large wooden sidewheelers in the mid-nineteenth century including the unfortunate *Lady Elgin*. She was sunk by collision on Lake Michigan in 1860 with the loss of 287 lives. *Frank E. Hamilton*.

The *H. J. Jewett* was the first iron hull designed by Marcus M. Drake and was built by the Union Dry Dock Company in Buffalo in 1882. *Frank E. Hamilton*

The *Owego* cost over $328,000 to build at Buffalo in 1888. She and her sister, the *Chemung*, "carried the broom" on the lakes for almost a decade. *University of Detroit Marine Collection.*

The "iron yard" of the Detroit Dry Dock Company at Wyandotte, Michigan, in the 1880's. *University of Detroit Marine Collection.*

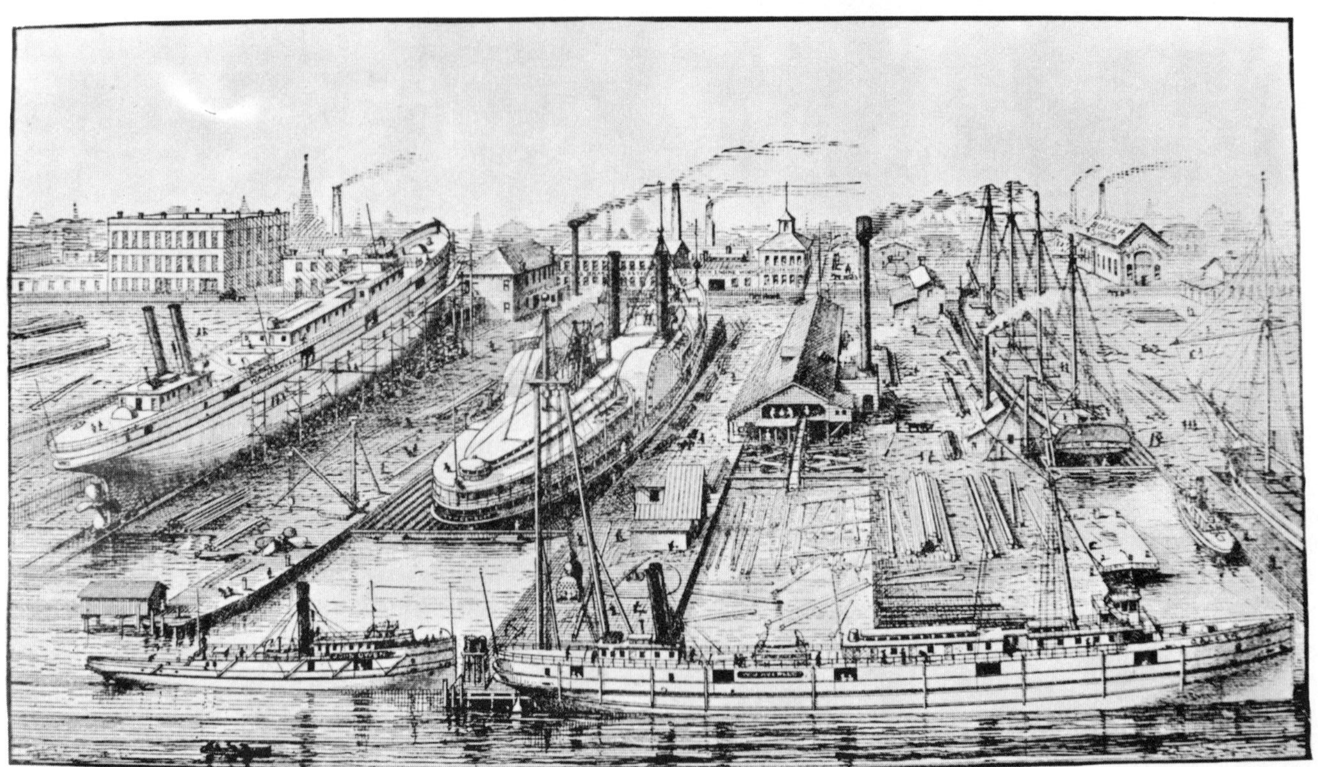

The Orleans Street yard of the Detroit Dry Dock Company in about 1884. The Dry Dock Engine Works and Dry Dock Hotel can be seen facing the shipyard. *University of Detroit Marine Collection.*

Frank E. Kirby designed the sidewheeler *City of Mackinac* in 1883. Her fine hull lines are hidden beneath the overhang of the deck. *University of Detroit Marine Collection.*

To the biased eye of a true ship lover, the modern clubhouse of the Columbia Yacht Club in Chicago lends little to the symmetry and curves of its platform—the hull of the *City of Mackinac. Author's Collection.*

Launching the bow half of the ocean
steamer *Keweenaw* at the Wheeler
shipyard, Bay City, Michigan, on May 2,
1891. The stern half had already been
launched. Notice the gantry crane in the
middle of the picture. *Michigan Pioneer
and Historical Collection.*

Frank Wheeler, Wheeler & Company,
Bay City, Michigan. *Author's Collection.*

The steamer *Keweenaw* shortly after both
sections were water-born. *Bay County
Historical Society.*

The four-masted schooner *John C. Fitzpatrick* ready to be dropped into her natural element at Wheeler's yard in Bay City, May 31, 1892. *Bay County Historical Society.*

The steamer *Merida*, another Wheeler-built ship, originally carried her boilers and engines amidship to equalize the strain in carrying iron ore. This proved impractical, and the machinery was later moved to the stern. *Author's Collection.*

The wooden freighter *Iosco*, built under the supervision of George F. Williams, ready for launching on April 25, 1891, at the Wheeler yard. *Michigan Pioneer and Historical Collection.*

The three-masted schooner *Moravia* being launched at Bay City in 1888. This was the only recorded stern launching at the Wheeler yard. Passenger steamer *Soo City* and the tug *Tempest* in the foreground. *Red Keg Press.*

The *Emily P. Weed* was the first steel ship built by Frank Wheeler at Bay City. She was later lost as the *Sevona*. *Robert J. MacDonald.*

Wheeler & Company built the tug *William H. Brown* in 1896 for New Orleans parties. She was sold to the Navy in 1898 and served in the Philippines. Later reduced to a barge, she was presumed sunk by the Japanese near Mindanao in 1941. *Michigan Pioneer and Historical Society.*

6.

Wheeler of Bay City

Chesley Wheeler learned the shipbuilding trade in Chaumont, New York. When, by 1865, a depleted timber supply had reduced Lake Ontario's shipbuilding role to almost nothing, Chesley and his wife, Eliza, with their two sons, moved to East Saginaw, Michigan. There he resumed his shipbuilding trade.[1] The Saginaw River was crowded with logs during the late 1860's and 1870's as the lumber boom reached its peak in that area. As soon as Chesley's oldest son, Frank Willis Wheeler, finished school, he went onto the river as a tug boatman. During the winters he helped his father in the ship repair business.

In the early 1870's, Frank left the river to join his father in the oper-

1. Augustus H. Gasser (ed.), *History of Bay County, Michigan, and Representative Citizens* (Chicago: Richmond & Arnold, 1905), p. 616; letter from Clarence M. Burton to Joint Committee on printing, Congress of the United States, March 22, 1926, Clarence M. Burton Papers, Burton Historical Collection, Detroit Public Library, Detroit, Michigan.

ation of a floating dry dock in Saginaw. They moved the dry dock further down river in 1876 to take advantage of deeper water at West Bay City. The following year, Frank left his father to go into the ship-building business with Albert A. Crane, a Bay City hardware merchant.[2] Frank borrowed $3,000 from a wealthy Bay City sawmill operator, H. W. Sage, to join the partnership.[3] The firm of Wheeler & Crane built four tugs, a barge, and a small passenger steamer in the next three years.

In 1880, Frank won the contract to build two large wooden package freighters, the *Lycoming* and *Conemaugh*, and sub-contracted them to Frederick Nelson Jones, who came out from Buffalo to build them.[4] In the next ten years, Frank Wheeler launched over fifty wooden ships.

As late as 1884, he was not ready to expand on the tremendous scale later evidenced. In that year he sub-contracted the barge *Alta* and steamer *Waldo A. Avery* to Thomas F. Murphy, a Cleveland ship-builder.[5] In January, 1886, Wheeler hired the former assistant superintendent of the Union Dry Dock Company of Buffalo, George F. Williams, as superintendent of his Bay City yard. Wheeler's success increased with this association.

George Williams served his apprenticeship under Frederick N. Jones in Buffalo. Later, he returned as Jones's superintendent after the latter moved to Tonawanda, New York. Williams and his brother, H. J. Williams, also ran their own yard in Buffalo for a short period of time. He had been with the Union Dry Dock Company since 1878.[6]

Under Williams's guidance, the yard, located directly across the Saginaw River from the present-day Defoe Ship Building Company plant, built seven large steamers and two schooners in the next two years. This was just a warm-up for 1888!

By April, 1888, Wheeler paid 670 employees over $7,000 every

2. *History of Bay County, Michigan, with Illustrations and Biographical Sketches of Some of its Prominent Men and Pioneers* (Chicago: H. R. Page & Co., 1883), p. 194.

3. *Bay City Daily Tribune*, October 3, 1889.

4. *Buffalo Commercial Advertiser & Journal*, September 17, 1880.

5. J. B. Mansfield (ed.), *History of the Great Lakes*, II, 671.

6. *Ibid.*, pp. 436-37.

other Saturday night.[7] He expected to increase the working force to 900 within a few weeks to cope with construction of several vessels at one time. Some of the vessels included the *Robert L. Fryer, Servia, Soo City,* and *Moravia.* The last-named vessel, a three-masted schooner, was unique in that she was the only Wheeler-built ship to be launched stern-first, so crowded was the yard.[8] But Wheeler was looking beyond the present crowded conditions. In May, he purchased a large tract of riverfront property adjacent to his shipyard, formerly occupied by a chemical company, and he ordered machinery for the construction of steel ships.[9] He hired Fred W. Ballin, chief draftsman for the Detroit Dry Dock Company for the past seven years, to take charge of the designing department.[10]

Frank appeared before the city council and made a proposition to benefit his blossoming shipyard. With the lumber trade falling off, he knew that the town was dependent in no small part for its livelihood upon the healthy condition of his shipyard. He also knew that he would have to go out on a financial limb to put his expansion program into effect. He proposed that the assessed valuation of his land and plant facilities be allowed to remain as it then was for a period of ten years.[11] This policy conflicted with the state charter, but the council appointed a committee to study the problem. Within a week the committee circulated a petition among the citizens of Bay City pledging themselves to this commitment, which they did.[12]

In the fall of 1888, Frank Wheeler was nominated to run as Republican representative to Congress from the Tenth District of Michigan. The district had been dominated by a Democrat, Spencer O. Fisher, for two terms. Fisher stood for free silver and a "reduction of taxation upon the clothing, blankets, shelter and other necessities of the laboring and producing classes."[13] Wheeler was pushed into the political

7. *Bay City Evening Press,* April 9, 1888.
8. *Ibid.,* April 18, 1888.
9. *Ibid.,* May 16, 1888.
10. *Ibid.,* June 14, 1888.
11. *Ibid.,* June 22, 1888.
12. *Ibid.,* June 27, 1888.
13. *Ibid.,* October 8, 1888.

arena by his own workmen, half of whom were Democrats.[14] By his own admission, Wheeler decided to accept the nomination after only a few days' consideration if it were tendered to him. He looked upon the issue as simply being one of free trade or protection, and he believed in the latter.[15]

"Bangor," in a letter-to-the-editor of the Democratic *Bay City Evening Press*, attacked Wheeler's exemption from the tax rolls that resulted from the petition circulated by members of the city council the previous spring. "Bangor" pointed out that Wheeler was paying a total of $190.59 in city and county taxes for personal property assessed at $5,000, or a 3 8/10 per cent tax, while the total value of boats, either under construction or recently launched, came to $545,000. Wheeler, he argued, should have been paying $20,710.00 per year in taxes.[16] This was the only charge that Wheeler's opposition could come up with that succeeded in reaching him. The Wheeler forces answered the charges by printing a pamphlet which showed that in 1883 Wheeler & Crane enjoyed a tax reduction, but they also showed that the deciding vote in favor of the reduction was passed by the mayor, Spencer O. Fisher, Albert Crane's brother-in-law. The pamphlet further showed that the petition circulated by the city council in 1888 was signed by Fisher, Thomas Toohey, S. P. Flynn, and other prominent Democrats.[17] It contained a petition signed by 350 members of the Ship Carpenters' and Caulkers' Union denouncing Fisher and supporting Wheeler. Thus the odd political situation developed in which workingmen crossed party lines to support the rising young capitalist in the aura of a benefactor rather than as an employer.

Wheeler swung into an old fashioned campaign that would make a hit in a small town such as Bay City. He gave the usual "if elected" speeches. He presented an elaborate banner to the Harrison & Morton

14. "Labor and Capital in Harmony," newspaper clipping, n.d., Frank W. Wheeler Papers, Michigan Pioneer & Historical Collection, Ann Arbor, Michigan.
15. "Frank W. Wheeler, Bay's Candidate for the Congressional Nomination," *Bay City Daily Tribune*, n.d., *Ibid.*
16. *Bay City Evening Press*, October 5, 1888.
17. "To the Laboring Men—Tenth District," October 26, 1888, pamphlet, Frank W. Wheeler Papers.

Republican Club which they strung across Midland Street. On it were pictures of Harrison and Morton and a large ocean vessel labeled "For Congress, F. W. Wheeler."[18] George L. Alexander, of the Grayling Glee Club, wrote a six-stanza campaign song to the tune of "When Johnnie Comes Marching Home." The first verse went:

Oh! Wheeler is the man for us, Hurrah! Hurrah!
Oh! Wheeler is the man for us, Hurrah! Hurrah!
He builds good ships. Don't slight the plan
And pays good wages to the workingman.
And they all feel gay when Wheeler comes home again.
And they all feel gay when Wheeler comes home again.[19]

It was a good thing for Frank that he did campaign for the election. When the results came in, it looked as if Fisher were the winner. A recount gave Wheeler 18,959 votes to Fisher's 18,844. Wheeler won by the scant majority of 115 votes![20]

By 1889, Wheeler was employing between 700 and 1,000 men, plus 300 teams of horses.[21] With the steel shipbuilding plant under construction, Wheeler took the next step in developing his shipyard. On January 18, 1889, the F. W. Wheeler & Company, a stock corporation, was organized with a capital stock of $350,000.[22] Wheeler was president; George F. Williams, vice-president; J. R. Goodfellow, a former Montana rancher, treasurer; and F. L. Gilbert, a Bay City lumberman, secretary.

On September 16, 1889, the new company laid the keel of their first steel-hulled ship, and the only sidewheeler built by Wheeler, the *City of Chicago*, for the Graham & Morton Line. She was launched amid festivities on March 18, 1890. But the real banquet was withheld until

18. *Bay City Daily Tribune*, October 2, 1888.
19. "The Wheeler Campaign Song," broadside, Frank W. Wheeler Papers.
20. "Official Canvass of Votes Given for State Officers and Representatives in Congress, at the Election Held on November 6, 1888," fold-out table in *Official Directory and Legislative Manual of the State of Michigan for the Years 1889-1890* (Lansing: Darius D. Thorp, 1889), ff. p. 424.
21. *The Industries of the Bay Cities* (Bay City: A. N. Marquis & Co., 1889), p. 86.
22. *Bay City Daily Post*, June 7, 1890; *Marine Review*, I (April 3, 1890), 1.

the launching of the second steel vessel from the Wheeler yard, the bulk freighter *Emily P. Weed*, named for the daughter of the famous New York editor and politician, Thurlow Weed.

As a switch, the shipyard workers sponsored the banquet to honor the employers. The Knights of Pythias band escorted the various company officers from their residences to the dining hall. Included in the culinary display were raw oysters, ham, veal, pickled lamb's tongue, three salads—lobster, potato, and shrimp—angel food, chocolate, and cocoanut cake, brandy and champagned jelly, fresh fruits, and many other delicacies. At the launching festivities, Wheeler's young daughter, May, clipped the ribbon suspending the christening bottle with a pair of golden scissors.[23] The yard and dining hall were elaborately decorated, but the decoration that would give the most unsettling thoughts at a later date to Frank Wheeler consisted of a representation of an arm and hammer with the motto "Labor conquers everything."[24]

The Wheeler yard built two vessels in 1890 that were unique to the lake shipbuilding industry. They were steel vessels designed for the ocean trade. Wooden vessels had been built for the ocean trade, but the unusual aspect of Wheeler's craft was that he had made them 290 feet long while the Canadian canals were only 185 feet long! When Wall Street vessel broker Samuel Holmes tried to find a major shipyard on the east coast to build the vessels, he found that they were filled with government and other contracts. He turned to Frank Wheeler for the ships. Two Saginaw men, Arthur Hill and James Jerome, along with Holmes, formed the Saginaw Steel Steamship Company. The hulls of the vessels were constructed in a series of twelve-foot steel plates. At the junction of each plate, on the inner side, was a steel strap wide enough for double rows of rivets. Temporary wooden bulkheads were installed at the junction ends of the ships.[25] They were launched in halves. The first of the two ships, the *Mackinac*, was joined, ran to Buffalo under her own steam, was cut in half at

23.   *Bay City Daily Post*, June 7, 1890; *Marine Review*, I (June 5, 1890), 1.
24.   *Marine Review*, I (June 12, 1890), 2.
25.   *Chicago Inter Ocean*, April 27, 1890.

Buffalo for the trip through the Canadian canals, and then was rejoined at Montreal. By towing the second vessel, the *Keweenaw*, in halves from Bay City to Montreal for joining, some of the cost to her builder was reduced. Considerable difficulty was experienced in joining the *Mackinac* because the Montreal dry dock was so shallow that the riveters could not take a full swing with their hammers. Great quantities of dirt had to be dug away before they could satisfactorily join her.[26] One of the vessels suffered the unusual occurrence of having a dent in her stern made by her own stem! The mishap occurred when the ship was being taken through the Lachine Canal with the stern section preceding the bow section.[27] Wheeler was able to compete with coastal shipyards on these contracts because of cheaper labor, despite the added expense of joining the vessels at Montreal.

In the spring of 1890, Frank Wheeler excited the Great Lakes region with news of another kind. His taking a trip to England caused rumors to float across the seas that he was selling out to an English syndicate. A Mr. Stephenson, representing some English capitalists, having visited Bay City in January, 1890, gave credence to the rumors. In March, 1890, Wheeler acknowledged that he was on the verge of accepting a proposition whereby the capitalization of a reorganized F. W. Wheeler & Company would be set at $3,500,000, with the Wheeler people retaining half of the new capital. The old Wheeler plant was set at $750,000.[28] At the last moment, Wheeler telegraphed the English syndicate that the deal was off. He said that he had decided that any business enterprise that would be a good thing for the English syndicate would be equally good for himself. He further concluded that

> the only way to make anything worth while out of such a
> syndicate arrangement is on the basis of fancy prices, and that
> sort of business is pretty certain to react eventually and cause no
> end of serious trouble for all concerned.[29]

26. *Marine Review*, II (November 6, 1890), 4.
27. Comments by J. E. Thayer and George L. Craig, in W. I. Babcock, "Longitudinal Bending Moments of Certain Lake Steamers," *Marine Review*, XXXII (November 30, 1905), 28.
28. *Chicago Tribune*, March 7, 1890.
29. *Marine Review*, I (May 15, 1890), 7.

The real reason was more deep-rooted. Frank learned that the trades' council had appointed a committee to determine whether he had violated the law by importing skilled labor from Canada under contract. This upset Frank, and he declared that he did not propose to build up a large business in a small town where "labor agitators cannot keep on their own side of the fence."[30] Another reason was that real estate flanking the shipyard property advanced about 100 per cent, which Wheeler considered neither "fair nor public spirited."[31]

Frank denied the charges of violating alien contract laws, and when real estate values returned to normal, he purchased more land with the idea of setting up his own engine shop. To accomplish this, he found it necessary to increase the capital stock in his company to $500,000.[32] When he finished his project, he had the largest and most modern shipyard on the Great Lakes.

The F. W. Wheeler & Company appeared to be on the threshhold of becoming the most productive shipyard on the lakes, but 1891 proved to be a disappointing year. The tone was set in January when Frank Wheeler sued James Davidson for $100,000 in damages for libel. Davidson operated a large wooden shipbuilding yard and dry dock a short distance upstream from the Wheeler yard in Bay City. Frank claimed that Davidson had persistently circulated reports among customers and business associates in Bay City, Detroit, and Buffalo that injured his credit and business. He further maintained that Davidson said that the Wheeler Company was insolvent, that they could not pay fifty cents on the dollar, that some creditors were being frozen out so that other favored ones could get security on the property. He charged that Davidson had told some of his men who had money deposited in a Bay City bank, which reportedly held Wheeler securities, that they had better withdraw their deposits.[33]

James Davidson countered by denying some of the charges. He did mention that the commercial agencies reported Wheeler's indebted-

<hr>

30. *Grand Rapids Leader*, March 14, 1890.
31. *Ibid.*; *Chicago Tribune*, March 14, 1890.
32. *Marine Review*, I (June 5, 1890), 1.
33. *Bay City Daily Tribune*, January 25, 1891.

ness at about $548,000, and that the parties in Buffalo and Detroit knew about Wheeler's security and his extension from creditors. Davidson added that he was willing to stand by anything he had said about Wheeler and that it would "take at least five years to settle the suit."[34] The court proceedings were ultimately dropped, but it showed the great strains under which Frank Wheeler was operating in order to enlarge his facilities. It also revealed the animosity that developed between the two local shipbuilding competitors.

The prospects for new steel shipbuilding contracts were not good in the winter of 1890-91. Wheeler employed only about 200 men. The only major steel job was lengthening the one-year old steamer *City of Chicago.*[35] In the spring, the company's capital was again increased—to $600,000. Rumors floated about that the Flint & Pere Marquette Railway Company was a large stock purchaser, and that the Michigan Car Works was going to establish a branch shop in Bay City through dealings with Wheeler. They all proved false. Wheeler announced that his steel shop was prepared to build cars, tanks, and bridges, as well as ships.[36] In November, Wheeler was forced to cut the wages of some of his men from as much as 12½ to 25 cents per day.[37] Standard wages varied depending on the skill, from $1.50 to $2.50 per day in 1891.

Late in 1891, Frank outbid other lake shipbuilders for contracts to build four lightships for the government. Hence, 1892 was guaranteed to be a better year at the outset. The employee roll crept up to about 600 workers again.[38] In January, 1892, George Williams, who had borne the brunt of the yard's management while Frank was in Washington, was forced to retire because of ill health brought on by overwork. He was fifty-seven. Other than the four lightships and the steel freighter *W. H. Gilbert,* the year was not, at first glance, as encouraging as the company had expected. They also built a steel tug

34. *Saginaw Courier-Herald,* January 27, 1891.
35. *Marine Review,* III (January 22, 1891), 4.
36. *Ibid.,* (May 14, 1891), pp. 5 and 10.
37. *Ibid.,* IV (November 19, 1891), 10.
38. Godfrey L. Garden, *Harpers' Weekly,* XXXVI (July 23, 1892), 708.

and three wooden vessels and had, either under contract or under construction, four large steel freighters and several wooden craft.

By the end of 1892, the long awaited engine works was ready for production. Most Wheeler-built ships prior to 1893 carried engines built in Detroit, either at S. F. Hodge & Company or the Frontier Iron Works. William Willis, formerly with the Hodge Company, was in charge of the new engine shop. Most of the boilers for the Wheeler ships came from the Wickes Brothers Boiler Works in Saginaw. The first Wheeler-built ship to carry a "home-grown" engine was the *William H. Gratwick*.

Of the four steel freighters built in 1893, the designs of three were influenced by the loss of the *Western Reserve*. Mr. H. A. Hawgood, owner of the *S. S. Curry*, explained the design changes:

> Our engines will be placed amidships, with 136 feet of shaft, and will be so located that we will have six hatches forward and four aft, with one trimming hatch between engine and boiler houses. The hatches are laid off with reference to 24 feet centers, the engines and boilers taking up space of two hatches. In this way we will have three-fifths of our cargo forward and two-fifths aft. . . . the great aim is, . . . to insure safety when running light.[39]

The keel-laying ceremony of the third vessel of this design held great significance to Frank Wheeler. It was to take place on March 2, 1893, his fortieth birthday, and the vessel was named the *Centurion*, the one hundredth vessel built by him. Invitations were sent out to many friends and business associates to attend the ceremony and banquet afterwards. Recently-retired George Williams sent the most original reply to the invitation:

> I hope to be present in the yard of Steel
> To view the laying of the Keel.
> And as the occasion will be a reunion
> Just christen the boy the noble Centurion.
>
> In the evening I will be there do not fear
> But I won't get wet on common beer.

39. *Marine Review*, VI (December 15, 1892), 12.

> But should the fates with me combine
> I will drink your health in sparkling wine.
>
> If all goes well, and no one has blundered,
> It will be the birth of Ship One Hundred.
> And with wit and wisdom the feast will be
> One joyous event of Ninety Three.[40]

The schooner *Mary E. McLachlan* was launched on the same day as part of the festivities. The steam barge *Kittie M. Forbes* was moored directly across the slip from the spot where the *McLachlan* would strike the water. Several people crowded onto the steam barge for a better view of the launching. The huge wave created as the schooner struck the water caused the ice in the slip to surge against the *Forbes.* The steam barge heeled over, and as she righted herself, the people were thrown against the railing. The railing snapped, and to the groans and shrieks of an estimated 6,000 launch spectators, several people on the *Forbes* fell into the water amid broken ice, planks, and other debris from the launching. Spectators and shipyard workers quickly rendered assistance, but veteran rivermen feared that some victims were trapped under the ice. A diver was sent under the ice along the bottom of the slip, but discovered no bodies. By the next day, after owners of a few floating hats were found and noses were counted around the town, everyone was accounted for. From five to eight people were injured, and one, Fred Babcock, a local painter, died from internal injuries.[41]

The year 1893 was also the year of the Panic. The Wheeler Company lived through the Panic because it had such a good year. The *Centurion* was the last steel vessel launched from the yard until April, 1895. The company launched two wooden boats in 1894, a Detroit River ferry and a steam barge. In 1895 Dame Fortune began to smile again, and the Wheeler yard produced five steel and two wooden hulls, with two more steel contracts that carried over to the next year. The total value of the contracts was estimated at around $2,250,000.[42]

---

40. Letter from George F. Williams to Frank W. Wheeler, February 27, 1893, F. W. Wheeler Papers.

41. *Ibid.*, Newspaper clipping, n.d.

42. *Marine Review,* XII (August 22, 1895), 11.

Frank Wheeler looked upon the general revival of the lake trade as a permanent thing. With future contracts in his hip pocket, the well-liked, stocky shipbuilder could again afford to stand in front of Saginaw's Bancroft House in the waning twilight, complacently puffing an expensive cigar, and say hello to his old time friends.[43] Indications early in 1896 seemed to vindicate Wheeler's predictions. His two contracts mushroomed into eight, all for large steel ships. One of the contracts was with John D. Rockefeller for the construction of a 400-foot steamer and two large barges.

In order to meet delivery dates on so many vessels, the yard again went through an improvement program. When Frank instituted steel building in the yard, he included cranes in his plans. Now he reorganized his yard plan to include the addition of five new cranes of varying types which would expedite the movement of steel plates and other heavy objects from anywhere in the yard to the building berths. He added a new machine shop well equipped with large tools for heavy steel fabrication.

The most productive year in the company's history, from the standpoint of steel ships, was 1896. The company had to increase production in order to meet financial obligations brought on by the improvement program. The improvements, in turn, were necessary if the company was to meet delivery dates as set down by contracts. It was a vicious cycle. In other words, Frank accepted too many contracts, some of which he could not fill if everything did not operate like clockwork. In the shipbuilding business, this is seldom possible. He found himself bedeviled by everything from late delivery of steel to labor problems. As a result, the company fell considerably behind schedule on the Rockefeller contracts. Demurrage charges were included in the contracts for each day of delay beyond the delivery date. When the contracts were filled, Wheeler faced a demurrage penalty of $40,000. The only real counter charge that Wheeler presented to Rockefeller's representatives was that he had given them three of the best-built ships on the lakes. With only this moral obligation involved, the Rockefeller interests assured him that his company would not be

43. *Saginaw Courier-Herald*, September 5, 1895.

the loser for following a liberal policy to turn out good ships. They completely wiped out the demurrage claims.[44]

Unfortunately, not all of Wheeler's creditors were so understanding. In 1897, he built a freighter, a barge, and two tugs, all of steel, but what little repair work he might have picked up was lost because the year started slowly for lake shippers. Wheeler's creditors held a meeting in Detroit in February, 1897, and made arrangements for the shipyard to continue operations by providing some working capital. The shipyard company filed a $250,000 trust mortgage with the Union Trust Company of Buffalo. The trust mortgage was to cover the payment of 6 per cent gold-bearing mortgage bonds that were payable in five yearly installments of $50,000 each.[45] This would also cover the $180,000 debt resulting from the improvement program. The principal creditor was the Carnegie Steel Company, suppliers of ship steel and plates.[46]

In one other move, John S. Porter, of Saginaw, replaced Charles W. Stiver as treasurer of the company.[47] Stiver had been both secretary and treasurer of the firm since 1895, and he continued to retain the position of secretary. Wheeler was still president and E. T. Carrington, who became vice-president when George Williams retired in 1892, continued in that position.

By January, 1898, the Wheeler Company had three more hulls under construction for Rockefeller's Bessemer Steamship Company. One of them, the steamer *Samuel F. B. Morse*, was to be the largest ship on the Great Lakes. Everything seemed to be moving well for Wheeler. Some English visitors remarked that the yard was better equipped with overhead appliances for handling steel plate than any yard on the Clyde.[48] The company was experimenting with a pneumatic riveting machine that was expected to cut labor and production costs.[49]

44. *Marine Review*, XIV (November 19, 1896), 7.
45. *Ibid.*, XV (March 4, 1897), 10.
46. *Ibid.*, (February 15), 1897, p. 11.
47. *Ibid.*, (May 13, 1897), p. 9.
48. *Bay City Times-Press*, January 4, 1898.
49. *Ibid.*, January 6, 1898.

The firm was getting much good publicity for its work on the new Bessemer giants. On January 9, the *Bay City Times-Press* announced that Wheeler expected to have 1,500 men at work by the beginning of February.[50] Two days later, lightning struck in the form of a strike by the riveters.

Back in the "good old days," Wheeler maintained almost a paternal or brotherly image with his workers. In 1885, his entire working force, numbering 150 men, walked out in a pay grievance. They were back at work the next morning with their demand of a 25 cents per day increase granted by Frank.[51] Real labor difficulties did not develop until the steel yard made its appearance, and Frank had to go outside the community to find skilled labor. In spite of the difficulties experienced over the hiring of alien labor in 1890, the labor force's feelings for Frank were evidenced in the launching festivities of the *Emily P. Weed*. But from that point on, a gradual deterioration set in until 1896, when the company almost had to pay demurrage charges to the Rockefeller interests because of time lost in labor disputes and other problems.

Up to January 11, 1898, the yard was an open shop, with about half of the 120 men involved in riveting non-union. But on that date "every mother's son of them joined the local branch" of the American Shipbuilders' & Boiler Makers' Union.[52] The riveters maintained that the strike was strictly over low wages. A company official said that if this was the case, it could be amicably settled. But if the walkout came because the company refused to make their yard a union one, under no circumstance would the company grant such a request.[53]

On January 14, the workers held a large rally at Jean's Hall in Bay City. Representatives from the Trades Council of the Bay Cities called for a tighter labor organization; a federal labor union was formed under the auspices of the American Federation of Labor, with 393 charter members.[54] Within two days, they signed up 196 more mem-

50. *Ibid.*, January 9, 1898.
51. *Bay City Daily Tribune*, April 21-22, 1885.
52. *Bay City Times-Press*, January 11, 1898.
53. *Ibid.*; *Marine Review*, XVII (January 13, 1898), 14.
54. *Bay City Times-Press*, January 15, 1898.

bers, nearly all of them being Wheeler & Company employees. Henry C. Bourdingno was elected president of the new organization and John Corrigan, vice-president.[55]

Riveters' wages were based on the number of rivets they drove in a designated number of hours per day, with a ten-hour day being considered standard. Variables included the size of the rivets and the type of riveting being done (i.e., the part of the ship, such as the shell, keel plate, spar deck plating, and so on). The Bay City yard was paying anywhere from 50 cents to $1.50 less per hundred rivets in 1898 than they did in 1895. As a comparison, the 1895 Wheeler pay scale ran slightly lower than the 1898 wage scales at the Wyandotte yard of the Detroit Dry Dock Company.[56] The dramatic rise in food prices in Bay City between 1897 and 1898 compounded the difficulty. The cost of a barrel of flour, for example, rose from $3.50 in 1897 to $5.00 in 1898; potatoes, from 10 cents to 60 cents per bushel.

The company increased laborers' wages in the yard from 10 to 12½ cents per hour. On the other hand, if the riveters failed to settle their grievance, the laborers would have to be sent home for lack of work. The company offered the riveters an increase of about 7 per cent above the pay scale in effect when they walked out, but this was rejected.[57] On January 19, the shipyard was completely shut down. About twenty-five riveters were reported to have departed for Superior, Wisconsin, in search of work.

L. M. Bowers, general manager of the Bessemer Steamship Company, appeared before the workers in late January to speak to them briefly about a possible advance in wages his company might pay in order to get its vessels completed.[58] The yard opened briefly on February 7, with about 200 workers signing a pledge to work on the Bessemer hulls, but it closed again the next day when the riveters refused to come back to work.

Membership in Local No. 90 of the American Federation of Labor

55. *Ibid.,* January 17, 1898.
56. *Ibid.,* January 18 and February 10, 1898.
57. *Ibid.,* January 19, 1898.
58. *Marine Review,* XVII (June 23, 1898), 10.

had now swelled to 868, but the unemployed shipyard workers were feeling the pinch. A three-act comedy, "Finnegan's Alley," was pre sented at the Bay Theater on February 9 for the benefit of the workers. About 300 tickets were sold at 25 cents each, which gave relief to a few of them. On February 12, the representatives of the company and those of the locked-out employees reached an amicable agreement to reopen the yard. The riveters still held out, but thirty of the seventy gangs showed a willingness to accept the 7 per cent increase offered earlier by the company.[59]

One of the reasons the yard reopened was the pressure exerted by L. M. Bowers, of the Bessemer Steamship Company. Acting as an official mediator between the shipyard and the employees, he was in a position to bring pressure on the shipyard officials to effect a settlement because of the contracts his company held. Another reason was Jerome W. Robbins, judge of the state Court of Mediation and Arbitration, who agreed to investigate and render a decision on the situation.

During the inquiry that followed, Sven Anderson, superintending engineer of the Wheeler Company, brought out some enlightening facts about the difficulties under which the company had been laboring. Freight rates on raw materials to Bay City cost an average of $5,000 per vessel above those of competitor shipbuilding companies in other lake cities. Because Wheeler & Company had no dry dock, they received little repair work. The company depended on new construction. Competition had become so keen that they were forced to make a 10 per cent wage reduction in 1897. There was a downward trend in the cost of vessel construction; the cost of a $250,000 vessel built in 1895 had been reduced by $50,000 by 1898. This reduction in material cost was seen in such set items as steel, freight rates, engines, and boilers. Labor constituted about half of the contract price of a new vessel. Although the amount of labor had been reduced by new machinery and techniques, this reduction did not correspond to the decrease in the material costs of vessel construction. Labor cost was

59. *Bay City Times-Press,* February 13, 1898.

the one area in which the Wheeler Company could still compete with other lake shipbuilders.[60]

The court decided that the wages of chippers and caulkers should be raised an additional 3 cents per hour, to 25 cents, and it supported the company offer of a 7 per cent increase for the riveters.[61] It looked as though Frank had squeaked through another serious situation. Then, on May 30, Secretary Charles Stiver announced that the company was shutting down for a few days to settle several important matters affecting certain parts of the shipyard. The following day, the Bessemer Steamship Company took over the operation of the yard.

Behind this sudden action was a visit of Treasurer John S. Porter to Cleveland. He had gone there to get money to meet a pay roll as well as other obligations of the company with the Second National Bank in Saginaw.[62] He secured $24,000 from the Bessemer Steamship Company to meet the pay roll and to pay for machinery that would not be delivered until it was paid for.[63] The bank applied the entire sum to certain other obligations that it held against the shipbuilding company. The Wheeler Company also executed a $28,000 chattel mortgage with Harry T. Wickes, of Saginaw, as trustee.[64]

Through a clause in its contract, the Bessemer Steamship Company took over the yard to complete the vessels then under construction for them. The yard reopened on June 10, and, after several delays, the workmen finally received their back pay. Frank Wheeler continued to superintend construction of the Bessemer vessels, but Robert Logan, a well known lake naval architect, came up from Cleveland to look after affairs for the Bessemer Company.[65]

The last of the Bessemer hulls was launched in August, but Frank Wheeler's financial problems did not end there. The bondholders of the first mortgage would have liked to take possession of the shipyard

60. *Ibid.*, February 18, 1898.
61. *Ibid.*, March 3, 1898.
62. *Ibid.*, May 31, 1898.
63. *Marine Review*, XVII (June 23, 1898), 7.
64. *Ibid.*, (June 2, 1898), p. 11; *Bay City Times-Press*, May 31, 1898.
65. *Bay City Times-Press*, June 15, 1898.

and sell it piecemeal to get their money safely returned. They were prevented from doing this by the Bessemer Company which held a claim for wages amounting to $23,000 that they had paid, plus an additional $24,000 labor claim that the Saginaw bank diverted to pay other Wheeler debts. The Bessemer firm also had demurrage claims of $70,000 that they could impose if they thought it necessary. In addition to these, about thirty-five lien cases were held against the three Bessemer hulls by supply concerns who maintained that they were unpaid. The Bessemer Company pointed to a clause in their contract with the shipbuilding company whereby all material and supplies were paid for by Bessemer to the Wheeler Company immediately upon delivery of goods to the yard.[66]

It looked as though Frank Wheeler was out of the shipbuilding business for good. He had gambled over the years to build his steel shipbuilding yard. Many creditors carried his first mortgage notes on the basis of friendship for him, and he was not the type of man to forget these things easily. Frank set out to purchase the first mortgage bonds. With assistance from the Bessemer Steamship Company, he hoped to settle claims with the numerous supply concerns. By December, he had secured about half of the bonds at prices as low as 20 cents on the dollar. He also succeeded in inducing many of the supply concerns to withdraw their claims against the Bessemer ships and himself. The *Marine Review* hinted that Wheeler was acting on a promise from the Rockefeller interests that if he succeeded in reducing the claims, he might gain another contract from them and so be enabled to reopen his shipyard.[67]

At the annual Lake Carriers' Association meeting in Detroit in January, 1898, vesselmen learned that Frank Wheeler had been so successful in dealing with his creditors that he had accepted a contract for a $100,000 steel lumber carrier from Chicago parties.[68] The West Bay City yard was going to reopen!

Wheeler had indeed gained possession of two-thirds of the first

66.   *Marine Review*, XVIII (October 13, 1898), 13.
67.   *Ibid.*, (December 15, 1898), p. 13.
68.   *Ibid.*, XIX (January 26, 1899), 9.

mortgage bonds, with the assistance of the Bessemer Steamship Company, and was again in control of his shipyard.[69] Even before the steel arrived to begin construction on the lumber carrier, Wheeler had a contract with the Bessemer Company for a 480-foot ore carrier. Bay City still had its steel shipbuilding plant, and Frank Wheeler was ready to open his yard in April, 1899.[70]

Frank Wheeler began with virtually nothing. He developed a reputation of turning out some of the finest wooden boats on the lakes at some of the lowest prices. By taking financial gambles, he did the same thing with steel ships and nearly ended up with nothing. During the course of his life, he was elected to Congress. He had built one hundred ships before he was forty years old. He relied chiefly on his talent as a shipbuilder and his ability to get along with people to pull him through the tough scrapes. Even when the going was roughest, business associates and friends were loath to permit Frank's walls to tumble about him. Frank had those qualities—honesty and sincerity—that made his creditors and his employees believe in him. As long as he was able to command the respect of his colleagues in the shipbuilding business, and as long as he was still able to build ships, any consolidation efforts that materialized would have to consider Frank Wheeler.

69. *Ibid.*, (February 16, 1899), p. 9.
70. *Bay City Times-Press*, April 9, 1899.

7.

Weekend at the Waldorf

Between 1897 and 1902, 2,722 business consolidations of manufacturing and mining companies were formed in the United States, representing a capitalization of almost $6.5 billion. In 1899 alone, 1,208 such consolidations, totaling $2.3 billion, took place.[1] After business settled down following the Panic of 1893, industrialists searched for methods to protect their holdings. They also had to combat an irritant in the form of government-sponsored antitrust laws. As business demands increased, so did the need for capital in sums beyond the means of individuals. Yet any system that developed as a solution to these demands and needs had to be flexible enough to provide finance and guidance. The corporate form of business with its parental hold-

1. Richard M. Abrams and Lawrence W. Levine, "The Coming of the Corporate Age," *The Shaping of Twentieth-Century America* (Boston: Little, Brown & Co., 1965), p. 62.

ing company seemed to provide the answers. Thus consolidations took place in every area of business from bicycles to tobacco.

All of the steel shipbuilding yards on the lakes were painfully aware of the downward trend of profits in new vessel construction brought on by keen competition among themselves for contracts with the major steel interests. They were able to counter this trend by improved techniques and machines that reduced labor costs, but even these had limitations. Frank Wheeler was a graphic example of relying on low labor costs. The next moves had to be an alliance with the eastern mining and financial interests and a consolidation among themselves.

In June, 1898, J. J. Lynn of Port Huron, Michigan, the Great Lakes regional representative for the General Electric Company, approached Alexander McVittie of the Detroit Dry Dock Company with the idea of a merging major lake shipbuilders. Lynn traveled extensively in eastern business circles and was familiar with consolidation trends and plans along the seaboard. McVittie had given some thought to such a proposition but had initiated no action. Lynn pointed out that although the vessel repair business was good, competition for orders for new ships had forced the prices so low that lake shipyards were building vessels cheaper than on the Clyde.[2] McVittie was receptive to Lynn's ideas, but he did not feel that his name should be used until he was sure how other lake shipbuilders would receive the scheme. With McVittie's advice, Lynn began to organize a consolidation movement among the major lake shipbuilders.

The going was not easy. The men involved were conservative in their views and were self-made men. They had struggled, some of them from humble beginnings, to attain the positions and wealth that they now enjoyed. They respected one another's position, but they would not take kindly to joining forces with those against whom they had competed for so long. It took from June to December before diminishing profits and fierce competition induced a nucleus of them to meet at the Waldorf Astoria Hotel in New York to discuss the plan.

At the initial meeting were James Wallace of the Cleveland Ship Building Company, Robert L. Ireland of the Globe Iron Works, Wil-

2. *Marine Review*, XIX (April 20, 1899), 15.

liam E. Fitzgerald of the Milwaukee Dry Dock Company, W. L. Brown of the Chicago Ship Building Company, Colgate Hoyt of the American Steel Barge Company, and Alexander McVittie of the Detroit Dry Dock Company. From this point, the deal took on a true business form as Lynn and McVittie played on the participants' practicalities.

Two appraisers, Robert Logan, marine architect from Cleveland, and Robert W. Hunt, machinery engineer and iron and steel expert from Chicago, were hired to establish the values of the physical holdings of the various shipbuilding concerns.[3] More meetings followed as problems were ironed out. All news of the proposed consolidation had to be kept ultra-secret to prevent inflation of stock and property valuations.

Because of the circumstances under which negotiations for the development of the incorporation took place, little is known of the specific problems that were encountered by the shipbuilders during those preliminary meetings. However, as early as February, 1899, some definite financial arrangements that ultimately were adopted were being discussed. The rate of interest on the preferred stock dividend was set at 7 per cent, non-cumulative, "the same as other companies of like character."[4] The preferred stock represented the values of the plant facilities that were turned into the combination, and the common stock was distributed at 20 per cent of its par value, thus deriving the working capital. Both common and preferred stock were established at $100 par value per share.[5] The only difference that arose between the heads of the companies was over the question of fixing management so as to avoid high salaries.

Some differences arose among the hierarchies of the individual companies that went into the consolidation. The most enlightening argument took place between Alexander McVittie and the McMillan in-

3. *Ibid.*

4. Letters from James McMillan to William C. McMillan, February 24 and March 3, 1899, McMillan Correspondence; Articles of Incorporation, American Ship Building Company, March 16, 1899, Minutes, American Ship Building Company, Lorain, Ohio. Cited hereafter as Minutes, ASBCo.

5. *Marine Review.* XIX (April 20, 1899), 14.

terest in the Detroit Dry Dock Company. McVittie offered to purchase the trustee stock of the Detroit Dry Dock Company at par, which would have netted the McMillans $113,000 and would have paid much of their 20 per cent cash payment for common stock in the new corporation. Senator James McMillan was willing to "help McVittie to make some money," but thought that half of the trustee stock "ought to suit him." McVittie pointed out that previous to "his working up this consolidation scheme," the McMillans would gladly have sold it at par or less. The Senator admitted this, but countered by saying that although he was not anxious to at the time, they had purchased the stock of John Owen at McVittie's urging. He concluded by pointing out that the McMillans had "carried the Trustee stock all through the panic period, and that it is only fair that those who have endorsed the paper should reap some little benefit."[6]

The small differences were obviously patched up because on March 16, 1899, the American Ship Building Company was incorporated under New Jersey law with an authorized capital of $30,000,000 divided equally into 150,000 shares each of preferred and common stock with a par value of $100 per share. The actual capital was set at $14,000,000, again equally divided between preferred and common stock. The legalities were worked out by James H. Hoyt, of the Cleveland law firm of Hoyt, Dustin & Kelley. The new corporation included the holdings of the Chicago Ship Building Company, the Cleveland Ship Building Company, the Globe Iron Works, the Ship Owners' Dry Dock Company, the Detroit Dry Dock Company, the American Steel Barge Company, and the Milwaukee Dry Dock Company.[7] The Detroit company, with its extensive riverfront property and subsidiary holdings, was considered the most valuable single company.

The reactions of the participants varied. William E. Fitzgerald

6. Letter from James McMillan to William C. McMillan, February 24, 1899, McMillan Correspondence.

7. The value of the individual companies was set as follows:

Detroit	$1,428,000
Superior	1,000,000
Cleveland (three companies)	1,400,000
Chicago	450,000
Milwaukee	413,000

placed a long-distance phone call to his wife to tell her of their good fortune. Long-distance telephoning was in its infancy, and his message had to be relayed by a telephone operator in Buffalo, New York. Some difficulty was experienced in getting the message through because the operator got the message confused. Knowing the cost of the call, Mrs. Fitzgerald, with the ability that only a wife can exhibit in returning her husband to solid ground, replied through the operator: "Tell him that a fool is soon parted from his money!"[8]

James McMillan was more concerned about legalities than in spreading the good news. He was afraid that the common stockholders would be liable for the difference between the $20 they paid for the share of stock and its $100 par value. In a letter to his son he explained that

> ... in case the company should be unable to pay its debts,
> then the stockholders could be called upon to pay the difference
> until the stock was fully paid up; hence all companies of this
> nature when formed have a preliminary company, like the construction company of a railroad, which makes a contract with
> the railroad company to build the line for so much in bonds
> and stock fully paid up.[9]

Actually, only two subsidiary companies needed to be set up. The old firm names in Chicago and Milwaukee were retained although there was a change of officers. The Superior Ship Building Company was organized to take over the shipbuilding activities of the American Steel Barge Company; the fleet of the latter was not included in the shipbuilding merger. In Detroit, all of the holdings of the Detroit Dry Dock Company were merged into the Detroit Ship Building Company. The Cleveland firms fell under the parent title of the American Ship Building Company.

On April 20, 1899, the principal stockholders held a meeting in Col-

8. Telephone conversation with Edmund Fitzgerald, son of William E. Fitzgerald and retired chairman of the board, Northwestern Mutual Life Insurance Company, Milwaukee, Wisconsin, February 25, 1968.

9. Letter from James McMillan to William C. McMillan, April 26, 1899, McMillan Correspondence.

gate Hoyt's office on Wall Street in New York and elected a board of directors, executive committee, and company officers. William L. Brown became president, Robert L. Ireland, vice-president, and Russell C. Wetmore, secretary and treasurer. Wetmore was affiliated with the American Steel Barge Company and, along with Colgate Hoyt, was close to the Standard Oil Company interests. James C. Wallace was appointed general manager and William E. Fitzgerald, assistant manager. It was expected that Fitzgerald would oversee the upper lake yards and Wallace the lower lake yards. The real governing body was the executive committee, even though they were responsible to the board of directors.[10] The transfer of property from the various shipyards to the new parent company went smoothly. The only serious hold up was a judgement amounting to $10,000 held by the Goodrich Transportation Company against the Milwaukee Dry Dock Company. This apparently stemmed from the "loss" of the *Muskegon*, and Fitzgerald and Andrew M. Joys furnished a penal bond to indemnify the new company against claims arising from it.[11]

A representative from each of the seven companies was appointed to act as a trustee for the stockholders. Each yard would be operated by a local superintendent, although a chief engineer and chief of the hull department would have headquarters in the Cleveland main office. A. V. Powell was hired as chief engineer and A. C. Diericx was transferred from Superior to head up the drawing room of the hull department.[12] For the most part, the local superintendents continued in their old capacities.

Some familiar faces, however, were lost in the shuffle as a committee reviewed personnel and needs of the various yards. Most of the high-salaried officers of the individual old companies resigned their

10. The executive committee was composed of Brown, Ireland, Fitzgerald, J. C. Wallace, Colgate Hoyt, Luther Allen, and Alexander McVittie. The board of directors was made up of all of the members of the executive committee plus H. H. Porter, Samuel Mather, Gilbert N. McMillan, Robert Wallace, Andrew M. Joys, H. M. Hanna, L. C. Hanna, and W. T. Coleman Carter. Board of Directors' Meeting, April 20, 1899, Minutes, ASBCo.
11. *Ibid.*
12. *Ibid.*, Executive Committee Meeting, June 8 and 27, 1899.

positions. Frank Jeffrey was placed in charge of the Lorain yard replacing William W. Watterson. The latter had succeeded Thomas Bristow in 1898 after the opening of the new dry dock there.[13] But the biggest loss came in Detroit where the Kirby Brothers resigned. Their resignations came as no surprise. In February, 1899, the Cramp & Sons Ship & Engine Building Company of Philadelphia made serious overtures to lure them away from Wyandotte. Frank Kirby was particularly interested because this would give him the opportunity to see how his vessel designs would fare against foreign competition.[14] He decided, however, to finish the plans on which he was then working, after which he planned to open his own office in New York. Joe Kirby retired from active participation in shipbuilding. As a memento, the employees presented Joe with a mahogany card table and a pair of gold cuff buttons mounted with emeralds and diamonds.[15] He was succeeded by Charles B. Calder, former superintendent of the Dry Dock Engine Works. J. J. Lynn also received recognition, but from the new parent firm, and in the form of $10,000 for "special services relating to the organization of the company."[16]

Meanwhile, the American Ship Building Company family continued to grow. In April, 1899, Frank Wheeler sold his old floating dry dock to James DeGrace, who had operated it for a number of years.[17] In May, the *Bay City Times-Press* published a report, denied by Vice-President Charles Stiver, that the Wheeler plant would be sold to the "shipbuilding trust."[18] Three days later, J. J. Lynn registered at the Fraser House in Bay City.[19] About a week later, when Robert Logan and Robert Hunt appeared, it was obvious that negotiations were being conducted between Wheeler and the American Ship Building Company.[20] On June 14, the West Bay City Ship Building Company

13. *Marine Review*, XXVII (March 26, 1903), 22 and XVIII (August 25, 1898), 14; *Wyandotte Herald*, September 30, 1898.
14. *Wyandotte Herald*, February 17, 1899.
15. *Ibid.*, July 7, 1899.
16. Executive Committee Meeting, May 3, 1899, Minutes, ASBCo.
17. *Bay City Times-Press*, April 25, 1899.
18. *Ibid.*, May 19, 1899.
19. *Ibid.*, May 23, 1899.
20. *Ibid.*, June 4, 1899.

filed its articles of incorporation with a capital stock of $500,000.[21] Frank Wheeler was vice-president and the parent firm held all of the stock except for one share per director of the subsidiary company.

Wheeler exchanged his yard and $120,000 in cash for $600,000 par value preferred and $600,000 par value common stock in the combination, plus $3,729, or the net balance after adjustments. He also retained the right of completing the steamer on the stocks, unless he failed to meet the delivery date of August 1, 1899, in which case the steamer would be sold to the shipbuilding corporation.[22] The Excelsior Foundry Company in Bay City was also included in the sale.[23]

When the consolidation of lake shipbuilders took place, negotiations were opened with the Union Dry Dock Company in Buffalo to include it. Because of corporate obstacles presented by its owner, the Erie Railroad, the Buffalo firm was unable to join. But its position, "in the new order of affairs" was "quite well defined."[24] Actually, negotiations were opened in April, 1899, for the possible purchase of the yard.[25] It took over a year of negotiations, but in October, 1900, the American Ship Building Company offered the Erie Railroad $260,000 cash for the yard machinery, and leased the property and dry docks for ten years with the right to purchase at any time within the term for a fixed price of $540,000 cash.[26] The proposal was accepted the following month with the railroad remaining liable for any demurrage claims on the steamer *Wilkesbarre*, then under construction in the yard.[27] The yard was not purchased outright until 1910.[28]

Another Buffalo shipyard, the Buffalo Dry Dock Company, merged with American Ship Building in April, 1900. The yard was adjacent to the Union Dry Dock Company on Buffalo Creek. It dated back to 1845 when Frederick Nelson Jones arrived from Black River, Ohio,

21. *Ibid.*, June 15, 1899.
22. Executive Committee Meeting, June 8, 1899, Minutes, ASBCo.
23. *Bay City Times-Press*, June 18, 1899.
24. *Marine Review*, XIX (April 20, 1899), 14.
25. Executive Committee Meeting, April 21, 1899, Minutes, ASBCo.
26. *Ibid.*, Special Executive Committee Meeting, October 19, 1900.
27. *Ibid.*, Executive Committee Meeting, November 21, 1900,
28. *Ibid.*, December 21, 1910.

GENEALOGY OF THE AMERICAN SHIP BUILDING COMPANY

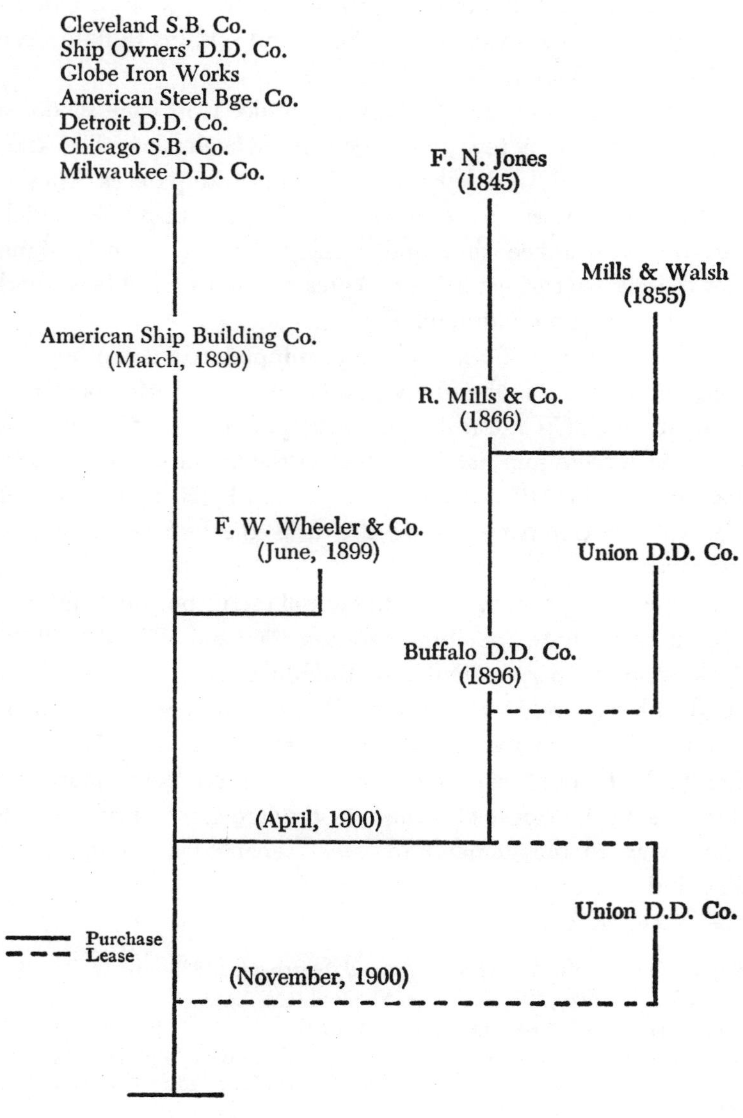

now Lorain, to begin building ships in Buffalo.[29] He apparently established a shipyard on Ohio Street between Wabash and Chicago Streets; but, about 1853, he moved across Buffalo Creek to a site north of and adjacent to the Bidwell & Banta shipyard.[30] In 1866, Jones decided to open a shipyard in Tonawanda, New York, and sold his Buffalo Creek yard to R. Mills & Company.

Frederick Jones built over 100 ships in Buffalo. Most were schooners or freight boats, but a few Jones-built sidewheelers rivalled those built next door by Bidwell & Banta as floating lake palaces. They included the *Mayfllower*, *St. Lawrence*, and *Mississippi*. Frederick's brother, the Milwaukee shipbuilder Benjamin Buel Jones, signed many of the master carpenters' certificates and must have been working in close connection with him.

Robert Mills, of R. Mills & Company, shipped as a cabin boy on a schooner out of Buffalo when he was a lad of twelve, He spent nineteen years on the lakes and rose to a position of command before coming ashore in 1855 to join Patrick Walsh in the operation of a floating dry dock in Buffalo. Mills & Walsh was joined by R. Rice in 1866 to form R. Mills & Company. Under this title, the firm purchased the Jones shipyard.[31]

The company was principally in the vessel repair business, although it did build a few ships. Sometime between 1866 and 1875, it built two dry docks running perpendicular to Buffalo Creek.[32] The yard was equipped to repair only wooden ships. During the eighties, the company built a few bulk freighters, such as the *Monteagle*, *Wyoming*, and *Robert Mills*; but even when times were good, never more than one ship was on the stocks at a time. In the late summer of 1890, the firm gave way to the demand for steel repairs by adding shears, punches, and rolls to its yard facilities.[33]

29.   *Buffalo Commercial Advertiser & Journal*, March 24, 1883.
30.   Frank E. Hamilton, "Notes . . . on Shipbuilding . . . ."
31.   *Buffalo Morning Express*, December 12, 1890.
32.   The first of the dry docks was 280 feet long, 41 feet wide, and had 11½ feet of water over the sill. The second dry dock was 370 feet long, 46 feet wide, and had 12½ feet of water over the sill.
33.   *Marine Review*, II (October 2, 1890), 7.

Patrick Walsh died in 1875 and Robert Mills continued the operations of the yard under the same firm name until he died in December, 1890. The yard was then operated by Hamilton J. Mills until 1896 when an alliance called the Buffalo Dry Dock Company was formed with the old Union Dry Dock Company. The latter firm merged with the parent Union Steamboat Company on June 6, 1896.[34] A New Yorker, Edward Corbin, secured a mortgage on the R. Mills & Company property and, together with the Union Steamboat Company, formed the Buffalo Dry Dock Company. George B. Drake, who gained his experience with the Union Dry Dock Company, was appointed general superintendent of both yards.[35]

On September 22, 1899, the Buffalo Dry Dock Company was reorganized with a capital of $575,000 by several prominent lake shipping people that included Robert R. Rhodes of Cleveland and E. D. Carter of Chicago.[36] Edward Smith was elected president, James Ash, vice-president, and Abner C. Adams, secretary-treasurer.[37] All of the officers were well known Buffalo shipping personalities. Their first move was to purchase the old Mills Dry Dock property from Edward Corbin for $674,500, including a transferral of stock, cash, and a five-year mortgage.[38] Seven months later, the Mills property became a part of the American Ship Building Company.

Formal transfer of the Buffalo Dry Dock Company to the combination occurred on April 24, 1900.[39] The Buffalo Dry Dock Company stock was exchanged for 3,000 shares of preferred American Ship Building Company stock and $6,250.[40] The American Ship Building Company now controlled every major steel shipbuilding yard on the

34. Letter from Department of State, State of New York, to the author, March 27, 1968.

35. *Marine Review*, XXVIII (July 16, 1903), 30.

36. First General and Special Meeting of Stockholders, September 22, 1899, Minutes, Buffalo Dry Dock Company Stockholders' Meeting Book, in possession of author.

37. Board of Directors' Meeting, September 25, 1899, Minutes, Buffalo Dry Dock Company Directors' Book, in possession of author.

38. *Ibid.*

39. *Buffalo Daily Courier*, April 25, 1900.

40. Executive Committee Meeting, April 24, 1900, Minutes, ASBCo.

Great Lakes, except the Craig Ship Building Company in Toledo. The operation involved seventeen dry docks on fourteen separate ship-building sites located at every strategic shipping point on the lakes!

The first year of the American Ship Building Company was one of the most remarkable years in the history of Great Lakes shipping. Because of a struggle precipitated between the major iron ore interests, virtually anything that would float carried a grossly inflated value. The shipyards could book no more new orders—not for a lack of building space, but for a lack of steel. The Carnegie Steel Company went as far as to furnish steel to the shipyards for the construction of half a dozen vessels for itself. In this way, it gained a slight advantage when other steel companies were refused contracts by the shipbuilding companies.[41] By the end of its first fiscal year, the American Ship Building Company launched twenty-nine ships, had sixteen under construction, and docked 1,072 ships for repairs![42]

Small wonder that work was pushed on a large new dry dock at the Superior plant! Work at the dry dock, begun under the old American Steel Barge Company management, was beset by strikes and bad weather. A large cave-in on May 25, 1899, caused considerable damage and further delay. More rain and strikes set the work back even further. Engineer Powell went to Superior in December to inspect a leak that developed. The dry dock was originally scheduled to be ready in August, 1899, but the first ship, the steamer *Nicaragua*, was not floated into the dry dock until May 21, 1900. In spite of the delays, the dock was completed in time to enjoy the boom times at the head of the lakes.[43]

A gala occasion of another sort at Superior in 1899 was the launching of the barge *John Smeaton* on June 17. The town fathers decided to use the occasion to promote the advantages of their town. The railroads provided excursion trains from as far west as Grafton, North

41. Waldron Fawcett, "The Most Remarkable Year in the History of the Great Lakes," *Harpers' Weekly*, XL (September 29, 1900), 915.

42. "First Annual Report of the American Ship Building Company for the Fiscal Year Ended June 30, 1900," American Ship Building Company, Lorain, Ohio.

43. The dry dock was 606 feet long on the blocks, 66½ feet wide at the gate, and had 19 feet of water over the sill.

Dakota, and as far south as Blue Earth City, Minnesota. Reception committees greeted the excursionists with martial airs and free box lunches when they alighted from some 100 coaches that were pulled into Superior by the puffing locomotives. All the streets between Third and Belknap were decorated with bunting, and the First National Bank boasted of an electric "Welcome" sign. The small passenger steamer *Bon Voyage* provided free excursions into the bay, four "world's champions" wrestled at the baseball grounds, and Superior beat Duluth in a baseball game. Some people even went to the laying of the cornerstone of the new Episcopal church. The Superior Fire Department gave an exhibition run, covering a half-mile route in four minutes with its ponderous horse-drawn steamer, to play streams of water on the Greek fire "consuming" the city hall. The *Smeaton* was launched at 4:15 in the afternoon. The weatherman cooperated by giving a display of "pyrotechnics with wind and rain as trimmings," in keeping with the rest of the spectacular events witnessed by the 15,000 people who poured into town.[44] The day was one that would linger fondly in the memories of many people for a long time to come. Those who experienced it agreed that it was a "Superior" day.

Despite festivities such as those displayed by the Superior town elders, the future of the American Ship Building Company appeared doubtful to some at its inception because of the great increase that had already been made in the lake fleet. Yet during the first five years of its existence, the company built 175 ships. Along with the vast increase in the number of large steel hulls came the need for the shipyards and dry docks to keep pace through modernization and addition of equipment. Some of the newer plants, such as Lorain and Chicago, were in good condition. But others, such as Buffalo and Cleveland, had fallen behind. William Knight remembered the condition of Buffalo when he arrived there in 1901.

> The impression upon my mind, . . . led me to question as to whether or not Noah constructed his ark at this place; . . . I think some of the designs of appliances and methods must have

44. *Inland Ocean* (Superior), June 17 and 24, 1899.

been handed down through the ages as they plainly bore the marks of extreme age and antiquity, . . .[45]

The Bay City yard was used as an overflow yard. If construction contracts filled the other yards, Bay City would be opened. Some of the equipment in Bay City was used to improve the other yards. Trestles for cranes were taken to Wyandotte.[46] A large steam hammer and half of a compound steam engine were taken to the Globe yard in Cleveland.[47] The executive committee recommended shutting down the Bay City yard completely because of the difficulty in obtaining material.[48] A month later, Frank Jeffrey was sent up as superintendent. As orders poured into the Cleveland office for new construction, the Bay City yard was reopened. As long as the building boom continued, Bay City was secure; but in 1904, when the bubble was quivering, the executive committee decided that Bay City should receive no new construction that the Buffalo yard could handle.[49] The Bay City shipbuilders continued to exist as though suspended by a thread.

In Cleveland, pneumatic machinery was installed in the Globe yard. The executive committee also purchased land for a dry dock extension at the head of the Old River Bed.[50] The old Cleveland Ship Building Company property along the Cuyahoga River was declared expendable. The property was sold in 1905 to the Erie Railroad for the construction of a coal dock.[51] Most of the other yards received additions to machinery shops and blacksmith shops or had other improvements made to them.

The greatest source of discomfort for the newly formed company was labor. Through 1900, labor problems were at a minimum. Labor seemed to be holding its breath until it could see some direction form-

45.   William Knight, "The Buffalo Dry Dock Company," *Live Wire*, I (March, 1915), 3.
46.   Executive Committee Meeting, September 26, 1899, Minutes, ASBCo.
47.   *Ibid.*, August 3 and September 26, 1899.
48.   *Ibid.*, August 3, 1899.
49.   *Ibid.*, January 20, 1904.
50.   *Ibid.*, December 17, 1902. Number One dry dock now measured 547 feet in length, 65 feet in width, and had 15½ feet of water over the sill.
51.   *Ibid.*, March 15, 1905.

ing on the part of the new corporation. In the summer of 1901, some time was lost because of a machinists' strike in Chicago; but, by October, it was broken, and the company was able to hire new men on its own terms.[52] In 1902, more time was lost because of the inability of steel suppliers to deliver their goods than was lost because of labor discontent.[53] But in 1903, the story was different.

In the early part of the year, 1,500 workers at the Lorain plant walked out over a pay grievance and failure by the company to recognize the union.[54] The Chicago yard experienced a similar strike by ship carpenters and caulkers at about the same time.[55] No sooner were the Lorain and Chicago strikes settled than the Buffalo yard was struck. The Buffalo strike originated with the holders-on in the riveting gangs but soon spread to other departments.[56] The plant was shut down and some of the men found work at the small rival Empire Shipbuilding Company.[57] The strike lasted about a month, and the launching of the steamer *P. P. Miller* was delayed by it.

A series of strikes occurred in the summer of 1903 at Bay City, Cleveland, and Buffalo. In July, in spite of an uneasy feeling among workmen at Superior, no strike resulted.[58] As an indication of the future, the Shipwrights, Joiners & Caulkers Association, at their annual convention, adopted a resolution calling for a nine-hour day and no Sunday work in all lake ports.[59] Not until November could President W. L. Brown report that threatened labor trouble at the Chicago plant could be avoided and that there were no labor troubles at any other plants.[60] The company had little labor trouble during the next two years.

52. *Ibid.*, August 21, and October 2, 1901.
53. *Ibid.*, October 29, 1902. The company lost an average of 60-75 days per contract because of supply delays.
54. *Buffalo Morning Express*, March 4 and 22, 1904.
55. *Marine Review*, XXVII (February 26, 1903), 23; and (March 19, 1903), 31.
56. *Buffalo Morning Express*, March 19 and 24, 1903.
57. *Ibid.*, March 27, 1903.
58. Executive Committee Meeting, July 15, 1903, Minutes, ASBCo.
59. *Detroit Journal*, October 29, 1903.
60. Executive Committee Meeting, November 18, 1903, Minutes, ASBCo.

Nor did the company have difficulty in keeping its building berths filled with new construction. Each year, more of the wooden ships succumbed to time and the elements and had to be replaced by steel-hulled ships. As the nation's blast furnaces demanded more and more iron ore, the deficit in hulls had to be filled by the steel shipyards. One editorialist, writing in 1903, noted that "no business venture . . . can look with complacency as far into the future as the lake ship builder."[61] Many of the new vessels were being built for large steel corporations on a cash basis. Many others were contracted for by independent operators or steamship syndicates on an individual steamer basis. Steamship bonds became the vogue among investors and financial institutions along the lakes.

The standard practice by the steamship company was to supply half of the contract price of a vessel in cash. Stock would be issued to the stockholders for the other half of the contract price, and a mortgage covering the entire value of the vessel would be given to the trust company as security for its loan. A provision in the mortgage usually stated that the vessel would be fully insured with the trust company as beneficiary. The bondholder was protected in several ways. Through the insurance clause, the bondholder was guaranteed his full return even should the vessel be lost. The trust company required that the steamship company furnish it with a quarterly statement of earnings and expenses that indicated how well the steamer was being managed. Also, the indebtedness of a vessel was limited by the mortgage, thereby forcing her to be operated on a cash basis. Finally, bonds were ordinarily made redeemable annually in 10 per cent lots. The steamship bonds usually would bear interest at the rate of 5 per cent per annum. The trust company often purchased the bonds at a low enough rate to provide them with a comfortable margin of profit when they resold them to investors. Many of the investors in steamship bonds were semi-public institutions such as universities, hospitals, and churches.

An example of this type of agreement existed between the Detroit Ship Building Company, as agent for the parent firm, and the Security

---

61. *Marine Review*, XXVIII (November 19, 1903), 17.

Trust Company of Detroit, Michigan. The West Bay City Ship Building Company built the steamer *W. R. Woodford* in 1908 for the Hawgood Steamship Company. The contract price was $430,000, and the steamship company issued 5 per cent interest bearing bonds for $215,000, securing them by a trust mortgage. The bonds matured in lots of $22,000 and $21,000, in even and odd years respectively, for a period of ten years. The Security Trust Company agreed to purchase the bonds at the rate of 91, or $910 for each $1,000 bond. There then followed several other minor considerations that further protected the trust company.[62]

Many ships were built on the basis of the "bonding business." In fact, launchings became so commonplace by 1903 that at Wyandotte the steamers *James H. Reed* and *A. D. Davidson* were merely dropped into the water without the benefit of christening ceremonies.[63] In Chicago, the *John Lambert* fared slightly better when someone went into the office and asked one of the stenographers to take enough time away from her job to break a bottle for the christening ceremony.[64]

Not all ships suffered such an austere beginning, despite the frequency of launchings during this period. The *Wilbert L. Smith* was launched at Lorain to strains sung by the Garden Theater Opera Company of Cleveland. The stage director of the opera company, J. J. Jaxon, wrote appropriate verses to the tune of "Sister Mary Jane's Top Note" from "The Girl from Paris." The company sang excerpts from "El Capitan" and Mr. Jaxon's verses as the vessel slid into the water. Yard superintendent Frank LaMarche prevailed upon his brother, manager of the Garden Theater, to bring the theater company to the launching. After the ceremony, everyone went to LaMarche's cottage for a party. On the way back to Cleveland, the chartered Lake Shore Electric car stopped at Avon Beach where the "players danced, sang, and did astonishing feats."[65] This must have

62. Agreement between Detroit Ship Building Company and Security Trust Company, March 19, 1908, Detroit Ship Building Company Papers.

63. *Marine Review*, XXVII (June 4, 1903), 31 and XXVIII (August 13, 1903), 25.

64. *Ibid.*, XXVII (May 14, 1903), 23.

65. *Cleveland Plain Dealer*, July 1, 1903.

been one of the most festive launchings that Lorain had experienced up to that time, especially when compared with the somber launching of the *Wilbert L. Smith*'s "sister," the *Hurlburt W. Smith*. The latter's flags were flown at half-mast in memory of her recently deceased managing owner, Captain W. W. Brown.[66]

In July, 1901, the American Ship Building Company suffered a great loss through the tragic death of its assistant general manager, William E. Fitzgerald. "Will" Fitzgerald maintained a family summer home on Lake Nagawicka near Milwaukee. On a hot summer night, his wife awoke to the smell of leaking gas. Fitzgerald went into the basement to inspect and found the leak. When he called a house servant, the servant came too close with a lighted candle. The resulting explosion caught Fitzgerald's clothing on fire and he died the following day.[67] The shipbuilding company was stripped of one of its most enthusiastic and talented younger men.[68]

The executive committee had two changes in 1902. L. M. Bowers and A. B. Wolvin replaced Colgate Hoyt and James C. Wallace. Bowers was manager of the newly formed Rockefeller-Carnegie combine, the huge Pittsburgh Steamship Company. A. B. Wolvin was the newly-elected president of the Superior Ship Building Company and an active vessel owner and operator in Duluth, Minnesota. Another important change in the company hierarchy occurred in 1903 when old Robert Wallace retired. He had wanted to retire when the consolidation took place but was prevailed upon by W. L. Brown to remain until the company was well established. One legend that developed around the venerable Wallace was his characteristic stovepipe hat. Whenever the hat was posted resolutely on his head everything was running smoothly. But should he be seen striding through

<hr>

66.   *Marine Review*, XXVII (February 19, 1903), 23.

67.   *Milwaukee Sentinel*, July 8, 1901.

68.   Fitting tributes were passed in the form of resolutions by the American Ship Building Company and especially by the Lake Carriers' Association and The Sea & Lake Insurance Company. The last two presented printed resolutions to Mrs. Fitzgerald and are now in the possession of Edmund Fitzgerald, retired chairman of the board of directors, Northwestern Mutual Life Insurance Company, Milwaukee, Wisconsin.

the shipyard with hat in hand, woe be unto any luckless shipbuilder whom he caught not hard at work. Fortunately, the hat was tall enough so that Wallace could be seen coming at a safe distance.

Also in 1903, Robert L. Ireland resigned as vice-president in order to devote more time to his duties with the Cleveland lake shipping firm of M. A. Hanna & Company. He was replaced by James C. Wallace. Robert Logan was hired to fill the post left vacant by Will Fitzgerald's death two years before, and Frank W. Hart, a large stockholder in the Gilchrist Transportation Company, was elected to the board of directors. The latter change would have future implications in dealings between the shipbuilding firm and the Gilchrist line.

As changes occurred within the American Ship Building Company, so did changes on the lake shipping scene that would have as much impact or more on the company. The greatest outside influence on lake shipbuilding at the turn of the century was the introduction of the hulett ore unloader. This giant machine, resembling a mechanical praying mantis, was the invention of George H. Hulett of the Cleveland firm of Wellman-Seaver-Morgan Company. The machine was radically different from the cable-supported unloading buckets in use up to that time. A large gantry, travelling on rails parallel to the dock, formed the base. A carriage travelled along the gantry at right angles to the dock. The carriage supported a tilting girder which, at the water end, supported a ram that carried a clamshell bucket. After the ram was lowered into the cargo hold the bucket could be rotated in any direction. This made it possible to reach not only the iron ore in the hatch opening but also that portion lying between the hatchways.[69] The machine radically reduced the unloading time at lower lake ports and cut down on the number of men required to clean up the cargo hold as the steamer became lightened.

One of the most immediate results of the new unloading machine on vessel design was cutting the hatch space centers on bulk freighters in half. The *James H. Hoyt* was the first lake freighter built with her hatches spaced with twelve feet centers.

---

69. Charles Piez, "The Handling and Storing of Iron Ore," *Marine Review*, XXVII (May 14, 1903), 26-27.

In 1900, the American Ship Building Company launched the first 500-foot ore carriers on the lakes, the steamers *John W. Gates, James J. Hill, William Edenborn,* and *Isaac L. Ellwood.* The company signed a contract in 1903 with A. B. Wolvin, representing the Duluth-based Acme Steamship Company syndicate, to build the first 550-footer. Before the huge freighter could be built, her building berth and the dry dock at Lorain had to be extended to accommodate her.[70] The steamer had several unique features that immediately afterwards became standard for lake bulk freighter construction. Her cargo hold was hopper shaped to accommodate the new hulett ore unloaders. The space between the sides of the ship and the sides of the hopper was used for water ballast and extended up the sides to the height of the main deck stringer. The supporting hold stanchions were done away with completely. In their place, a system of girder arches was substituted to provide support to the main deck and the sides of the ship. The thirty-three hatches were spaced with twelve feet centers. She was flush-decked, with only the pilothouse and texas deck forward and the coamings around the engine and boiler openings and dining room skylight aft to break the continuous line of the spar deck. The ship was named the *Augustus B. Wolvin,* but she was quickly dubbed the "Yellow Kid" because her barn-like hull was painted a brilliant yellow that verged on orange. Her bottom was painted a brilliant green to the waterline. There could certainly be no mistaking her far out on the lake!

The *Wolvin's* launching, on April 9, 1904, brought expressions of astonishment from H. G. Mull, general manager of the famous Cramps' shipyard of Philadelphia. He could not believe that such a large ship could be launched in so simple an operation with such a minimum of danger.[71] At the chicken salad and champagne luncheon held in the mould loft following the launching, A. B. Wolvin gave credit for the *Wolvin's* design to James C. Wallace. He added

70.   The dimensions of the enlarged dry dock were 550 feet on the blocks, 60 feet wide at the gate, and 18 feet of water over the sill.

71.   *Marine Review,* XXIX (April 14, 1904), 26.

that "Jimmy Wallace wanted to build the boat and . . . he [Wolvin] had never been able to keep up with the ideas of Jimmy Wallace."[72]

The first five years of the American Ship Building Company had eclipsed the expectations of even those who were involved in its incorporation. The pace that had been set in shipbuilding could not possibly continue, but the next decade would still see many exciting changes. And "Jimmy" Wallace's ideas would continue to guide the American Ship Building Company for several years to come.

72. *Ibid.*, p. 27.

The Lull before the Storm

At the annual election of company officers in October, 1904, William L. Brown retired from the presidency to become chairman of the board of directors of the American Ship Building Company. His position was filled by thirty-nine year old James C. Wallace. Jim had a varied background in the steamboat and shipbuilding business. He learned the machinist trade from his father, Robert Wallace. In 1884, he went with the Globe Iron Works where he worked as a machinist and later moved into the drafting room. Later, he sailed as assistant engineer on the *Onoko*. When the Cleveland Ship Building Company was formed in 1887, he took charge of its drawing room and became vice president and general manager of the firm by 1893. In 1899, he became general manager of the new shipbuilding consolidation.

Wallace's vacated position of general manager was filled by Robert Logan, a River Clyde Scotsman who came to Canada in 1888 to supervise construction of the steamer *Manitoba* for the Canadian Pacific Railway. He came to Cleveland in 1893 and had been associated with that city's marine interests ever since. Russell Wetmore assumed the position of vice-president. Ora J. Fish, who joined Globe in 1887 as bookkeeper and cashier, became the new secretary.[1]

The newly installed officers inherited a company with a surplus of over $3,600,000 that had built thirty-six vessels during the past fiscal year and had contracts for nine more for the ensuing fall and winter.[2] The *Marine Review* lucidly noted that "of all the combinations organized in the United States during the past five years there is none so conservatively organized as the American Ship Building Co. and none so well entrenched financially."[3] Business was so good that the company was able to retire the $150,000 mortgage on the old Mills Dry Dock property in Buffalo and to continue the maintenance fund of $200,000 established two years earlier.[4]

By the following June, the company built twenty more vessels and had an additional twenty-one under contract. The tendency of vessel owners to increase the size and carrying capacity of their ships continued. The 5,000-ton capacity steamer of 1900 had stretched to 11,500 tons by the summer of 1905 and was expected to reach 13,000 tons by the spring of 1906.[5]

Although the word "stretch" was used figuratively, it comes close to describing what was actually done. Vessel owners discovered that the small steel freighters of the nineties could just meet operating expenses. During the winter of 1903-04, the American Ship Building Company lengthened the Hanna freighter *Republic* in its Cleveland shipyard. This set the mode. During the next two winters, other owners rushed to lengthen their smaller ships. Some vessels, such as the *G. J. Grammer*, were only three years old but already were bordering on economic obsolescence. The cost figures of the *Republic* were hard

1. *Marine Review*, XXX (October 13, 1904), 25.

2. Fifth Annual Report of The American Ship Building Company, for the Fiscal Year Ended June 30, 1904.

3. *Marine Review*, XXX (December 1, 1904), 27.

4. Fifth Annual Report of The American Ship Building Company, for the Fiscal Year Ended June 30, 1904; Third Annual Report of The American Ship Building Company, for the Fiscal Year Ended June 30, 1902.

5. Sixth Annual Report of The American Ship Building Company, for the Fiscal Year Ended June 30, 1905.

to dispute. Before she was lengthened, she represented an investment of $100,000. The addition of a 72-foot midsection increased her capacity by 1,300 tons, or 26,000 tons for an average season—at no greater operating expense. The "stretching" project, which cost about $70,000, increased her annual earning power by $13,000.[6]

Most of the bulk freighters lengthened during this period carried a new 72-foot section amidships. The new length was determined by the hatch multiple: the older ships had 24-foot spaced hatch centers, and the new midsection represented three hatches. Vesselmen thought that this would provide considerably more carrying capacity without making the length disproportionate to the beam. Nevertheless, the specters of the *Western Reserve* and *W. H. Gilcher* were not banished.

Some marine men felt that the 43-foot beam of the older ships would not lend the necessary support to the increased length of the reconstructed freighters in a heavy sea. The additional length was not considered a danger in the newer vessels since they had 50-foot beams. The skeptics were soon provided with ammunition. The steamer *Sevona* was lengthened in the Buffalo yard during the winter of 1904-05. Her owners were thought to be more cautious than necessary in providing strength to the rebuilt freighter.[7] In a terrific gale on September 2, 1905, the *Sevona* was driven onto the rocks off Sand Island in the Apostle Islands of Lake Superior. The vessel broke in half, and seven unfortunate crew members trapped in the forward half of the ship perished.

Vesselmen were quick to point out that the disaster was the result of circumstances and not construction. Insurance underwriters were not so sure. They made a tour of inspection of the lengthened vessels during the winter of 1905-06.[8] While nothing came of their inspection, still, there was no rush that winter by vessel owners to have their ships lengthened. The fact that the *Sevona* was the only loss sustained by the "stretched" ships justified the faith of their owners in the reconstructions.

6. *Marine Review*, XXX (December 15, 1904), 24.
7. *Ibid.*, XXXI (June 8, 1905), 17.
8. *Ibid.*, XXXII (November 2, 1905), 20-21.

One unique contest that unofficially developed during the "stretching boom" was the speed with which the halves of the to-be-lengthened ships could be separated. The Craig Ship Building Company at Toledo pulled the steamer *L. C. Waldo*'s forward half the required 72 feet in twenty-three minutes, but the Superior Ship Building Company claimed the record by separating the barge *Constitution* in just seventeen minutes!

As vessel owners demanded larger vessels, American Ship Building continued to keep its building berths filled with giant new ships under construction. Profits, however, were not so great as might be expected under the existing favorable circumstances that then existed. Actually, the situation developed into a vicious cycle. When ship sizes increased, the company was forced to increase its dry dock and repair facilities accordingly. In late 1904, the executive committee announced the purchase of nineteen acres adjoining the Lorain shipyard. Preparations were made for the construction of a second dry dock there.[9] In May, 1906, President Wallace presented to the executive committee plans and estimated costs for additional dry docks or extensions of older facilities at Cleveland, Detroit, Chicago, and Buffalo.[10] Also the maintenance fund was increased to $500,000.[11]

In 1905, two American Ship Building Company plants suffered fires that might have proved disastrous. In the afternoon of March 30, a fire started in the main engine room of the Buffalo Dry Dock Company. Four hundred men were at work in the yard at the time. The water main under Buffalo Creek was broken, and the pumpers lined up to pump water directly from the river. Nonetheless, what ap-

9. Executive Committee Meeting, November 10, 1904, Minutes, ASBCo.

10. *Ibid.*, May 16, 1906. Estimated costs for the new or improved facilities were:

Cleveland	$70,000
Detroit	90,000
Chicago	30,000
Buffalo	132,000

The new dry dock at Lorain measured 684 feet on the blocks, 75 feet wide at the bottom, and had 14½ feet of water over the sill.

11. Seventh Annual Report of The American Ship Building Company, for the Fiscal Year Ended June 30, 1906; Executive Committee Meeting, July 25, 1906, Minutes, ASBCo.

peared at first to be a fire of major proportions was quickly brought under control with a minimum loss of work time. Weber's Saloon, next door to the dry dock, was extensively damaged by the flames and by the forty customers as they made a hasty exit.[12] The temporary loss of this recreation center must have been as distressing to the shipyard workers as the loss of three machine shops to the dry dock management.

The second major fire occurred shortly before midnight on December 30 at the West Bay City Ship Building Company. The 720-foot-long main building which housed the saw mill and large machine shops was nothing more than a framed shell, and it collapsed in a smoldering heap in less than an hour. The new steamer *James B. Wood* was uninjured, but only the strongest exertions saved the half completed *John Sherwin*, sitting on the stocks, from injury.[13] Wallace, Logan, and Frank Jeffrey hurried up from Cleveland to assist local superintendent Hugh L. Timm in letting contracts to replace the machinery and building.[14] Despite a loss of nearly $250,000, there was practically no loss of time on new construction because of the prompt action by company officials. The *John Sherwin* was not so fortunate four months later when she departed from the shipyard on her maiden voyage. One of the Michigan Central Railroad bridges failed to open for her so that before she got out of the Saginaw River, she was back at her birthplace to have four broken plates repaired.[15]

American Ship Building Company money was used to purchase bonds from steamship companies for which it was building ships. One of the most ambitious projects involved the formation of the Lackawanna Steamship Company and the construction of eight steamers for an aggregate price of $2,250,000. The steamship company was formed by the Pickands, Mather & Company, Kean Van Cortlandt & Company, and Robert J. Dunham. American Ship Building agreed to purchase at par 4,400 shares of stock in the company and received in

12. *Buffalo Morning Express*, March 31, 1905.
13. *Bay City Daily Tribune*, December 31, 1905.
14. *Marine Review*, XXXIII (January 4, 1906), 59.
15. *Ibid.*, May 3, 1906, p. 34 and XXXV (January 10, 1907), 34.

exchange all of the assets of the Ship Owners' Dry Dock Company in Chicago.[16]

The Ship Owners' Dry Dock Company was located on Goose Island in the North Branch of the Chicago River. The company had three dry docks, the earliest of which dated back to the middle of the nineteenth century. E. M. Doolittle and Jordan Miller purchased the interests of George Wicks about 1855 and built a dry dock near the North Halstead Street bridge.[17] In the 1860's, Andrew Miller joined his brother in the operation of the yard. In 1871, the firm, now called Miller Brothers' Dry Dock Company, built a second dry dock as the Chicago grain market swelled the city's lake trade.[18] By 1895, the elder Millers had dropped from the scene. The yard was run by Thomas E. Miller, president, Brice A. Miller, treasurer, and Thomas L. Miller, secretary. A smaller third dry dock was later added to accommodate the growing Chicago River fleet of tugs and canal boats.[19]

Because of the huge volume of grain traffic at Chicago, the shipyard drew most of its business from local repairs. The Chicago River was narrow and was spanned by many swing bridges. The towing business was good. Miller Brothers' contributed several tugs to the local towing fleets over a period of fifty years. The firm also built a few freighters and schooners, but new construction was always secondary to the repair business.

In December, 1900, the locally financed Ship Owners' Dry Dock Company was incorporated with a capital of $5,000.[20] In April, 1901, the capitalization was increased to $300,000.[21] In the same month, Gabriel F. Slaughter, representing the Miller Brothers' Dry Dock

16.   Board of Directors' Meeting, October 10, 1906, Minutes, ASBCo.

17.   This dry dock, later called Number One, was 275 feet long, 44 feet wide, and had 8 feet of water over the sill.

18.   Number Two dry dock was 285 feet long on the blocks, 44 feet wide at the gate, and had 12 feet of water over the sill.

19.   Frank E. Hamilton, "Notes . . . on Shipbuilding . . . ." Number Three dry dock was 160 feet long on the blocks, 40 feet wide at the gate, and had 10 feet of water over the sill.

20.   Articles of Incorporation, December 21, 1900, Minutes, Ship Owners' Dry Dock Company, in possession of the author.

21.   *Ibid.*, Special Stockholders' Meeting, April 16, 1901.

Participants in the incorporation of the American Ship Building Company (other participants are pictured elsewhere in the book). *Left to right, top row:* J. J. Lynn, advisor. *Author's Collection.* Alexander McVittie, Detroit Dry Dock Company. *Author's Collection.* James H. Hoyt, legal advisor. *Author's Collection. Middle row:* Robert L. Ireland, Globe Iron Works. *Author's Collection.* Colgate Hoyt, American Steel Barge Company. *Author's Collection.* Russell C. Wetmore, American Steel Barge Company. *Author's Collection. Bottom row:* Luther Allen, Globe Iron Works. *Author's Collection.* Robert W. Hunt, appraiser. *Author's Collection,* Robert Logan, appraiser. *Author's Collection.*

The steamer *Isaac L. Ellwood*, built in 1900, was one of the first 500-foot ore carriers on the Great Lakes. She is shown here entering Conneaut, Ohio, in about 1901. *Author's Collection.*

The *L. C. Waldo* received a 72-foot midsection at the Craig Ship Building Company during the winter, 1904-1905. *Author's Collection.*

The *Emily P. Weed* was lengthened during the winter of 1904-1905 and came out as the *Sevona*. She was lost in September, 1905, on Lake Superior. *Robert J. Mac Donald.*

By adding a 72-foot midsection to the *Republic,* her earning capacity was increased $13,000 per year, *Smithsonian Institution.*

Augustus B. Wolvin, "The Yellow Kid," was the first 550-foot lake freighter. Her hopper-shaped cargo hold and girder arches were built to accommodate the new hulett ore unloaders. *Frank E. Hamilton.*

The steamer *Republic*, later the *North Pines*, showing the older stanchion type cargo hold. Here the vessel is being rebuilt for ocean service in World War I. *American Ship Building Company.*

Arch-type cargo hold of the steamer *Elbert H. Gary*, built to facilitate the hulett ore unloaders. *Author's Collection.*

The steam-powered hulett ore unloader at Conneaut, Ohio, was later replaced by an electrically-operated hulett. *Author's Collection.*

American Ship Building Company dry dock No. 1 at Cleveland, Ohio. Tug *Alva B.*, named for Alva Bradley, in dock. *Author's Collection.*

Wilbert L. Smith's launching party included The Garden Theater Opera Company in 1903. *Richard D. Bibby.*

A stenographer took time from her job at the Chicago Ship Building Company to christen the *John Lambert* in 1903. The *Lambert* was one of several canal-size freighters built for the Great Lakes and St. Lawrence Transportation Company. *Frank E. Hamilton.*

Left to right: James C. Wallace, president, 1904-1914. *Author's Collection.* Merton E. Farr, president, 1916-1928. *William H. Gerhauser*; James S. Dunham, Ship Owner's Dry Dock Company, Chicago. *Author's Collection.*

Frank L. Lamarche, superintendent of the Lorain yard, and Omar M. Steele, general superintendent in 1905. *Author's Collection.*

The *Alexis W. Thompson* launched by the West Bay City Ship Building Company on April 2, 1908. *Bay County Historical Society.*

Self-propelled repair scow *Robert J. Close* serviced vessels at Duluth-Superior ore docks with the least possible delay. *Author's Collection.*

The *Noronic* was built by Western Ship Building & Dry Dock Company at Port Arthur, Ontario, in 1914. *Author's Collection.*

American Ship Building's first "fleet," the wooden steamer *Mary H. Boyce,* carried ship's plates, rolled in Cleveland, to Port Arthur for the building of the *Noronic. American Ship Building Company.*

American Ship Building's Cleveland Globe yard about 1916. *Left*, collier *Marquette & Bessemer No. 1* and steamer *John W. Moore*; right, sidewheeler *City of Erie. American Ship Building Company.*

The *Danebrog*, a "Frederickstadt" type ocean steamer, built at the company's Chicago yard, ran into neutrality problems before she ever sailed for the Atlantic. *American Ship Building*.

The *War Banner* was one of the thirty-three ships to be built under contract for the Cunard Steamship Line, Ltd., of London, in early 1917. She was requisitioned by the Shipping Board as the *Lake Worth* at Chicago prior to being commissioned. *J. A. Skodny.*

The Federal Home Building Corporation developed a housing project for shipyard workers in Lorain during World War I. It included two combination stores-apartments at the corner of Iowa and E Streets. Pictured above in 1967. *Author's Collection.*

Ready . . .

Over . . .

And up! The *Lake Fernando* rolled at the greatest angle ever recorded at a lake ship launching when she was dropped eight feet into the water at the Buffalo Dry Dock Company in 1919. *Author's Collection.*

The *Lake Aurice* struck the water at the Superior Ship Building Company on July 4, 1918, at 12:01 a.m., the first of ninety-two ships launched nationally in a show of patriotism. *American Ship Building Company.*

One of Dr. Eaton's speakers, Mr. Templeton, drives home a point during a Liberty Loan address at Buffalo in 1918. The shipyard band contributed to the enthusiasm. *Christian J. Stellrecht.*

The panic created by the submarine menace in early 1917 is illustrated by this impractical and costly blockade runner designed by the American Ship Building Company. *Painting by Rev. Edward J. Dowling, S. J., University of Detroit, based on profile plans in the National Archives.*

AMERICAN SHIP BUILDING COMPANY GENEALOGY
1905 – 1915

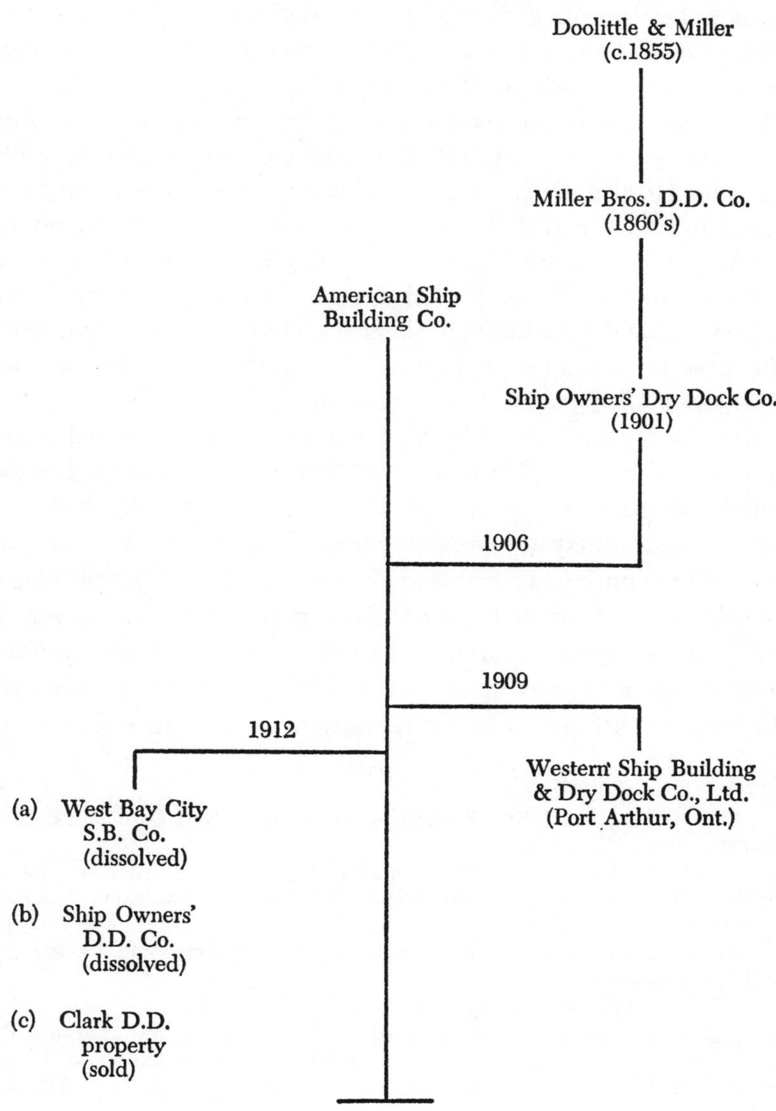

Company, offered to exchange that company's holdings and a cash settlement of $130,000 to the Ship Owners' firm for all of the Ship Owners' stock and $300,000 in bonds.[22] The offer was accepted, and the new firm acquired a shipyard and three dry docks.[23] The Ship Owners' company hired William W. Watterson as its first superintendent and James Mowatt as its yard manager.[24]

Watterson had bounced around the globe considerably in his forty years. He came from the Isle of Man, where he learned the shipbuilding trade. He also served on English full-riggers engaged in the South American trade. In 1885, he came to Cleveland, where he found employment with the earlier Ship Owners' Dry Dock Company and with William Radcliffe. He succeeded Thomas Bristow as superintendent of the Cleveland Ship Building Company's big Lorain plant in 1898.[25] When the consolidation of shipyards took place, he left the combine to engage in independent marine surveying.

After hiring Watterson, the Ship Owners' company signed a contract with Edward Gillen of Racine, Wisconsin, to enlarge Number One dry dock according to plans drawn by A. V. Powell, chief engineer of the American Ship Building Company.[26] The company showed a net profit in its first year of operations of only $4,389. One of the tribulations it suffered was a strike during October and November by the carpenters and caulkers, who objected to a nine-hour working day. Watterson replaced the union men by hiring, from the Ohio and Mississippi rivers, men whose slack season was the late fall and win-

22.   *Ibid.*, Letter from Gabriel F. Slaughter to Directors, Ship Owners' Dry Dock Company, March 28, 1901.

23.   Charles A. McDonald, a Chicago marine insurance underwriter, was elected president, James J. Rarden, vice-president, and Daniel J. Smallwood, secretary-treasurer.

24.   Executive Committee Meeting, April 23, 1901, Minutes, Ship Owners' Dry Dock Company.

25.   J. B. Mansfield (ed.), *History of the Great Lakes*, II, 1096.

26.   Executive Committee Meeting, April 23, 1901, Minutes, Ship Owners' Dry Dock Company. The enlarged dry dock was 480 feet long on the blocks, 60 feet wide at the gate, and had 16 feet of water over the sill. It was opened on March 5, 1902.

ter. This added the expense of a restaurant within the company yard because of threatened violence by the union carpenters and caulkers.[27]

The next two years were fraught with financial difficulties and a change in management. The capitalization was raised to $600,000. Although the company realized an undivided profit of $35,161 and docked 91 vessels in 1902, the cost of the dry dock improvement and purchase of machinery for steel repairs was so high that the company did not have sufficient working capital.[28] The company did not qualify for cash discounts, consequently, and had to pay excessive prices for material. The board of directors decided to raise $30,000 by asking stockholders to purchase three-year, 6 per cent promissory notes, but this move realized only $16,500.[29]

The tight financial condition of the company prompted a change of officers and the hiring of Robert J. Dunham as president and general manager.[30] Shortly after, Watterson resigned to accept the more stable position as Superintendent of Repairs for the Pittsburgh Steamship Company and Master Mechanic J. T. Radcliffe was elevated to superintendent of the dry dock company.

The only new construction built by the company under Watterson's supervision was the steel-hulled Milwaukee fire tug *M.F.D. No. 15*. She was designed by Chicago naval architect W. J. Wood and was appropriately christened with a bottle of Blue Ribbon beer.[31] Unfortunately, the company lost $10,352 on the contract.[32]

Dunham's first year as general manager was by no means an easy one. His first move was to increase by 25 per cent the bids that Wood

27. *Ibid.*, Report to the Stockholders, April 15, 1902.

28. *Ibid.*, Special Stockholders' Meeting, October 22, 1902, Annual Meeting of Stockholders, April 21, 1903, and Special Meeting of the Board of Directors, October 22, 1903.

29. *Ibid.*, Special Meeting of the Board of Directors, October 22, 1903, and Executive Committee Meeting, November 13, 1903.

30. *Ibid.*, Meeting of the Board of Directors, November 6, 1903. Dunham replaced McDonald as president. Daniel Smallwood resigned and was replaced by H. B. Watson as secretary and McArthur Young as treasurer. James Rarden remained as vice-president.

31. *Marine Review*, XXVII (June 4, 1903), 22.

32. Annual Meeting of Stockholders, April 19, 1904, Minutes, Ship Owners' Dry Dock Company.

drew up for prospective contracts for a government lightship and two wooden lighters for the Lehigh Valley Transportation Company. The North Branch firm won both contracts and the company severed its contract with Wood.[33] Dunham tried to negotiate with the Ship Carpenters' Union for a nine-hour day. The "old regime" had given in to the union's demand for an eight-hour day, and this yard was the only one on the Great Lakes that had done so. Dunham simply stated that failure to arbitrate meant that he would either close the yard or "co-operate with non-union carpenters."[34] A lock-out resulted, with the added expense of $1,200 for guards and a boarding house for the non-union carpenters within the yard.[35]

By the spring of 1906, the board of directors considered the advisability of selling their holdings. The net surplus showed a decrease of $6,173 from the year before, commerce on the narrow North Branch of the Chicago River was down by 30 per cent, and the firm needed to borrow $25,000 to meet expenses until the incoming winter accounts could catch up with it.[36] It managed somehow to weather the storm until the organization of the Lackawanna Steamship Company cruised to its rescue.

The Ship Owners' Dry Dock Company experienced five years of rough financial and labor difficulties. Now it was the American Ship Building Company's turn. The year 1907 began with "labor in fair supply, [and] material coming forward according to schedule."[37] By March, the situation changed as the yards in Superior, Chicago, Wyandotte, Lorain, and Cleveland went out on strike. The workers' resistance in the strike-bound yards everywhere, except Chicago, was beginning to weaken by June. President Wallace reported that he

33. *Ibid.*, Executive Committee Meeting, February 19 and 26, 1904. During this period, J. DeKoven Towner succeeded H. B. Watson as secretary of the firm. Number Two dry dock was extended to 350 feet in length.

34. *Ibid.*, October 11, 1904.

35. Annual Meeting of Stockholders, April 18, 1905.

36. Annual Meeting of Stockholders, April 18, 1905 and April 17, 1906, Executive Committee Meeting, January 25, 1906, and Board of Directors' Meeting, March 27, 1906.

37. Board of Directors' Meeting, December 12, 1906, Minutes, ASBCo.

was doing everything he could to break the strike including, "at large expense to the Company," importing new men, boarding and sleeping them at the plants, "in order to hasten the progress of the work."[38]

Shuffling of contracts was necessary. The 600-foot steamer *Thomas Lynch* was launched in Chicago at the outset of the strike. In May, she was fitted out sufficiently to be towed to the Lorain yard by the little wooden steamer *Mary H. Boyce* for the installation of her machinery.[39] Chicago yard number 76 (*Arthur H. Hawgood*) and Detroit yard number 173 (*Caldera*) were transferred to the Bay City yard, which was not on strike. Much of the repair work was shunted to the Buffalo yard. As a result, the new construction in that yard was delayed.[40]

Fortunately for the company, the local yard superintendents, who usually operated autonomously, held one of their rare meetings at the company's general offices in Cleveland just before the beginning of the strike. They discussed the maneuvering which might be possible should a general strike occur. The local officers recommended a policy for their individual yards, and the merits were discussed by all present.[41]

William L. Brown and James Wallace decided that an attempt to import non-union men into South Chicago would result in bloodshed and possible death. Rather than precipitate violence the company closed the yard to all new construction, throwing about 1,800 men out of work.[42] All of the yards, with the possible exception of Bay City, suffered in one form or another as a result of the strike. The Wyandotte yard, for example, lost $150,683 on six contracts because of late delivery; in addition, one of its contracts was transferred to Bay City.[43]

38. Executive Committee Meeting, June 18, 1907.

39. *Marine Review*, XXXV (May 9, 1907), 31.

40. Executive Committee Meeting, June 18, 1907, Minutes, ASBCo.

41. John H. Smith, "Views of an Ex-Manager," *Live Wire*, I (March, 1915), 3.

42. Executive Committee Meeting, June 18, 1907, Minutes, ASBCo.; *Marine Review*, XXXVI (October 31, 1907), 20-21.

43. "Contract Data, 1899-1915, Detroit Ship Building Company," William A. McDonald Collection, Dossin Great Lakes Museum, Belle Isle, Detroit, Michigan.

Part of the loss sustained by the Detroit Ship Building Company was the result of the greatest single underwriter loss experienced on the lakes up to that time. The ornate passenger sidewheeler *City of Cleveland III* was launched at Wyandotte in January, 1907. She was considered the crowning achievement among Frank E. Kirby's many creations. The vessel's name was kept a secret almost up to launch time because her owner, the D & C Company, offered a $10 prize and an annual pass to the person suggesting the best name. Clevelander J. R. Manning, the recipient of the prize, wrote convincingly that for sentimental and business reasons the leading steamers in the line should bear the names of the cities in the company title. Her launching was one of James Wallace's most skillful feats because her width over the paddlewheel guards was three feet wider than the slip into which she was launched![44] It was accomplished without a hitch! Her interior was richly decorated in hand-carved Mexican mahogany with splashes of gold, red, verd antique, and gleaming white. The Great Lakes fraternity awaited her appearance with a parental eagerness.

On May 13, 1907, the lakes community was shocked to learn that the *City of Cleveland III* had gone up in smoke early that morning. She was moored at the Orleans Street yard in Detroit with everything except her carpets and furniture aboard. The lavish decorations were almost completed and she was to have gone into commission on June 30. The fire that succeeded in completely gutting her was thought to have started from defective temporary wiring near her port paddle box. Since none of her pumps or fire fighting apparatus was available for use, she soon burned out of control with the splendorous wood and paint contributing to the flames.[45] The ship was rebuilt and came out the following year. The underwriters made a cash settlement with the shipbuilding company of $525,000, but the company still lost $34,794 on the contract.[46]

In the summer of 1907, new construction orders ran considerably

---

44. *Marine Review,* XXXV (January 10, 1907), 18.

45. *Ibid.,* May 16, 1907, pp. 24-25.

46. Finance Committee Meeting, January 7, 1908, Minutes, ASBCo.; "Contract Data, 1899-1915 . . . ," William A. McDonald Collection.

behind those of the year before. The general unrest of labor in the Great Lakes region made vessel owners hesitant to invest in new ships. When the Panic of 1907 struck in the fall of that year, the conservative directors of the American Ship Building Company curtailed expenses by temporarily suspending construction, except on repair work and new construction that was nearly completed, and deferred payment of the regular quarterly dividend on preferred stock.[47] Despite the strikes and depression that adversely affected the steel industry and lake carrying trade, the company launched twenty-three ships and showed an increase of over $3,000,000 in its working capital.[48] By the summer of 1908, the lake trade was falling back into its normal patterns of traffic, even though the season ran considerably below that of the year before for lake shippers.

The brief interlude in the frantic construction pace that the shipbuilding company maintained since its inception gave the officers an opportunity to draw a deep breath and reflect on future needs. They deemed the Bay City and Chicago North Branch yards expendable and decided that the dry docks at terminal points could be enlarged without the purchase of more property.[49] The older dry dock at Superior was enlarged. Two dry docks in Buffalo were filled so that a large one could be constructed, cutting across the original sites at about a 45 degree angle to Buffalo Creek.[50]

In April, 1908, the Parliament of the Doninion of Canada passed an act which imposed a duty of 25 per cent on all repairs of Canadian vessels in the United States. It became effective on July 1 of the same year.[51] During the fiscal year of 1907-08, the company repaired fifty-

47. Board of Directors' Meeting, November 14 and December 28, 1907, Minutes, ASBCo.

48. Ninth Annual Report of The American Ship Building Company, for the Fiscal Year Ended June 30, 1908.

49. Board of Directors' Meeting, July 15, 1908 and Executive Committee Meeting, July 27 and September 16, 1908, Minutes, ASBCo.

50. The enlarged Superior dry dock was 620 feet overall, 60½ feet wide at the bottom, and had 17½ feet of water over the sill. The new Buffalo dry dock was 600 feet long on the blocks, 79 feet 4 inches wide at the bottom, and had 14½ feet of water over the sill.

51. Tenth Annual Report of The American Ship Building Company, for the Fiscal Year Ended June 30, 1909.

six Canadian vessels; after July 1, 1908, practically none.[52] When James Wallace and W. L. Brown investigated the possibility of building a subsidiary Canadian plant, they determined that the most advantageous site was at Port Arthur, Ontario, on Lake Superior. The Canadian government would grant a 3 per cent yearly bonus for twenty years on the cost of all machinery, dry docks, buildings, and real estate. Wallace and Brown also discovered that the property would be exempt from all but the school tax for the same period of years. They recommended that the parent company retain 80 per cent of the stock with the remainder being held by Canadian parties.[53] Brown, Wallace, A. B. Wolvin, Robert L. Ireland, and H. H. Porter composed the committee to make the necessary arrangements.[54]

The Western Ship Building & Dry Dock Company, of Port Arthur, Ontario, was organized with a capital stock of $600,000, of which the parent firm was to acquire $500,000 worth of stock at $120 par value per share. The Canadian share of the investment was headed by James Whalen of Port Arthur.[55] Construction was begun immediately, and the City of Port Arthur accepted the dry dock on January 1, 1911.[56]

While American Ship Building Company was investing in Canadian property, some of its American holdings began to slip. The temporary lull in the iron ore carrying trade in the latter half of 1907 and in 1908 proved disastrous to one of the largest independent steamship companies on the lakes. The Gilchrist Transportation Company of Cleveland operated a large fleet of wooden and steel bulk freighters, many of the latter class built on a "bond basis." The ore carrying trade suffered the most on the lakes because of the Panic of 1907. Iron ore tonnage through the Sault Locks decreased by 38 per cent in 1908 from that of the year before.[57] When the steamship company defaulted, the

---

52. *Ibid.*

53. Executive Committee Meeting, December 12, 1908, Minutes, ASBCo.

54. *Ibid.*, Board of Directors' Meeting, May 19, 1909.

55. *Ibid.*, October 9, 1909.

56. *Ibid.*, Executive Committee Meeting, June 22, 1911. The dry dock was **661** feet 9 inches long on the blocks, 72 feet 3 inches wide at the bottom, and had 16½ feet of water over the sill.

57. "Comparative Traffic—Years 1907 and 1908," table in *Statistical Report of*

American Ship Building Company was placed in a bad position. The failure of a company of this size usually impaired the sale of vessel bonds as an investment in other markets because of the loss of confidence that was sure to follow. Secondly, the shipbuilding company had extended credit to the Gilchrist company for repairs that were awaiting insurance claim settlements. James H. Hoyt, representing the finance committee of American Ship Building, reported that his firm had claims amounting to $598,000 against Gilchrist. On the other hand, the steamship company required $540,000 to meet bond obligations, insurance premiums, and current bills to prevent its falling into the hands of a receiver.[58] The insurance claim settlements would not be released until the premiums were paid.

The American Ship Building Company had to throw good money after bad if it hoped to realize any money that was due it. The company huddled with some Cleveland banks, which also held an interest in the Gilchrist company. The banks advanced the $540,000, of which American Ship Building contributed $295,000. The loan was secured by the deposit of $3,000,000 in second mortgage bonds; the shipbuilding company's repair claims were secured on a two-for-one basis after the other debts were reduced. The steel-hulled Gilchrist ships represented an equity of over $4,000,000. The management of the steamship company was placed in the hands of a five-man directorate: two men appointed by the banks, two by the Gilchrist company, and one by American Ship Building.[59]

The second mortgage bonds matured on January 15, 1910, but the Gilchrist Transportation Company needed $300,000 to cover floating debts until its annual stockholders' meeting three days later. There were liens on the ships, and they were subject to seizure. James Hoyt met with Frank W. and J. C. Gilchrist and F. M. Osborne of the steamship company and proposed that they personally sign a joint

---

Lake Commerce Passing Through Canals at Sault Ste. Marie, Michigan and Ontario During Season of 1908 (Washington: Government Printing Office, 1909), p. 12.

58. Executive Committee Meeting, December 12, 1908, Minutes, ASBCo.
59. *Ibid.*

promissory note for that amount and assign all outstanding claims to a trustee. This would give the steamship company breathing space until March. Frank W. Hart, a major stockholder in the Gilchrist Transportation Company and a member of the board of directors worked effectively behind the scenes.

After much consultation, the banks and American Ship Building agreed that a promissory note from the individuals would not increase their chances of collecting the debts, so they advanced the $300,000. Of that amount, $37,000 was due on insurance premiums. The shipbuilding company's proportion of the loan amounted to $82,600. It would realize $103,500 in adjusted insurance repair claims.[60]

The financial muddle of the Gilchrist line was too much for the Gilchrist stockholders to cope with, and American Ship Building agreed to the appointment of a receiver.[61] Before the vessels could be sold, American Ship Building had to invest another $170,000 so that it might acquire one-third of the first mortgage bonds. Through a stipulation in the mortgage, the shipbuilding company guaranteed all of the outstanding bonds of that issue.[62] The shipbuilding company was able to exchange its part of the settlement for stock in the Interlake Steamship Company (a Pickands, Mather & Company subsidiary) and ultimately sold the stock at a profit over a period of years.[63]

The Gilchrist dealings illustrate the precarious position in which the American Ship Building Company could find itself. Business transactions of a similar nature occurred over the next few years as shipping rates fluctuated. The most serious blow to the lake trade after 1908 occurred in 1914, when iron ore receipts dwindled by 35 per cent.[64] Although tonnage figures showed an increase during most of

60. *Ibid.*, Finance Committee Meeting, January 15, 1910.

61. *Ibid.*, Executive Committee Meeting, January 19, 1910.

62. *Ibid.*, December 20, 1911.

63. *Ibid.*, Finance Committee Meeting, July 28, 1913. The eight steamers involved in the foreclosure were the *Joseph C. Gilchrist, Perry G. Walker, Henry S. Sill, Frank W. Gilchrist, R. S. Schuck, J. L. Weeks, R. L. Ireland,* and *Lewis Woodruff* (*Ibid.*, January 6, 1912).

64. "Comparative Traffic—Years 1913-1914," table in *Statistical Report of Lake Commerce Passing Through Canals at Sault Ste. Marie, Michigan and Ontario During the Season of 1914* (Washington: Government Printing Office, 1915), p. 9.

the years between 1909-1914, they did not show the seasonal fluctuations within each year. The summer months were hardest on both vessel operators and the shipyards. New vessel construction continued, but not at the pace maintained prior to 1909. Although giant new bulk carriers were built, the carrying supply had about filled the demand of the iron ore industry. The company turned instead to more varied and specialized craft such as tankers and tank barges, tugs, and passenger steamers.

Changes occurred in the physical holdings of the American Ship Building Company as the patterns of lake freighters changed. Since there was no longer a demand for huge new ore carriers, and small wooden freighters were rapidly disappearing, more property became expendable. The Clark Dry Dock property in Detroit was filled in even with the dock line in 1906.[65] Since the expense of taxes and watchmen over the years was a luxury the company could not afford as lake trade slumped, it began to seek a buyer "at not less than $70,000."[66] The Bay City yard was closed down in 1908, and, by 1910, most of the machinery had been removed.[67] The West Bay City Ship Building Company was dissolved in 1912.[68] In 1909, new tax laws passed in Illinois made it advantageous to transfer the assets of the Ship Owners' Dry Dock Company to those of the Chicago Ship Building Company. The transfer did not take place until 1912.[69] Between 1909 and 1915, the yard continued to operate at a profit because of the multitude of small craft in and around the Chicago waterway system. In 1913, the board of directors decided to build a large new dry dock at South Chicago at about a 45 degree angle to the Calumet River and to close down the North Branch yard.[70] The

65. *Marine Reivew*, XXXIV (July 19, 1906), 25.

66. Executive Committee Meeting, January 19, 1912, Minutes, ASBCo. The property was sold in 1912 for $85,000 (*Ibid.*, January 15, 1913).

67. *Ibid.*, January 10, 1910. The property was sold in 1911.

68. *Ibid.*, May 15, 1912.

69. *Ibid.*, Board of Directors' Meeting, July 28, 1909 and Executive Committee Meeting, May 15, 1912.

70. *Ibid.*, Board of Directors' Meeting, November 26, 1913 and letter from Henry L. Christy and Frederick A. Brown of Chicago to Board of Directors, November

smaller dock in South Chicago was to accommodate the business formerly conducted by the other Chicago yard. As a free dump, the dry docks on the North Branch property were filled.[71]

The repair business fluctuated with the vagaries of the lake trade but generally remained good. As a consequence, the company was forced to keep its operating facilities in good repair. It updated the Globe yard in Cleveland by building several new buildings and shops at a cost of $300,000.[72] The Number Three dry dock in Buffalo was in such need of repair that the Deputy Labor Commissioner notified the company that it was too dangerous to use until it was repaired.[73] In another consolidation move, the company's main office at 120 Viaduct Street in Cleveland were removed to the shipyard at the foot of West 54th Street.[74]

The Superior yard also reflected the mood of consolidation that was taking place within the company holdings. The yard buildings were rearranged so that isolated units were brought closer together for a more efficient and economic operation. Emphasis was placed on repair rather than new construction potential. The yard also built the 86-foot self-propelled repair scow *Robert J. Close*. It facilitated repairs to vessels at loading or unloading docks with the least possible delay and without steamers having to enter the shipyard for minor repairs.[75]

Several changes in the company hierarchy were made. William L. Brown resigned as chairman of the board of directors in 1913 and was temporarily replaced by James C. Wallace. The most significant resignation was that of Wallace in 1914. He was succeeded as president by Edward Smith of Buffalo. In December, 1913, Henry L. Christy of Chicago was elected chairman of the board of directors, replacing

---

25, 1913. The new dry dock at South Chicago was 667 feet 9 inches long on the blocks, 79 feet 10 inches wide at the bottom, and had 15 feet 2 inches of water over the sill.

71.   *Ibid.*, Board of Directors' Meeting, June 23, 1915.
72.   *Ibid.*, Executive Committee Meeting, January 19, 1910.
73.   *Ibid.*, June 25, 1913.
74.   *Ibid.*, Board of Directors' Meeting, September 22, 1915.
75.   F. A. Miller, "Efficiency in Repair Work," *Live Wire*, I (January, 1915), 1.

Wallace. Russell Wetmore died in January, 1914, and Ora J. Fish assumed the position of treasurer. Merton E. Farr, president of the Detroit Ship Building Company, succeeded Edward Smith as vice-president when the latter moved up to the presidency. Robert B. Wallace, James Wallace's younger brother, replaced Robert Logan as general manager in 1909. Wallace resigned in 1914 and Alfred G. Smith of Chicago became the new general manager. The ranks of the original members of the corporation were dwindling. A few could still be found on the executive committee and board of directors, but only Edward Smith and James H. Hoyt, general counsel, remained as officers. The cohesiveness among the officers began to give way.

In April, 1915, Henry Christy reported to the board of directors that in 1910 James Wallace had entered into a license agreement with the distinguished British naval architech Sir Joseph W. Isherwood for the use of his type of internal ship construction. According to Christy, royalties exceeding $64,000 were paid even though the contract was not signed by any of the officers, nor was the company seal affixed to the paper. Wallace had exceeded his authority as president, and the contract was not binding.[76] The situation produced disagreement among the directors which came to a head the following year.

In the Isherwood construction, the side framing was longitudinal instead of the traditional transverse framing that prevailed upon the lakes. The great advantage was a saving in weight, but ships that were longitudinally framed were supple. In a good sea, they resembled a slithering snake as they twisted and rolled with the seas. For a period of four or five years, the Isherwood style of construction was in vogue just as the whaleback, turtleback, and other innovations enjoyed a short popularity from time to time.

The company settled with Isherwood in 1916 and built several vessels under his license. As a result of the argument that ensued over this and other matters among the directors of the shipbuilding firm, however, Henry Christy resigned as chairman of the board.[77] The older members of the board of directors stood firm behind James Wallace. Christy bitterly expressed his feelings in his letter of resignation:

76. Board of Directors' Meeting, April 13, 1915, Minutes, ASBCo.
77. *Ibid.*, June 28, 1916.

The action of President Smith, who was chosen President
at my request in throwing in his lot with certain directors of the
Company, whom I believe have other interests at heart than the
interests of the American Ship Building Company, . . . makes
it apparent to me that I am unable to complete the reforms
inaugurated during the past two years.[78]

Christy's position remained unfilled, and Edward Smith died one
month later. Merton E. Farr became the new president of American
Ship Building at a crucial period in the company's history.

War had erupted in Europe the previous year. The Port Arthur
shipyard was producing 200 shrapnel shells per day and was ready
to build Bull tractors to aid the Canadian and British war effort in the
wheat fields of Western Canada.[79] The shipbuilding fraternity on the
southern side of the Great Lakes realized that soon they would be
called upon to play either a neutral or combatant role in the drama
that was unfolding. Merton E. Farr was capable of handling the tasks
that were heaped upon him.

78. *Ibid.*, Letter of resignation from Henry L. Christy to Ora J. Fish, November
3, 1915.
79. "Port Arthur," *Live Wire*, I (July, 1915), 4.

9.

Tonnage and the Farr Shore

As noted in the last chapter, the Port Arthur shipyard already was engaged in war production by 1915. The war shell contract was profitable, but the manufacture of Bull tractors was a failure. Furthermore, the company built only thirteen new hulls in five years, most of which were of a minor nature. J. S. Gorman, auditor of the parent firm, wrote to Merton E. Farr early in 1916 that "business general conduct here is not satisfactory because of a disorganized situation affecting officials, principal and minor." He recommended the hiring of a "strong man in the operating department, and cooperation throughout all departments" to remedy the situation.[1]

But the decision had already been made to dispose of the facility should the proper offer be made.[2] In the spring of 1916 the large Can-

---

1. Letter from J. S. Gorman to Merton E. Farr, January 25, 1916, Minutes, ASBCo.
2. *Ibid.*, Finance Committee Meeting, October 26, 1915.

ada Steamship Lines, Limited, in the persons of R. M. Wolvin and J. W. Norcross, purchased about $350,000 worth of the Western Ship Building & Dry Dock Company stock and expressed an interest in purchasing the remainder within the year.[3] This was accomplished in October of the same year.[4] In order to consummate the deal American Ship Building accepted 900 shares of Canada Steamship Lines stock and credited the buyers with $60,000 to obtain a more suitable cash settlement.[5] When the shipyard was incorporated in 1909, the venture appeared promising. Over the years, however, and including the sale of the yard, the American Ship Building Company lost over a half million dollars.[6]

Meanwhile, the situation on the American side of the lake was rapidly changing as a result of changes in international trade. British shipyards cut off their contracts with neutral nations. This was reflected in New York ship brokers' offices as prices of ships soared correspondingly with transoceanic freight rates. It cost $1.25 per 100 pounds to ship cotton from New York to Liverpool whereas it had formerly cost 20 cents per 100 pounds. Provisions rose from $4.85 per ton to $1.25 per 100 pounds. All other commodities showed similar increases.[7] The Scandinavian nations—Norway in particular—turned to the United States to fill the void created by the loss of British shipyards.[8] The bulk of the world trade was conducted by smaller-tonnage vessels. For instance, the British mercantile fleet in 1915 totalled 10,218 steamers aggregating slightly under 21,000,000 tons and averaged only 2,100 tons per ship.[9] The Baltic and North Sea trade of the Norwegians was particularly adaptable to the smaller vessels.

3. *Ibid.*, Board of Directors' Meeting, March 24, 1916.

4. *Ibid.*, October 31, 1916.

5. *Ibid.*

6. *Ibid.*, Statement of Loss Sustained by American Ship Building Company Through Its Accounts and Investments in the Stock of the Western Ship Building & Dry Dock Company, Ltd., September 26, 1917.

7. "Finance: Fortunes of the Shipping Industry," *The Nation*, CII (March 9, 1916), 294.

8. Winthrop L. Marvin, "American Shipbuilding—A Real Renaissance," *The American Review of Reviews*, LVI (July, 1917), 64.

9. "Mobilizing the Shipyards," *The Nation*, CIV (April 12, 1917), 423.

The first contracts that American Ship Building received as a result of the world shipping situation required some nautical surgery. The old iron-hulled freighters *George F. Brownell, Owego, Binghamton,* and *John G. McCullough* were sold to East Coast interests. The Buffalo Dry Dock Company cut off the stern of the *McCullough* so that she would fit into the Canadian canals. It cut the other vessels in half; they were then towed to Lauzon, Quebec, for joining in July and August, 1915. They were towed one at a time by the tug *Petrel,* with the bow section following the tug and the stern section following the bow section stern first.[10] The *McCullough* and *Brownell* later were victims of an enemy submarine.[11]

In October, 1915, as a result of the inflationary world shipping conditions, the shipbuilding firm received its first new construction contract. A. G. Smith announced that he had signed contracts with Norwegian parties for the construction of two ocean steamers of Welland Canal size for $225,000 each and that he was negotiating with New York ship brokers for four more vessels of the same type.[12]

The American Ship Building Company followed a basic ship design called the "Frederickstadt" type. It had been developed by Norwegian naval architects to conform to the rules of the Norwegian Board of Sea Control, the national classification society comparable to Lloyds of London.[13] The vessels were limited in length to 261 feet overall by the Canadian canals. They were "three-islanders," that is, they had raised forecastles and poop decks with their machinery and cabins amidships.

As the submarine war raged and the acquisition of ships became more acute, the shipbuilding company purchased more land adjacent to its Wyandotte plant in anticipation of salt water contracts.[14] It also

---

10. "Buffalo," *Live Wire,* I (August, 1915), 2.

11. The *Brownell,* under her original name of *Chemung,* was the subject of an international incident when an Austrian submarine reportedly machine-gunned her crew after sinking her in the Mediterranean Sea on November 26, 1916.

12. Finance Committee Meeting, October 26, 1916, Minutes, ASBCo.

13. George B. Turnbull, "General Cargo Ships—Single-Deck Type," *Great Lakes Engineering Works, Detroit, Michigan* (catalog; Battle Creek: Gage Printing Co., c.1916), p. 90.

14. Board of Directors' Meeting, March 24, 1916, Minutes, ASBCo.

began to stockpile ship steel before the steel prices soared.[15] In the spring of 1916, the company signed contracts for $342,000 per ship for seven more ocean vessels.[16] In July, prices levelled temporarily at $337,000 per ship, with Norwegians building most of them.[17] James E. Davidson, a Bay City ship owner and recent addition to the company's board of directors, also was building some for speculative purposes.[18] In December, 1916, the company closed three more contracts for ocean-going ships at $525,000 per ship.[19]

Norwegian ship owners invested over £40,000,000 sterling by 1917 when a new force entered the field. In late 1916 and early 1917, the British Government began buying up every available building berth in this country to construct cargo carriers.[20] In March, 1917, President Farr announced the signing of a contract with the Cunard Steamship Line, Ltd., of London, for the construction of thirty-three vessels at an aggregate price of $19,690,000.[21] Simultaneously, the board of directors approved a $500,000 expenditure for yard improvements, more land, and more tools.

The Cunard Line began its dealings with American Ship early in 1917 when it purchased the interests in four Norwegian steamers still on the stocks.[22] The contracts were indicative of the times. The original contract for the *War Tune* was $420,000, as agreed upon by Christen Gran of Bergen, Norway, in September, 1916. Circumstances were so favorable for the shipbuilding company that it was able to include contingency clauses in the contract making it possible to collect a bonus for early delivery even though the vessel was accepted by the owner after the delivery date! If construction of the vessel was delayed by strikes, weather, or late arrival of material, the lost time was to be

15. *Ibid.*, April 26, 1916.
16. *Ibid.*, April 26 and June 28, 1916.
17. *Ibid.*, July 26, 1916.
18. *Ibid.*, March 24, June 28, July 26, and September 27, 1916.
19. *Ibid.*, December 20, 1916.
20. "America's Shipbuilding Resources," *Living Age*, CCXCIII (June 17, 1917), 700.
21. Board of Directors' Meeting, March 28, 1917, Minutes, ASBCo.
22. These were the steamers *War Patrol*, *War Major*, *War Tune*, and *War Cross*.

added to the fixed delivery date. The company was to receive $200 for each day the vessel was completed before the delivery date, and a like amount for each day of delay in payment beyond the fixed payment dates. After the Cunard Line purchased the vessel, it was late a total of nine days in making payments. The shipbuilding company gained fifteen days because of time lost to strikes and cold weather at Wyandotte, and the vessel was completed eighty-five days ahead of schedule. Thus the American Ship Building Company received $435,000 instead of the contracted price of $420,000, for building the *War Tune!*[23]

The phenomenal rise of prices for ships was matched by a rise in construction costs. The company was unaccustomed to working on ocean vessels, and new plans, forms, and molds were costly. American Ship Building lost a total of $43,000 on the first six Norwegian vessels it built but on the next three it realized a total profit of $137,500.[24] Once the pattern of construction was formed, it became profitable! These high-flying contracts were about to have their wings clipped.

On April 6, 1917, the United States entered the First World War. Ten days later, the government-sponsored United States Shipping Board came into being. For three months, the neophyte agency and its functionary, the Emergency Fleet Corporation, struggled with growing pains and internal dissension. They attempted to strengthen America's merchant marine by straightening out its long-neglected problems. Finally, the antagonism within the agencies and the resulting bad publicity caused President Woodrow Wilson to accept the resignations of their leaders. He appointed Edward N. Hurley, a former Chicago industrialist, as their dual chairman. One week later, Hurley requisitioned all steel-hulled ships over 2,500 deadweight tons under construction in American shipyards. The order was issued primarily to prevent inflationary tonnage prices and to insure the proper mobili-

23.   Letter from Ora J. Fish to Ernest Ketcham, July 26, 1917, *War Tune* File, Detroit Ship Building Company Papers.
24.   Statement of Construction Accounts to Close in May, 1917, Board of Directors' Meeting, May 23, 1917, Minutes, ASBCo.

zation of economic resources of the nation's merchant marine.[25] Of the
431 ships commandeered, thirty-eight were under contract to the
American Ship Building Company. Three ore carriers, however, a
tanker, and two ocean vessels, were later released to their owners.[26]

There were many anxious moments among shipbuilders and foreign
vessel owners after June 13, 1917, when the Urgent Deficiencies Act
was adopted. This gave President Wilson the power to requisition
ships under construction for foreign interests.[27] The Chicago Ship
Building Company was building one such ship, the *Danebrog*, which
was scheduled to sail during this frenzied period. The departure date
was June 28, but because of engine trouble, which could conceivably
be attributed to the builder, the captain of the *Danebrog* delayed in
accepting the vessel on the part of his employer. Since the delay prevented him from getting to the customs collector, who closed his office at noon on Saturdays, he had to wait until Monday before trying
to obtain clearance papers. A question arose as to whether James E.
Davidson, the original owner, or The Steamship Company "Dana" of
Denmark, to whom Davidson was selling the ship, was the owner. The
customs collector referred the question to Washington. An eight-day
lay-over followed while an answer was awaited.

Kellogg Fairbank, president of The Chicago Ship Building Company, told Ora J. Fish that Davidson should go to Washington with
the Danish representative of the steamship company to consult with
the Danish ambassador and the Shipping Board or some other official.
Davidson was unable to go to Washington but did write to the New
York agent of the Danish owner. By July 2, no answer was forthcoming from Washington. The captain of the *Danebrog*, who maintained
that his company was losing $2,000 per day as a result of the delay,

25. Edward N. Hurley, *The Bridge To France* (Philadelphia: J. B. Lippincott &
Co., 1927), p. 38.

26. Norman L. McKellar, "Steel Shipbuilding Under the U.S. Shipping Board,
1917-1921," *The Belgian Nautical Ship-lover*, No. 87 (May-June, 1962), 278-79,
281, 283; No. 88 (July-August, 1962), 392. The released ocean ships were the
Choctaw and *War Song*. The ore carriers were the *Louis W. Hill, Carmi A.
Thompson*, and *William A. Amberg*, and the tanker was the *William P. Cowan*.

27. Edward N. Hurley, *The Bridge To France*, p. 31.

talked of retaining a lawyer. Fairbank wrote to Merton E. Farr, "I think Davidson is fast asleep and needs waking up. It may prove expensive if he does not [go to Washington]."[28] The clearance papers arrived eventually, and the Danish company filed suit for $16,000 damages. The suit later was withdrawn by the plaintiff.[29] The Steamship Company "Dana" suit was a minor incident in the history of the shipbuilding company, but it shows the tensions that existed during the transition period before the axe of requisition fell.

During the fall months of 1917, the company had to content itself with the contracts on hand and added yard construction and improvements while Farr sparred with the Shipping Board for new contracts and a settlement on the requisitioned ships. Ten of these vessels were being constructed to builder's account. Admiral W. L. Capps, general manager of the Emergency Fleet Corporation, gave Farr authority to sell six of them to American steamship companies for $817,852 each. Farr was also negotiating for the construction of ten 360-foot cargo vessels that would have to be taken to the coast in halves.[30] There was much talk but no new contracts. Finally, with a touch of sarcasm, Farr wrote to Capps:

> Through the courtesy of you gentlemen, we are permitted to build ten ships of ocean type, but unfortunately without the cooperation of the Fleet Corporation, by being denied priority class in obtaining certain materials, which may delay production of not only these ten ships, but other hulls which are to follow.[31]

Even though American Ship Building received contracts for forty ocean cargo steamers of Welland Canal size in November, Capps continued to stall on the multitude of legal and construction details that necessarily had to be worked out until illness and old age obliged him

28. Letter from Kellogg Fairbank to Merton E. Farr, July 2, 1917, S.S. *Danebrog* Suit File, Chicago Ship Building Company Papers.

29. Board of Directors' Meeting, April 24, 1918, Minutes, ASBCo.

30. *Ibid.*, October 24, 1917.

31. Letter from Merton E. Farr to Admiral W. L. Capps, November 10, 1917, Construction Organization Decimal File No. 300, Records of the United States Shipping Board, Record Group 32, National Archives, Washington, D.C. Hereafter cited as USSB Records.

to resign in December, 1917.[32] He was replaced by Charles Piez, a Chicago businessman.

In the meantime, the Fleet Corporation began to fill its local organization. Henry L. Penton became the Fleet Corporation district officer, with offices in the Perry-Payne Building in Cleveland.[33] Captain R. W. England was hired as Penton's assistant. Most of the technical questions and problems that arose between the shipbuilding firm and the Fleet Corporation were handled by them.

The contract for Emergency Fleet Corporation ships did not occur simply as a result of Merton E. Farr's persistent communication with Shipping Board officials. Negotiations were under way as early as May, 1917. The Shipping Board needed American Ship Building as badly as American Ship Building needed the Shipping Board. The coastal yards could not begin to fill the maritime needs of a land war that was being fought across the ocean, three thousand miles away. Many of the East Coast building ways were filled with naval construction and skilled workmen were at a premium. The most destructive period of submarine attacks, during which the British lost 916 ships, was the ten months prior to December 29, 1917.[34] For one of the few times in the history of the United States, the nation was in a shipbuilding panic.

The seriousness of the panic was exemplified by the diagram of a proposed blockade runner presented to the Fleet Corporation by the American Ship Building Company in May, 1917. The vessel was of Welland Canal dimensions but could carry only 900 to 1,000 tons of

32. Board of Directors' Meeting, November 28, 1917, Minutes, ASBCo. Of the forty steamers, the first six were contracted to be built at $705,875 net per ship, and the other thirty-four ships at $730,000 net each, exclusive of war zone equipment.

33. Henry L. Penton left the Chicago Ship Building Company in 1903 to become Chief Engineer of the Great Lakes Engineering Works at Detroit, Michigan. He left that firm in 1907 to join Washington I. Babcock in the firm of Babcock & Penton, consulting engineers and naval architects, with offices in the Perry-Payne Building in Cleveland and in New York. Babcock left the Chicago firm after the consolidation in 1899 and set up an office in New York as a naval architect. He remained there until his death on August 7, 1917.

34. Roy W. Kelly and Frederick J. Allen, *The Shipbuilding Industry* (Boston: Houghton Mifflin & Co., 1918), p. 16.

cargo. She had a low silhouette, good speed, presented a small target—reminiscent of the blockade runners of the Civil War. Consideration was given to "other increased chances of 'getting through' as well as utility en route as a submarine destroyer." She was to carry two three-inch deck guns for protection.[35] Fortunately, the costly vessel of small capacity was never built!

During May and June, 1917, American Ship Building Company personnel conferred with Theodore E. Ferris, naval architect for the Fleet Corporation, and Daniel H. Cox, general manager of the Division of Steel Construction. They went over plans of the ocean ships that the shipbuilding company was producing and discussed changes needed for the contemplated building program. On June 13, Farr met with Ferris, and they decided that the most adaptable plan was the Frederickstadt. Farr said his company could built upwards of twenty ships by the close of navigation in 1918. Farr was also willing to turn over his plants and organization to the Fleet Corporation but wanted a clear 10 per cent cash profit for the work produced. Ferris wrote to George W. Goethals, then general manager of the Shipping Board, that the price was going to be high, but that Farr would try to cut down on the price or control it in a way more pleasing to Goethals. Ferris personally felt that Farr wanted to do the "very best he can for you in this matter," but that he did not want to lose money. Ferris added:

> I have always found Mr. Farr amiable to do business with
> and he is most fair and straight in all his dealings . . . . It seems
> to me we ought to try and line up ships with him if it is possible
> to do so. They will be sure ships and there is not much doubt
> but that you will get them by the specified delivery dates.[36]

Also in June, since the Fleet Corporation was considering granting contracts to other lake shipyards, Ferris asked Farr for a set of de-

---

35. Diagram of a Proposed Blockade Runner, American Ship Building Company, May 7, 1917, USSB Records.

36. Letter from Theodore E. Ferris to George W. Goethals, June 13, 1917, American Ship Building Company Papers, in possession of author. Hereafter cited as ASBCo Papers, author.

tailed drawings of the Frederickstadt ships for distribution to them.[37] When asked what the charge would be for the right to distribute the plans, Farr pointed out that they represented great value and that a duplicate set recently had been sold to a Canadian shipyard for $10,000 with the restriction that they be used only in that yard.[38] Ferris forwarded the offer to Admiral Frederick T. Bowles, manager of the Division of Construction, who countered with an offer of $7,500 and no restrictions.[39] Ruled by patriotism and better judgement, Farr sent the valuable set of plans to Washington with the comment, "whether the shipbuilding concern using this data pays for it or not, is left entirely to you."[40] Thus the Frederickstadt plans became the prototype design for the Emergency Fleet Corporation vessel construction program on the Great Lakes.

Although Farr had authority to sell the ten ocean freighters constructed on builder's account to a domestic steamship company, he failed to do so. In January, 1918, he sold them to the Shipping Board for $780,000 per ship. He also closed a contract to install the military equipment on all fifty freighters then under contract to the Shipping Board. Military equipment included gun foundations, gun crew quarters, radio, searchlight, ice machine, and additional life saving equipment.[41] That same month, the American Ship Building Company received contracts for ten more ocean ships from the Shipping Board.[42]

Several lake shipbuilding companies were constructing the "Laker" type of ocean vessel following the Frederickstadt design. These included the Globe Ship Building Company and McDougall-Duluth Ship Building Company at Duluth-Superior; the Manitowoc Ship Building Company at Manitowoc, Wisconsin; the Saginaw Ship

37. *Ibid.*, Letter from Theodore E. Ferris to Merton E. Farr, June 5, 1917.

38. *Ibid.*, Letter from Merton E. Farr to Theodore E. Ferris, December 1, 1917.

39. *Ibid.*, Letter from Admiral Frederick T. Bowles to Merton E. Farr, December 8, 1917.

40. *Ibid.*, Letter from Merton E. Farr to Admiral Frederick T. Bowles, December 12, 1917.

41. Board of Directors' Meeting, January 23, 1918, Minutes, ASBCo. The contract for installing military equipment on the ten requisitioned ships was $28,500 per ship; the total contract price for the forty ships was $1,026,000.

42. *Ibid.*, February 27, 1918.

Building Company at Saginaw, Michigan; the Toledo Ship Building Company at Toledo; and the Great Lakes Engineering Works with plants at Ecorse, Michigan, and Ashtabula, Ohio. There was a strong likelihood that the companies would have similar problems as they were building the same type of vessel and were all in the same region of the country. At the suggestion of Edward N. Hurley, representatives of all the firms met at Detroit on January 3, 1918, and formed the Association of Lake Shipbuilders. Their avowed object was to "cooperate and coordinate in the production of ships for deep sea service." They elected Merton E. Farr their president.[43] On January 29, Charles Piez suggested that the organization hold monthly meetings. Farr thought the suggestion a good one but dropped it back into Piez's lap. He suggested that "if the conferences can be had with one of high authority, good results will obtain; otherwise, in my opinion, very little good will result."[44]

Farr also told Piez in the same letter that although the several plants of American Ship Building were in splendid condition, a shortage of hull and boiler material could necessitate closing the plants unless relief came at once. He described the situation as "discouraging." Piez immediately sent this information to Bernard Baruch, chairman of the Raw Materials Committee for the Council of National Defense.[45]

But a shortage of materials was not the only discouraging situation with which shipyard officials had to contend. The Emergency Fleet Corporation was born under difficult conditions and had expanded so rapidly that inefficiency and confusion were inevitable. The shipyard personnel, accustomed to working independently, reacted unfavorably to the bureaucratic technicalities and paperwork. Yard superintendents and their assistants soon found themselves spending the major part of their time making out reports to satisfy local Shipping Board inspectors. The situation was not tempered by the high tensions

43. *Ibid.*, January 23, 1918.
44. Letter from Merton E. Farr to Charles Piez, January 31, 1918, USSB Records.
45. *Ibid.*, Letter from Charles Piez to Bernard Baruch, February 5, 1918.

under which the shipyards operated in meeting deadlines and delivery dates.[46]

The trouble came to a head when one of the district inspectors threatened to use his influence to break a major contract between the company and the Shipping Board on the grounds that the company was not living up to its commitments. The immediate problem concerned estimates that were too low. Unfortunately, the inspector vented his wrath on Merton E. Farr. Farr, in a letter to Hurley, said that theory made a good story but seldom delivered the goods. He then wrote of a tombstone inscription of a well-known man who had suffered financially: "Sacred to the Memory of a Man who was ruined by the Estimates of his Engineers." Farr acidly commented, "I don't want this inscription on mine."[47]

Hurley assured Farr of his intention to cooperate and passed the situation on for Charles Piez to handle. Farr thought that the inspection of the ships was too exacting and wanted his men to have more leeway in building the ships. Many of the inspectors were so technical that they actually were retarding progress.[48] He felt that the shipbuilders must "have a better understanding of motives underlying [the] activities of your late district officer and associates or [the] present program cannot be carried out."[49] Piez must have clarified the position of his inspectors because the situation was not repeated.

Shipping Board inspectors were not the only vexatious problem. The draft also contributed its share of annoyances, although it appeared to be localized in Chicago. Perhaps the importance of the shipbuilding business was lost in the great metropolis, whereas in other cities where American Ship Building maintained a plant, the maritime industry was better publicized and thus was more important to the community. Whatever the reason, it did not sooth "Ked" Fairbank's demeanor when he lost hard-to-replace riveters, shipfitters, and tin-

46.   Letter from A. G. Smith to Henry L. Penton, December 20, 1917, ASBCo Papers, author.

47.   Letter from Merton E. Farr to Edward N. Hurley, January 5, 1917, USSB Records.

48.   *Ibid.*, Memoranda from Edward N. Hurley to Charles Piez, January 21, 1918.

49.   *Ibid.*, Telegram from Merton E. Farr to Edward N. Hurley, January 14, 1918.

smiths. The Fleet Corporation could grant exemptions to skilled ship-yard workers, but the lists of names had to be sent to Washington for approval and then sent back to local draft boards. The exemptions had to be renewed every thirty days. The president of the Chicago Ship Building Company simply could not understand why "we [should] be harrassed with uncertainty and red-tape and correspond-ing with Washington and God knows what all, which is quite unne-cessary."[50] He wrote to General Counsel Henry A. Kelley, "I don't think the Shipping Board means to ball things up, but they are hor-ribly muddleheaded and don't see how it works at the other end of the line."[51]

Meyer Bloomfield, Head of the Industrial Service Department of the Division of Labor, wrote a beautifully-worded four-page reply in response to Fairbank's stinging letter and explained the problems en-countered by his office in Washington. Fairbank merely penciled across the top of it, "not to administer meticulous equity, but to build ships."[52] The best advice came from Henry Kelley who counseled that "extreme care should be taken not to place it [the draft] on the ground that it will serve to induce men more readily to enter the ship yards" lest the shipbuilding industry gain publicity as currying fa-vor.[53] The advice calmed Fairbank somewhat, but in late February, Chicago Ship Building still lost ninety-seven men for whom it had claimed exemptions.[54] The problem plagued the Chicago plant throughout most of the war.

In October, 1918, Fairbank had to meet a problem of a different sort. The sprawling Hog Island shipyard near Philadelphia was shanghaiing skilled labor from the Chicago plant! An ex-foreman from the Chicago yard, now employed by Hog Island, appeared in

50.   Letter from Kellogg Fairbank to Edward B. Burling, December 28, 1917, Chicago Ship Building Company Papers. Burling was a counsel with the Shipping Board and a friend of Fairbank's.
51.   *Ibid.*, Letter from Kellogg Fairbank to Henry A. Kelley, December 28, 1917.
52.   *Ibid.*, Letter from Meyer Bloomfield to Kellogg Fairbank, January 5, 1918.
53.   *Ibid.*, Letter from Henry A. Kelley to Kellogg Fairbank, January 14, 1918.
54.   *Ibid.*, Letter from D. H. Filson to Kellogg Fairbank, February 25, 1918. Filson was Chief of Employment at the Chicago Ship Building Company.

saloons outside the Chicago plant and promised higher wages than those established by the Great Lakes District of the Wage Adjustment Board. He also offered free transportation to Philadelphia. The "agent" became so bold as to contact men within two blocks of the shipyard and meet them at Peterson's Saloon at 101st Street and Ewing Avenue, as well as other saloons on 106th Street in South Chicago. He induced seven out of forty gangs of riveters to "desert." The situation was demoralizing the yard, to say nothing of threatening delivery of two vessels that fall.[55]

Henry Penton told A. G. Smith that there was nothing the Labor Department could do to intervene. Smith wired Fairbank that it "looks as if [the] matter were in our own hands to take such action as we legally can or otherwise."[56] Fairbank telegraphed Hurley to inform him of the situation. Hurley passed the information on to Charles Piez. Fairbank also hired a private detective to learn more and possibly to document the circumstances. By this time, however, the United States Employment Service was becoming inquisitive. The "agent" ceased operations and the detective tailed him to Philadelphia to the Hog Island yard. The detective was sure of the unethical recruiting methods but was unable to implicate positively the Philadelphia shipyard.[57] But Fairbank's actions brought results. Early in November, Charles Piez ordered the curtailment of advertising for shipyard labor; later in the month, the Fleet Corporation discontinued the practice of paying transportation expenses for newly recruited labor.[58]

Labor constituted a major problem nationally for the shipyards. At the outset of the war, shipyard workers received adverse publicity as the result of strikes. The Shipping Board granted wage increases of as much as 40 per cent over those of the preceding year and resorted to a 10 per cent war premium to promote a full six day work week in the

---

55. *Ibid.*, Telegram from Kellogg Fairbank to Edward N. Hurley, October 31, 1918.

56. *Ibid.*, Telegram from A. G. Smith to Kellogg Fairbank, October 30, 1918.

57. *Ibid.*, Reports of Chicago Investigator No. 45, October 31 to November 8, 1918.

58. *Emergency Fleet News*, November 14, and December 12, 1918.

yards.[59] The Fleet Corporation was charged unofficially with supporting management and promoting an open shop.[60] Talk of possible labor conscription, or at least of federal regulation of employment and wages, became stronger.[61] The major problem on the lakes was difficulty in obtaining skilled workmen rather than an attitude detrimental to the war effort.

A government observer reported in March, 1917, that the lake shipyards were only 40 per cent unionized and suffered from poor housing and transportation facilities. He added that the presence of saloons and disorderly houses made the district a fertile ground for the "Woolies" and German propaganda.[62]

The memories of old-timers are strangely vague on the topic of disorderly houses—perhaps from fear of being quoted—but they do recall taverns located near the shipyards. In Cleveland, "Shipyard John" ran a saloon on West 54th Street in a predominately Romanian area just south of the shipyard. He and barkeepers along Detroit Avenue were only too willing to extend credit to the thirsty shipbuilders. They tallied the drinks on pay day, adding a little for "interest," to the anguish of the irate shipbuilders' wives. Representatives of the International Workers of the World would find difficulty in being heard in such establishments, much less in gaining an audience! Similar conditions existed in all of the lake shipbuilding cities. Actually, there were almost no strikes in the lake shipyards. Crawford Vaughan, former premier of South Australia, during a tour of the lakes in 1917, commented that "the man who talked strike would be regarded as an

59. "Speeding Up the Shipbuilding Program," *New York Times Current History,* VII (February, 1918), Part 2, p. 256.

60. "Ships and Organized Labor," *The New Republic,* XIV (March 2, 1918), 132-33.

61. Homer L. Ferguson, "The War's Effect on Merchant Shipbuilding, The Standard Ship and Momentous Problems of Production," *Scientific American Supplement,* LXXXIV (December 8, 1917), 359; Burton J. Hendrick, "Can We Build Those Ships in Time?," *The World's Work,* XXXV (December, 1917), 185.

62. S. M. Evans, *A Discussion of Conditions Affecting Ship Production: Together with an Estimate of Ship Deliveries (Steel and Wood), April to December, 1918* (Washington: Government Printing Office, 1918), p. 52.

agent for the Kaiser, and he would probably be tipped into the ice-cold lake waters, to get out as best he could."[63]

In March, 1918, President Farr reported that a wage increase in the Great Lakes District conforming to those of the Delaware River District was necessary, but that the Fleet Corporation would bear the cost of the increase.[64] The cost of living in the Great Lakes District increased by 15 per cent from December, 1917, to August, 1918. Using this as a basis, the Shipbuilding Labor Adjustment Board approved a 15 per cent wage increase in October, 1918. This meant a basic wage increase of 10 cents from the existing 70 cents an hour.[65] The same ruling established joint shop committees to air grievances. It also prevented discrimination against both union and non-union men, provided better sanitary conditions in the shipyards, and established standard piece rates for riveters, fitters, chippers, and other skilled workmen. A 10 per cent war bonus was added to piece rates at the close of each pay period.

Increased wages and better sanitary conditions did not make for greater production. Shipyard workers were unaccustomed to the money they now carried in their pockets. One East Coast riveter remarked "we just got to getting so much money that nearly all the boys would knock off two days a week, because we made enough in four days to give the Missus and still have plenty left."[66] Frederick Lewis Allen pin-pointed the difficulty when he said that the man in the shipyard must "feel a soldier's pride, a soldier's sense of duty. The shipbuilder's badge must be a badge of honor to him—as full of meaning as a uniform."[67] A former Cleveland minister, Dr. Charles A. Eaton,

---

63.   Crawford Vaughan, "The Shipyards of the Great Lakes," *The Outlook*, CXIX (June 9, 1917), 382.

64.   Board of Directors' Meeting, March 27, 1918, Minutes, ASBCo.

65.   U.S., Shipbuilding Labor Adjustment Board, *Decisions as to Wages, Hours and Other Conditions in Atlantic Coast, Gulf and Great Lakes Shipyards, October 1, 1918* (Washington: Shipbuilding Labor Adjustment Board, 1918), p. 4.

66.   P.T.C., "A Labor View of the Shipbuilding Programme," *The New Republic*, XIV (February 23, 1918), 111-12.

67.   Frederick Lewis Allen, "Building the Bridge to France; Why the Government is Calling for United States Shipyard Volunteers," *The Outlook*, CXVIII (February 20, 1918), 285.

pastor of New York's Madison Avenue Baptist Church, was of the same opinion. The Shipping Board and Dr. Eaton formed the National Service Section and began sending public speakers and printed materials to the shipyards telling the workers of the vital importance of their role in the total war effort. British, Canadian, Anzac, French, and Italian soldiers and airmen were paired with laymen and toured the shipyards to give enthusiastic and encouraging speeches on company time.[68]

A by-product of Dr. Eaton's programs was the national and international riveting contests. In March, 1918, "Finner" Shock and his riveting gang at the Baltimore Dry Dock & Ship Building Company drove 1,414 3/4-inch rivets in nine hours. Two weeks later, a gang at American Ship Building's Buffalo yard drove 1,624 7/8-inch rivets. Top honors and national recognition fell to riveter John Corrigan, heater John O'Donnell, and holder-on Jack Roiski, who drove 3,415 3/4-inch rivets in nine hours at the Wyandotte plant of the Detroit Ship Building Company. Slightly behind Corrigan was Bill Hartz, riveter at the Chicago plant, who drove 3,055 rivets in nine hours.[69] Eventually, the riveting contests had to be called off because too many workers left their jobs to watch the contestants in action. These contests aroused national interest in shipbuilding and raised the standard of good rivet driving averages that were vital to production.[70] In July of that year, 1918, the Wyandotte plant, with sixty-three gangs, was second only to the Newport News Dry Dock & Ship Building Company in the national averages for rivets driven per week. They drove just under 2,700 rivets a day per gang. Of the American Ship Building plants, only the Buffalo yard fell under the national average of 1,400 rivets per gang.[71]

The greatest show of patriotism by the shipbuilders was held on July 4, 1918. Secretary of Navy Josephus Daniels announced that "we

68. Douglas H. Cooke, "S.O.S.—Send Out Ships!; How the Spirit of Adventure Has been Put into Industry," *The Outlook*, CXX (September 4, 1918), 28-9.
69. *Wyandotte Herald*, May 10, 1918.
70. W. C. Mattox, *Building the Emergency Fleet* (Cleveland: Penton Publishing Co., 1920), p. 59.
71. *Emérgency Fleet News*, September 26, 1918.

are launching this day far more tonnage than that of all the American vessels sunk by submarines since the war began."[72] American shipyards launched ninety-two ships totalling 450,000 deadweight tons on that day. The Great Lakes District contributed fourteen ships of 47,700 total tons.[73] Each of the American Ship Building Company construction yards contributed a boat to the launching parade. Superintendent John Sinclair had the men of his Superior Ship Building Company come to work early. They had the honor of launching the first boat on that ceremonious holiday. The *Lake Aurice* struck the water at 12:01 A.M. and A. G. Smith telegraphed Daniel Cox, "we think this launch will probably carry off the banner as being the first vessel of the Great American Fleet launched this day."[74] The Cleveland yard set a triple record by delivery of a ship, launching of a ship, and laying of the first keel plate of a third ship within five minutes after the berth was vacated.[75]

Most of the major problems of coastal shipyards were reflected in the Great Lakes District to some degree. One of the most critical problems on the East Coast was housing the thousands of shipyard workers and their families. Although the problem was not critical on the lakes, Lorain and Wyandotte did receive Fleet Corporation housing developments. Edward N. Hurley announced that the community sites were being planned to provide all the social, moral, and artistic features that would add to the social, moral, and physical well-being of the employees.[76] In other words, the agency was going to try to get away from the uninspiring type of company homes familiar to industrial America.

The increased shipbuilding facilities at Lorain were creating problems for the community as housing was difficult for the shipyard workers to find. Many workers lived in Cleveland and rode the Lake

72.   "Our Answer to the U-Boat; Our Great Shipbuilding Victory," *Literary Digest*, LVIII (July 13, 1918), 11.

73.   "July Fourth in Our Shipyards," *Scientific American*, CXIX (July 6, 1918), 3.

74.   Telegram from A. G. Smith to Daniel H. Cox, July 4, 1918, ASBCo. Papers, author.

75.   *Ibid.*

76.   "Houses for Shipyard Workers," *Survey*, XXXIX (January 5, 1918), 399.

Shore Electric to Lorain every day. The shipbuilding company noted a great increase in absences because of a justifiable fear of the Spanish influenza epidemic sweeping the country. The interurban company failed to alleviate the crowded conditions of the cars by providing more service.[77]

The American Ship Building Company entered into an agreement with the Fleet Corporation to form The Federal Home Building Company and purchased forty-two acres of land within walking distance of the shipyard. It constructed about 200 homes housing 150 families.[78] This housing area was between D and F Streets and stretched from Iowa Avenue to Alexandria Street. Two large two-storied frame stores with balconied apartments were built on Iowa Avenue, facing Danley Square.

J. W. Butler was manager of the Lorain project. He found that workmen were paying $15 to $22 per month for a single room. Yet when he charged $9.25 monthly rental for a five-room house, one man raised such a fuss that Butler looked up his wages and found that he earned over $400 a month! Another problem that Butler faced was the large influx of foreigners attracted to the shipyard by high wages. He was warned by his superior of the danger of trying to rent to "foreigners and Americans promiscuously, inasmuch as it has been my experience that the two elements cannot be mixed successfully."[79] Butler continued to "integrate" the project successfully and had no trouble renting the homes, as was exemplified by the following desperate letter:

Dear Sirs:
  I hereby make the application for one of the Government houses containing five rooms.

77. Letter from F. A. Hubbard to Charles C. Marshall, State Public Utility Board, Columbus, Ohio, October 15, 1918, USSB Records. Hubbard was Housing Project Superintendent for the Shipbuilding company.

78. Board of Directors' Meeting, June 26, 1918, Minutes, ASBCo. The home building firm had an authorized capital stock of $75,000.

79. Letter from Frederick Apel, District Representative, Property Bureau, U.S. Shipping Board, to Harold G. Aron, Chief, Property Bureau, December 2, 1918, USSB Records.

I have lived in Lorain for the past 8 months in furnished rooms,
a tent, and have also boarded but have not been able to find
a house for my self.

It has cost on an average of $6.50 a week to live this way
just for a roof over my head alone.

My wife and I have just about gone the limit living like this
and there by appeal to you for a house . . . .

Geo. D. Wood
c/o Spademan Grocery Co.
East Erie Ave.
City[80]

The housing project in Wyandotte was not so large nor so elaborate
as the one in Lorain. The Detroit Ship Building Company purchased
thirteen acres of land about a mile and a quarter from the shipyard. It
was bordered by Cedar Street and North Line Road between Fourth
and Fifth Streets. The shipbuilding company formed The Wyandotte
Home Company and built seventy-eight houses on the site.[81] The
manager, Fred A. Dunmire, rented them as rapidly as they were completed.[82]

While houses were being built to accommodate the shipyard workers, negotiations were being carried on to provide more contracts for
the yards. Charles M. Schwab, former head of Bethlehem Steel
Company and new Director-General of the Fleet Corporation, tried
to induce Merton Farr to build 5,000-ton cargo steamers and send
them in halves to St. Lawrence River shipyards for completion.[83] Farr
conferred with the Association of Lake Shipbuilders who felt that the
plan was impractical. They suggested a 4,200-deadweight ton cargo
steamer of Welland Canal size that could be lengthened to 5,000-tons
after the war.[84] Schwab was disappointed in the reaction but agreed

80.   *Ibid.*, Letter from George D. Wood to J. W. Butler, April 2, 1919.

81.   Board of Directors' Meeting, September 18, 1918, Minutes, ASBCo. The company had an authorized capital of $75,000.

82.   Letter from Frederick Apel to Harold G. Aron, November 2, 1918, USSB Records.

83.   *Ibid.*, Telegram from Charles M. Schwab to Merton E. Farr, May 14, 1918.

84.   *Ibid.*, Telegram from Merton E. Farr to Charles M. Schwab, May 15, 1918.

to Farr's entreaties that disruption of the standardized methods used on the "Lakers" and the poor facilities along the St. Lawrence River would actually create more of a loss in tonnage than what would be gained by building larger vessels in halves.[85] A week later, the American Ship Building Company received contracts to build sixty 4,200-ton Welland Canal size steamers for $820,000 a ship and an additional $20,000 a ship for plant additions to accommodate the new construction.[86] The ships were to be delivered in 1919.

Naval architects expressed concern over the stability of the newly-contracted-for ships. They were designed along the same lines as the ships then being constructed for the Fleet Corporation on the lakes, but deeper. The beam remained the same which made them likely to be top-heavy, particularly when they were unloaded but had full coal bunkers. Naval architect Laurens N. Prior stated that only the limitations of the canals would justify the adoption of a vessel "with as small initial stability as this one has, and a certain amount of care would always have to be taken that the vessel shall be loaded in a suitable manner."[87]

The fiscal returns of the company for 1917-18 showed a remarkable net addition of $6,626,265 transferred to surplus account. The company built forty-five cargo ships and two navy tugs during the year. It also had contracts for building and delivering 172 cargo ships to the Fleet Corporation between July 1, 1918, and the close of navigation in 1919. The company contributed over $3,500,000 to the Liberty Loan and appropriated $410,000 for patriotic war funds in cities where its plants were situated.[88] A copy of the annual report was forwarded to Charles M. Schwab at Merton E. Farr's request. The effect was that of a stick of dynamite.

85. *Ibid.*, Telegram from Charles M. Schwab to Merton E. Farr, May 16, 1918, and Merton E. Farr to Charles M. Schwab, May 17, 1918.

86. *Ibid.*, Letter from Charles Piez to American Ship Building Company, May 25, 1918; Board of Directors' Meeting, May 24 and June 26, 1918, Minutes, ASBCo.

87. Letter from Laurens N. Prior to Division of Steel Ship Construction, Emergency Fleet Corporation, June 14, 1918, ASBCo. Papers, author.

88. Nineteenth Annual Report of The American Ship Building Company for the Fiscal Year Ended June 30, 1918, ASBCo. Records.

In September, after looking over the annual report, General Counsel Chester W. Cuthell of the Shipping Board, wrote to Schwab. He noted sardonically that "it would seem that Mr. Farr's fears so frequently and so earnestly expressed . . . were entirely without foundation."[89] Cuthell felt that the Fleet Corporation was almost too generous in agreeing to a two-thirds absorption of plant improvement in its latest contract. Schwab's reaction was immediate. He wanted to see Farr and Samuel Mather in Washington the following week for an explanation of the extremely high profits ostensibly made at the expense of his organization.[90]

Samuel Mather was unable to attend the meeting, so Farr had to represent the company alone. He claimed that the Fleet Corporation paid the full original contract price. Schwab pointed out that this carried little weight since the six "contract" ships that were delivered during the company's fiscal year were more expensive than the requisitioned ships. He contended that if American Ship Building made as much profit per ton during the coming year as it did during the last one, the net profit would exceed $20,000,000! Schwab did not mince words. The shipbuilding company held Fleet Corporation contracts for 176 contract ships and thirty-two requisitioned ones. He demanded that Farr at once agree to reductions in price on all of the contracts.[91]

Farr had agreed the year before to limit company profits on government contract work to 10 per cent. In the resulting contract shuffle, the Fleet Corporation honored the absorption of two-thirds of the $1,200,000 improvement program, but the last sixty vessel contracts were reduced by $20,000 per ship.[92] Schwab thought that the readjustment was fair and that it would provide an object lesson to any other contractors who thought they could take advantage of the Fleet Corporation. It also saved his agency $12,000,000.[93]

89.   Letter from Chester W. Cuthell to Charles M. Schwab, September 26, 1918, USSB Records.

90.   *Ibid.*, Telegram from Charles M. Schwab to Merton E. Farr and Samuel Mather, September 27, 1918.

91.   Letter from Charles M. Schwab to Edward N. Hurley, October 2, 1918.

92.   *Ibid.*; Board of Directors' Meeting, October 9, 1918, Minutes, ASBCo.

93.   Letter from Charles M. Schwab to Edward N. Hurley, October 2, 1918,

However, Charles Schwab was too good a businessman to lose confidence in an efficient organization just because he had caught it with its fingers in the sugar bowl. The following spring, the Fleet Corporation asked American Ship Building to staff and complete contracts in coastal yards that were financially weak and which did not have the technical and managerial capacity to complete contracts.[94] Alfred G. Smith visited the Pennsylvania Ship Building Company and the New Jersey Ship Building Company to investigate the possibilities. The Fleet Corporation offered American Ship Building a fee, based on the unexpended balance of each contract, to superintend finishing the vessels.[95] The company was completing Fleet Corporation contracts and could spare part of its organization, but the war ended before this move was realized.

Meanwhile, the yards continued to turn out ships at an amazing rate. The ships were usually accepted by the Fleet Corporation long before the contracted delivery dates. The combination of speed and inexperienced labor took its toil on quality. Although the Shipping Board inspectors consistently gave American Ship Building Company plants good ratings, they were based on a national standard which was not so good as the yard superintendents would have liked. The important thing was to get the tonnage on the board; thus, quality was sacrificed. The vessels were put through a series of dock and acceptance trials, but no one really knew how they would perform until they were actually on the run. The relaxation of thorough testing became a nightmare for Martin Peterson, the Shipping Board agent at Montreal.

As the vessels passed through Montreal, the captains and chief engineers came to him with long lists of things that needed adjustment. They all told the same story—they were hurried away from the shipyard with the promise that whatever was unfinished would be fixed at Montreal. The promises occasionally took a humorous twist as

---

USSB Records. This figure was apparently a secretarial error. The author's computation is one-tenth that amount.
94. *Ibid.*, Letter from Charles Piez to Merton E. Farr, April 3, 1919.
95. *Ibid.*, April 16, 1919.

in the case of the captain of the Toledo-built *Lake Chelan* who was promised "a Pilot House here as his ship had none."[96] Shoddy workmanship often led to more serious consequences as in the case of the *Lake Wimico*:

> Chief Engineer Anderson reports that upon receiving a bell to go astern, while going down the Lachine Canal, the tail shaft backed out until the coupling came against the stuffing box gland studs, bending them badly. This was due to the engineering crew on the run down, the nuts having come off all of the coupling bolts in the after coupling without being noticed by the engineers. All three piston rods were roughly turned, deep tool marks being in each of them. The H.P. and I.P. valve rods had quite a bend in the thread just above the valves, in fact, this engine was the roughest job from the American Ship Building Company that has passed through here.[97]

By early January 1919, the tonnage situation was thought to be under control by the Shipping Board. The war shipbuilding boom obviously was over. The Association of Lake Shipbuilders was dissolved after Charles Piez announced that the Shipbuilding Labor Adjustment Board was about to disband.[98] Shortly thereafter, the working day was reduced to eight hours, and all overtime was eliminated.[99] With the cutbacks, some shifting of hulls was necessary by American Ship Building to meet delivery dates. In March, the steel and materials of two hulls were moved from Buffalo to Cleveland for construction because of the poor showing of the Buffalo yard in workmanship and construction time.[100] In July, one hull was transferred from Lorain to Cleveland because a shortage of riveters threatened the delivery date.[101] On October 4, 1919, all remaining contracts between the

96. *Ibid.*, Letter from Martin Peterson to W. M. Williams, July 1, 1918, Correspondence of Montreal Office. Williams was the Shipping Board agent in Cleveland, Ohio.
97. *Ibid.*, August 28, 1918.
98. Board of Directors' Meeting, January 22, 1919, Minutes, ASBCo.
99. *Ibid.*, February 26, 1919.
100. Letter from A. G. Smith to Henry L. Penton, March 4, 1919, USSB Records.
101. *Ibid.*, July 24 and 26, 1919.

Fleet Corporation and the company reverted from a cost plus basis to a lump sum basis.[102] A few Fleet Corporation vessels were delivered in 1920, but by then the shouting was over.

During the four fiscal years from 1916 to 1920, the American Ship Building Company delivered 250 ships with an aggregate deadweight capacity of 1,010,500 gross tons.[103] Most of these ships were in the Welland Canal size ocean class with the "Lake" surname: *Lake Inaha, Lake Ennis, Lake Narka, Lake Fugard.* Mrs. Woodrow Wilson selected their names and must have been hard-pressed to find enough bodies of water to go around.[104] A few were built with funds set aside from Liberty Loan drives and received names of towns or counties that were regional contest winners: *Vinton County, Henry County, Bartholomew.*

At the time of their construction, the "Lakers" were thought of as a war-time emergency measure. After the war, most of them were laid up as the United States again permitted her merchant marine to fall into decay. A few years later many were sold to foreign buyers, and the Ford Motor Company scrapped 130 of them. Several were lost during the submarine onslaught at the beginning of the Second World War. There is scarcely a port in the world where a "Laker" has not gently nosed her bow into a slip or made a dock sometime in the past fifty years. Merton E. Farr had wired Charles Piez in the spring of 1918 that his men were "with you heart and soul but want a chance to demonstrate what middlewest shipbuilders can do."[105] The American Ship Building Company and its lake colleagues could boast of a job well done.

102. Board of Directors' Meeting, November 26, 1919, Minutes, ASBCo.

103. Twenty-First Annual Report of The American Ship Building Company for the Fiscal Year Ended June 30, 1920, ASBCo Records.

104. Letter from A. C. Wilkies, Acting Manager, Ship Construction Division, U.S. Shipping Board, to Dr. A. L. Fugard, Pueblo, Colorado, October 1, 1919, ASBCo Papers, author. Dr. Fugard wrote an inquiry to the Shipping Board asking for the source of the *Lake Fugard*'s name.

105. Telegram from Merton E. Farr to Charles Piez, April 5, 1918, USSB Records.

10.

The In-between Years

The years between the two world wars were similar to the years preceding the First World War. In all but three years between 1920 and 1940, the American Ship Building Company enjoyed a yearly profit. The profits did not show the seasonal fluctuations of generally poor lake shipping seasons. This made the shipbuilding and repair business uncertain at best. Only consistently conservative leadership enabled the company to survive the recessions of the twenties and the depression of the thirties.

Even before the Fleet Corporation contracts were completed, the company began to revert to a more subdued role. In August, 1919, Merton E. Farr recommended that the plants at Buffalo, Chicago, and Superior be reduced to repair yards as soon as was practicable. Those at Cleveland, Lorain, Detroit, and Wyandotte were to be "reduced so far as possible to their respective normal requirements."[1]

1. Board of Directors' Meeting, August 27, 1919, Minutes, ASBCo.

The housing projects at Lorain and Wyandotte were turned over to the Shipping Board for the nominal consideration of one dollar each, and a company-owned frame boarding house adjoining the Lorain yard, the American House, was sold.[2] Farr asked that the West Yard at Milwaukee be abandoned and the repair work in that city be shifted to the South Yard.[3]

He also suggested the building of four 12,000 ton bulk freighters and ten 3,500 ton ocean-type freighters on company account for speculative purposes.[4] Five months later, the board of directors approved the formation of a subsidiary steamship company to take ownership of the vessels.[5] On March 9, 1920, the Independent Steamship Company, a Delaware corporation, was incorporated with a capital stock of $500,000.[6] The ore freighters were named the *Merton E. Farr, James Davidson, L. M. Bowers,* and *H. H. Porter.* Four of the ocean vessels were named after battles or places where American troops had distinguished themselves in the late war: *Juvigny, Romagne, Montfaucon,* and *Baccarat.*[7] The six remaining steamers were given names of American Indian tribes: *Chippewa, Onondaga, Cayuga, Oneida, Kiowa,* and *Seneca.* Captain R. W. England, formerly with the Shipping Board, was appointed operating manager of the steamship company.[8] The bulk freighters were sold before they were completed, but the ocean-type vessels represented problems to the company for several years because of the glutted condition of the world tonnage market.

Five of the ships were taken to the Altantic Coast where the company hoped they would soon be sold.[9] The vessels remained there for

2.   *Ibid.,* June 22 and August 25, 1920.

3.   *Ibid.,* February 20, 1920.

4.   *Ibid.,* August 27, 1919.

5.   *Ibid.,* January 29, 1920.

6.   Articles of Incorporation, March 9, 1920, Minutes, The Independent Steamship Company, in possession of the author.

7.   Board of Directors' Meeting, March 24, 1920, Minutes, ASBCo.

8.   Board of Directors' Meeting, October 29, 1920, Minutes, The Independent Steamship Company.

9.   Board of Directors' Meeting, November 24, 1920, Minutes, ASBCo. These ships were the *Juvigny, Chippewa, Baccarat, Romagne,* and *Seneca.*

three years. Despite these vain hopes, the shipbuilding company was prepared when the recession that followed the war set in.

Dry dock Number Three at Cleveland was declared obsolete and closed down.[10] The plants at Superior, Milwaukee, Detroit, and Wyandotte were closed until repair prospects brightened. The Wyandotte plant never reopened. The office building was sold to the City of Wyandotte and the site is occupied today by the city's police station. The shipbuilding company became enmeshed in a tax assessment argument with the town officials and decided to dismantle the plant.[11]

By 1922, the repair business was decreased by 40 per cent from that of the year before, and the company had no new construction contracts.[12] When grain prices rose in the fall of 1922, five of the Independent Steamship Company vessels lying in ordinary at Detroit were brought out. They operated for only forty days at a net loss of $133, but for the first time since the end of the war, the company horizon began to brighten.[13] In 1923, the company continued to operate the five vessels in the lake coal and grain trade. It was even able to charter two of the ships laid up on the East Coast, the *Juvigny* and *Romagne*, to the Lind Navigation Company of New York.[14] In the same year, the iron ore fleet resumed full operation, a sure sign that the shipbuilding company's fortunes would increase. American Ship Building built four bulk freighters in 1923 and had contracts for two more. It also had under construction the "largest and most expensive" sidewheelers ever ordered for inland water service.[15]

The sidewheel passenger ships *Greater Buffalo* and *Greater Detroit* were built for the Detroit & Cleveland Navigation Company for

10. *Ibid.*, April 27, 1921.

11. *Ibid.*, October 11, 1922; *Wyandotte Weekly Herald*, August 11, 1922.

12. Twenty-Third Annual Report of The American Ship Building Company for the Fiscal Year Ended June 30, 1922.

13. Board of Directors' Meeting, March 23, 1923, Minutes, ASBCo.

14. *Ibid.*, May 23, 1923.

15. Twenty-Fourth Annual Report of The American Ship Building Company for the Fiscal Year Ended June 30, 1923.

$3,500,000 each.[16] They were the last steamers designed by Frank E. Kirby. He designed them originally as turbine-driven propellers, but J. P. Wells, Superintendent of Engineering for the owners, objected that he would have to retrain his engineers, who were accustomed to sidewheelers.[17] Construction was delayed by a shipyard fire at Lorain in January, 1923, but they were finally launched that fall. The "arks" were towed to Detroit for their machinery, and made their appearances the following summer. One writer described the sister steamers as resembling "a white summer resort hotel that has unexpectedly found itself adrift."[18] This was an apt description of the multi-tiered steamers with their large glassed-in pilothouses perched high on the forward portion of the top deck and the many minaret-like ventilators popping up from the long clerestory roofs. They were a fitting tribute to Frank E. Kirby, but they were a plague to the profit and loss section of the shipbuilding company's annual report.

The year 1924 should have been a profitable one for American Ship Building. The Independent Steamship Company sold the *Oneida* and *Onondaga* to the Ford Motor Company on a cash basis.[19] The chartered *Romagne* and *Juvigny* remained in service on the coast. The year before, over 59,000,000 tons of iron ore were shipped in lake freighters, and early spring predictions called for 55,000,000 tons to be moved in 1924. Only the war years of 1916 and 1918 were better. By the time navigation opened, a slight national recession set in, and estimates for iron ore dropped to 35,000,000 tons. By July and August, normally the best months of the iron ore trade, over 100 ships were laid up. Although the trade picked up in the fall, only 42,600,000 tons of ore were moved by the lake fleet.[20] Vessel operators availed themselves of the opportunity to have necessary repairs done on their inactive vessels with profits gleaned from the year before. Thus the total

16.   Gordon P. Bugbee, *The Lake Erie Sidewheel Steamers of Frank E. Kirby*, p. 12.

17.   *Ibid.* Kirby died in New York on August 26, 1926, at the age of eighty.

18.   Francis Duncan, *Inland Seas*, XIII (Winter, 1957), 281.

19.   Board of Directors' Meeting, May 28, 1924, Minutes, ASBCo.

20.   *Annual Report of the Lake Carriers' Association, 1924* (Detroit: P. N. Bland Printing Co., 1925), p. 141.

amount of dry docking and repairs done by American Ship Building increased by 20 per cent over that of 1923.[21]

On June 28, 1924, the company suffered a severe setback to its Lorain plant. On a hot, muggy Saturday, at 5:12 in the afternoon, the yellowish-black funnel of a killer tornado struck Lakeview Park, demolishing the bathhouse and throwing its victims into the lake. In eight minutes, it cut a swath of destruction from the park across the Black River, through the east side, and twisted the Erie Avenue bridge out of use on its way. When the funnel cloud lifted, it left behind seventy-eight dead, over a thousand injured, and property damage estimated at $6,500,000. The shipbuilding plant was a shambles. The roofs were torn off most of the buildings, wooden structures demolished, cranes toppled and twisted, and fencing torn down. The steamer *J. S. Ashley* was torn loose from her moorings and smashed the concrete dock in Number One slip. The freighter *Henry Ford II*, nearing completion at the fit-out dock, broke her lines and was adrift in the Black River for several hours, but miraculously escaped serious damage. Number Two building berth was so severely damaged that it was abandoned. Because so many of the shipyard workers suffered damage to their homes and were in serious distress, the company donated $10,000 to the Ohio Relief Commission to aid the community.[22] Company officials estimated that $375,000 was required to restore the shipyard to its full working capacity, and little of the loss was covered by insurance.[23]

The tornado set the tone for the remainder of the year for the company. Labor costs were high, skilled workmen hard to obtain, and material was late in arriving. These factors caused the loss of almost $500,000 in new ship construction accounts, wiping out current operating earnings for the year and seriously depleting the year's total earnings.[24] A great part of the construction loss came from the side-wheeler accounts.

21. Twenty-Fifth Annual Report of The American Ship Building Company for the Fiscal Year Ended June 30, 1924.

22. Board of Directors' Meeting, July 23, 1924, Minutes, ASBCo.

23. Twenty-Fifth Annual Report . . . American Ship Building Company . . . June 30, 1924.

24. *Ibid.*

At the end of the disastrous year, Merton E. Farr retired as president of the firm and was succeeded by Alfred G. Smith. Farr had been president of the Detroit Ship Building Company for several years before he took over the reins of the parent firm in 1915. He had guided the company through the strains of the World War. A testimonial resolution drawn up by the board of directors read in part:

> His record as President, particularly during the war years, has been one of conspicuous achievement. During the actual period of the war . . . , the Company delivered to the United States Government one-fourth in number and one-seventh in tonnage of the total ships delivered to it from all sources in the United States. During the four years of the war activity the Company built and delivered more than one million tons deadweight of steel freight-carrying steamships. This record, accomplished under Mr. Farr, is unsurpassed by any American builder.[25]

As if passenger ship contracts and internal yard problems were not enough to contend with, Kellogg Fairbank heard rumors that another shipyard was going to locate on the Great Lakes. Charles M. Schwab's name was prominent in the rumors, and Fairbank suggested to Merton Farr that a "timely word might help the situation" to find out whether there was "anything in the wind."[26] Curiously enough, on the same day that the tornado struck Lorain, Farr replied:

> I have heard similar prophecies by an individual who is only happy when he is raising the devil, but I cannot recall one instance when his statements or prophecies have come true. This may be an exception. I think perhaps an alienist or a "Lord High Executioner" could perform a great service if he would get busy.[27]

It is not known if the person spreading the rumor was in Lorain that fateful day, but Farr did wire Schwab at Loretto, Pennsylvania, to

25. Board of Directors' Meeting, November 19, 1924, Minutes, ASBCo.
26. Letter from Kellogg Fairbank to Merton E. Farr, June 26, 1924, Chicago Ship Building Company Papers.
27. *Ibid.*, Letter from Merton E. Farr to Kellogg Fairbank, June 28, 1924.

find out if he was involved in the rumor. Schwab wrote back that he already had far too many shipyards which, "in the present unfortunate state of affairs," were not profitable. He suggested that he and Farr get together to renew old acquaintances and talk over the busy days of the war.[28]

The next few years were generally good for lake shipping as the nation rode toward the crest of its prosperity. As long as the ore fleet started in the early spring and bucked ice and ran late into the fall and fought heavy seas, the company's repair business remained constant. As prosperity continued, contracts for new vessels also trickled in. All vessel construction by American Ship Building was done now at the Lorain plant. Between 1925 and 1929, the yard produced fifteen ships, most of them 600-foot bulk carriers. One of them, the self-unloader *Carl D. Bradley*, was the largest American vessel on the Great Lakes. The company also built two tank barges, two tankers, and a tug during this period.

In other company areas of business, the Independent Steamship Company sold its eight remaining steamers.[29] The shipbuilding company bought the tools and equipment of a small ship repair concern, The Kraft Ship Yard & Dry Dock Company, located at 94th Street and the Calumet River in South Chicago, not far from the American Ship Building Company yard.[30] The Kraft equipment was moved to the parent yard and the small yard was closed.

In June, 1928, President Alfred G. Smith died and was succeeded by W. H. Gerhauser. The year presaged what Gerhauser would face throughout the first ten years of his presidency. Ice in the St. Marys River and Whitefish Bay in Lake Superior delayed the opening of navigation by a month, the season ended about twenty days early, and many vessels were laid up early. The repair business decreased, and

28.   *Ibid.*, Letter from Charles M. Schwab to Merton E. Farr, June 30, 1924.

29.   The *Juvigny* and *Romagne* were sold to Edward P. Farley & Company of New York in 1926. In 1927, the *Baccarat* and *Seneca* were sold to The Hammond Lumber Company of San Francisco; the *Cayuga* and *Kiowa* to O. W. Blodgett of Bay City; the *Chippewa* to The Pioneer S.S. Company of Cleveland; and the *Montfaucon* to The Mid-West Transportation Company of Detroit.

30.   Board of Directors' Meeting, October 13, 1926, Minutes, ASBCo.

new construction dropped off by nearly $4,000,000.[31] The following year told basically the same story.

Fortunately, by selling some of its non-productive shipyard properties, the company cut down operating expenses before the depression set in. The Number Three dry dock property in Cleveland was sold to the Great Lakes Cement Corporation and today is still the slip for a cement elevator. Merton E. Farr purchased the land belonging to the Detroit Ship Building Company. The South Yard of the Milwaukee Dry Dock Company was sold to the Chicago & North Western Railway Company.[32] Two other abandoned properties, the North Yard at Chicago and the West Yard at Milwaukee, were also sold.[33] This left the company with repair yards at Superior, Buffalo, Chicago, and Cleveland, and a construction-repair yard at Lorain.

In order to utilize more profitably the heavy machinery while it was sitting idle, the company entered the industrial machine and structural steel business. A small subsidiary, The Lakeside Engineering Company, was formed to execute the field work made necessary by contracts secured in this line of work.[34] In other moves, several clerical employees were released to effect a savings in salaries, and John E. Steinman was appointed General Superintendent of the company.[35] The latter move would benefit the company throughout the Second World War.

Gerhauser pursued such a conservative course that he appeared to be guided by a sixth sense warning him of the impending economic crisis that was about to strike the nation. A proposal was presented to him in 1929, however, that was too tantalizing not to investigate. He presented a plan to the board of directors in March whereby the ship-

---

31.　Twenty-Ninth Annual Report of The American Ship Building Company for the Fiscal Year Ended June 30, 1928.

32.　Board of Directors' Meeting, April 25, October 28, and December 19, 1928, Minutes, ASBCo.

33.　*Ibid.*, August 21 and October 9, 1929.

34.　*Ibid.*, February 5, 1930; Thirtieth Annual Report of The American Ship Building Company for the Fiscal Year Ended June 30, 1929. The subsidiary firm had an authorized capital stock of $500 divided into 250 shares with a par value of $2.00 each.

35.　Board of Directors' Meeting, July 25 and August 22, 1928, Minutes, ASBCo.

building company might purchase some of the bulk carrying fleets of the Great Lakes. He was granted authority to carry on negotiations and, along with General Counsel G. W. Cottrell, met with James A. Farrell, president of the United States Steel Corporation. The plan called for the formation of a stock corporation by Otis & Company of New York. The shipbuilding company was called upon to invest $6,000,000, but the directors balked at investing such a large sum of the stockholders' money without their approval.[36] Further negotiations lowered the company's commitment to $2,500,000, but the response of vessel owners, when representatives of the New York approached them, did not warrant further consideration at that time.[37]

A month later, Kellogg Fairbank wrote to Gerhauser that a finance company, The Chicago Corporation, had recently been formed in that city and "some of the keenest and strongest men in town" were directors. The firm had $60,000,000 actual cash in hand which they had been lending on call in New York. Fairbank was approached about the possibility of acquiring a large block of American Ship Building Company stock. He informed them that he thought the Rockefeller interests owned about one-fifth of the stock and that Brown Brothers interests also owned a considerable amount, either of which might be purchased. "Ked" suspected a connection with Otis & Company.[38] He expected to be reached shortly by New Yorker Edward P. Farley, chairman of the Shipping Board during the Harding administration.[39] Gerhauser advised Fairbank that negotiations in Cleveland were rapidly taking on "a definite form" and suggested that it would be "quite embarassing [sic] at this stage to have another interest negotiating for our stock." He recommended that Fairbank refrain from giving further information until the plan then being negotiated in Cleveland was either concluded or rejected.[40] Negotiations never reached a final stage because the financial panic struck, but it is interesting that Ed-

36. *Ibid.*, March 27, April 24, and May 22, 1929.
37. *Ibid.*, June 26, 1929.
38. Letter from Kellogg Fairbank to W. H. Gerhauser, June 1, 1929, Chicago
39. *Ibid.*, June 5, 1929.
40. *Ibid.*, Letter from W. H. Gerhauser to Kellogg Fairbank, June 6, 1929. Ship Building Company Papers.

ward P. Farley was elected to the board of directors of the shipbuilding company in October, 1929.[41]

A few months later, a major stock revision took place. For several years, the finance committee had recommended a plan for reconstructing and reducing the company's capital. On March 26, 1930, stockholders approved a plan for the conversion of old $100 par common stock into new no-par common stock, an increase of the authorized number of common shares, and the payment of $40 per share in cash to the common stockholders. About $6,000,000 was involved in the distribution, but whether or not the maneuvering was connected with the negotiations of a few months past is a matter of speculation.[42]

Although the depression years that followed the stock market crash were difficult, the conservative nature of the shipbuilding company again enabled it to survive. New construction between 1930 and 1940 amounted to a railroad car float, two tugs, two bulk freighters, a dredge, and a few dump scows. Repair work was restricted to the barest needs of the lake fleet, much of which was laid up. Even so, the firm experienced a yearly deficit in only three years—1932, 1933, and 1937.

Under Gerhauser's leadership, the company picked up contracts when and how it could. Several vessels that had been laid up for a long period showed signs of rusting on their bottoms. The company offered special rates for dry docking, scraping, and painting.[43] Several bulk carriers were converted to self-unloaders and one of them, the *John J. Boland*, was lengthened.[44]

Some property bounced back to the company as a result of the de-

41.   Stockholders' Annual Meeting, October 9, 1929, Minutes, ASBCo.; *Cleveland Plain Dealer*, February 27, 1930.

42.   Thirty-First Annual Report of The American Ship Building Company for the Fiscal Year Ended June 30, 1930. The number of authorized common shares of stock was increased from 155,000 to 230,000, each with a par value of $60.

43.   Board of Directors' Meeting, December 7, 1932, Minutes, ASBCo.

44.   The American Ship Building Company converted the following vessels to self-unloaders during this period: *Hoover & Mason* (1928); *Empire City* (1929); *Louis R. Davidson, William T. Roberts, Theodore H. Wickwire, Jr.* (1932); *J. F. Schoellkopf, Jr.* (1933); *Harry Yates* (1934); *John J. Boland, George F. Rand* (1936); *J. S. Ashley* (1937). In addition, the company converted the *Frank C. Ball* to a sand dredge (1930) and the *G. G. Post* to a crane ship (1936).

pression. A subsidiary of the Construction Aggregates Corporation defaulted, and the shipbuilding company was saddled again with the Chicago North Yard. In 1930, the American Ship Building Company built the large open-lake tug *T. L. Durocher* for the T. L. Durocher Company of DeTour, Michigan. Two years later, that firm defaulted on payments and the tug became the property of the Independent Steamship Company.[45] The shipbuilding company succeeded in chartering her on two occasions during the thirties. The Great Lakes Towing Company chartered her in 1933 for ten trips between Tonawanda, New York, and East Chicago, Indiana, to tow the oil barges *L.T.C. 8* and *L.T.C. 9*. The steamship company realized $4,000 per trip, but the charter was cancelled after five trips because the Lake Tankers Corporation was unable to provide enough gasoline to keep the barges in business.[46] In 1937, the big tug was chartered to the Nicholson-Universal Steamship Company for $75 per day to tow the oil barges *Gotham 84* and *Gotham 85* between Cleveland, Bay City, and other lake ports.[47] American Ship Building had several inquiries about the tug but was unable to sell her.

O. W. Blodgett defaulted on payment of the ocean-type steamer *Cayuga* in 1930 and she also came back to the Independent Steamship Company.[48] The company went as far as to charter her to T. L. Durocher to give him an opportunity to save his tug, but in the end, both vessels reverted to the shipbuilding company subsidiary.[49] Kellogg Fairbank talked of possibly selling the *Cayuga* to Japanese shipbreakers in 1935 when he learned that they were buying ships cheaply, loading them with scrap steel, and scrapping the ships when they arrived in Japan.[50] The possibility never materialized. The last survivor of the original Independent Steamship Company was sold in 1937 through Cleveland marine insurance broker William L. Fitzgerald to

45. Board of Directors' Meeting, August 24, 1932, Minutes, ASBCo.
46. *Ibid.*, June 28, 1933.
47. *Ibid.*, August 17, 1937; *Great Lakes News*, XXII (September, 1937), 1.
48. Board of Directors' Meeting, August 30, 1930, Minutes, ASBCo.
49. *Ibid.*, May 27, 1931.
50. Letter from Kellogg Fairbank to W. H. Gerhauser, January 24, 1935, Chicago Ship Building Company Papers.

Panamanian buyers.[51] She was lost ten months later off the coast of Cornwall, England.

American Ship Building had several opportunities to purchase struggling shipyard companies during the thirties. The most tempting offer came from Charles C. West, president of the Manitowoc Ship Building Company at Manitowoc, Wisconsin. Because of the recent deaths of his two original partners, West felt that it was necessary either to strengthen his organization or combine in some manner with another shipbuilding company.[52] A committee appointed by Gerhauser to look into the matter decided, after visiting the Manitowoc facilities, that the plant arrangement made it a very expensive one to operate on a small volume of business and declined West's offer.[53]

In 1939, Adam E. Cornelius, of the Buffalo vessel operating firm of Boland & Cornelius, offered American Ship Building the two small repair yards of a Boland & Cornelius subsidiary, The Lake Erie Shipbuilding Company. The Buffalo repair yard was at the foot of Michigan Avenue. The Toledo yard was at 902 Water Street on the Maumee River. Cornelius accepted an offer of cash and stock in the American Ship Building Company. American Ship Building Company directors W. J. Conners, Jr., J. S. Wood, and John J. Boland did not vote on the matter because of their personal interests in Boland & Cornelius.[54]

Early in the depression, Gerhauser took measures to reduce company expenditures. Some have already been noted. In 1931, the Cleveland work force was reduced to carry only the business that the Lorain yard could not handle.[55] At a meeting held in most incongruous surroundings—aboard the palatial passenger liner *President Coolidge*, docked at Pier Nine in Jersey City, New Jersey—the board of directors reduced by about 10 per cent the salaries of all salaried employees.[56] The same employees received another 10 per cent pay reduc-

51.   Board of Directors' Meeting, March 24, 1937, Minutes, ASBCo. The *Cayuga* was renamed *Alba* and lost on January 31, 1938.

52.   *Ibid.*, January 30, 1931.

53.   *Ibid.*, W. H. Gerhauser, Report to Committee on Proposed Manitowoc Acquisition, January 30, 1931.

54.   *Ibid.*, October 11, 1939.

55.   *Ibid.*, May 27, 1931.

56.   *Ibid.*, October 14, 1931.

tion in 1932.[57] American Ship Building joined other lake shipbuilders in 1933 in forming an association pursuant to the National Industrial Recovery Act. The code of fair practice assured shipyard workers a minimum wage of 45 cents and a maximum work load of not more than thirty-six hours per week during a period of six months.[58] In April, 1934, a wage raise of 10 cents an hour for skilled labor and 5 cents an hour for unskilled gave the workers the highest hourly wages in company history. Employment was intermittent, however, and weekly earnings were unsatisfactory to "employees and management alike."[59]

The lake shipping doldrums began to lift in 1936, and shipyard business picked up correspondingly. By the following year, shipyard wages increased by about 12 per cent, but the job situation had not improved. To provide work for themselves, machinists in Lorain accepted a 15 cent per hour wage reduction in order to permit the company to bid on a contract for the construction of two engines for the Inland Waterways Corporation.[60]

Also in 1936, the parent company dissolved most of its subsidiary corporations when a new revenue act provided that gain or loss did not have to be determined until the property was disposed of by the parent firm.[61]

As the doldrums lifted, American Ship Building picked up some contracts when it became the sole licensee in the United States for a reciprocating compound steam engine, the Lentz engine, patented by Willy Salge & Company of Berlin, Germany.[62] In effect, this engine was two compound engines joined at the HP cylinder ends of each. The arrangement of cylinders so that steam passed directly through a valve from the HP cylinders to the LP cylinders with a minimum loss of heat through radiation provided a more efficient use of the steam

57. *Ibid.*, August 24, 1932.

58. *Ibid.*, August 23, 1933.

59. Thirty-Sixth Annual Report of The American Ship Building Company for the Fiscal Year Ended June 30, 1935.

60. Board of Directors' Meeting, March 24 and April 27, 1937, Minutes, ASBCo.

61. *Ibid.*, March 18, 1936.

62. *Ibid.*, March 11 and June 24, 1936.

in the LP cylinder. The company built few Lentz engines but it did Lentzify several lake freighter engines. Lentzifying involved installing a new HP cylinder equipped with a Lentz valve gear in a conventional steam engine. The valve gear, designed to act as a booster, got more steam to the last cylinder by using the steam to greater advantage.

With the apparent end of the depression in 1937, the lake trade seemed to regain its sound footing. Such was not the case. Business the next season was the worst since 1932 and continued so into September, 1939, when the world situation stimulated the nation's steel industry. Almost half of the lake fleet was laid up by mid-summer in 1939. The shipbuilding company's repair business declined 25 per cent during the fiscal year—this after a poor showing the year before.[63] With German armies on the march in Europe, the second half of the year was as different from the first as night from day.

By October, President Gerhauser was negotiating with French representatives for the construction of small trawler-type vessels and submitting bids on engine parts for ice-breaking tugs for the Canadian Government.[64] Nothing came of either proposal, but they were signs of things to come.

In 1940, the ore fleet operated on a full basis for only the second time since 1928. Much neglected repair business came into the company yards. In June, a representative from the United States Maritime Commission suggested that American Ship Building rehabilitate the idle William Cramp Ship & Engine Company plant at Philadelphia and build two large combination passenger/cargo vessels. While the board of directors decided that the company would cooperate with the government to the fullest extent in carrying out its defense program, it would accept the contract only on a fee basis and only if the company was not called upon to invest money or assume any financial risks on the project. This decision was based on an examination of repairs needed by the Cramp facilities.[65]

63.   Fortieth Annual Report of The American Ship Building Company for the Fiscal Year Ended June 30, 1939.
64.   Board of Directors' Meeting, October 11, 1939, Minutes, ASBCo.
65.   *Ibid.*, June 12, 1940.

In August, 1940, the shipbuilding company successfully bid $6,300,000 on a contract to build twelve net tenders for the Navy Department.[66] This was the only government contract landed by the company in 1940 but several inquiries were being studied with an emphasis placed on minesweeper construction. In anticipation of the role that the company would play in the turbulent days ahead, space was rented on the fourteenth floor of the Terminal Tower Building in downtown Cleveland to house some executive offices and the purchasing and accounting departments.[67] Also the engine of the tug *T. L. Durocher* was converted from coal to oil and she was moved to New York to facilitate her possible sale.

The depression was over and American Ship Building emerged in a stable financial condition. Rather than relying on lending institutions, the company paid its own way by selling government securities purchased during better times.[68] The last of the patriarchs on the board of directors, H. H. Porter, passed from the scene in 1933. But the "younger" generation had proven themselves capable. Harry Gerhauser took over the presidency during difficult times and succeeded through conservative and wise management. Like Merton E. Farr in 1915, he worked in a time of economic difficulties and hovering war clouds. When the storm struck, Gerhauser and the American Ship Building Company were ready.

66. *Ibid.*, August 14, 1940.
67. *Ibid.*, December 18, 1940.
68. *Ibid.*, March 23, 1932.

11.

Gumbo Mud
and Yankee Ingenuity

When World War II came to the nation, only the manner of its beginning was a shock. Government-sponsored programs such as Lend-Lease expressed the anti-Nazi sentiments of the nation. The same water-distance problem and shortage of ships faced by the country in World War I again stared it in the face. In this case, however, Congress had already attempted to rectify one of the great weaknesses, tonnage shortage, by passing the Merchant Marine Act of 1936. The act gave birth to the United States Maritime Commission under the chairmanship of Joseph P. Kennedy. The Commission, originally intended to be a quasi-judicial body, took on a more functional role as Kennedy battled mail subsidy scandals.

In 1938, Kennedy was succeeded as chairman by Rear Admiral (Retired) Emory Scott Land, who aggressively pursued a policy of

1. Frederick C. Lane, *Ships for Victory, A History of Shipbuilding Under the U.S. Maritime Commission in World War II* (Baltimore: Johns Hopkins Press, 1951), pp. 12-13.

awarding private subsidies to private industry for building ships. Land was a close friend of President Franklin D. Roosevelt and thus enjoyed an almost czarist position as chairman. As he jokingly said of himself, "You know, I don't believe in the commission form of government; I think you ought to have a one-man show and shoot him at sunrise if he doesn't run it right."[2] Despite Land's apparent salty and hard-bitten attitudes, he was a diplomat and successfully ran the Maritime Commission activities throughout the war. One of his first moves as chairman was to arrange for Commander (later Vice Admiral) Howard L. Vickery, of the Naval Bureau of Construction and Repair, to become his assistant. Together, these two men headed the agency that had to conquer the tonnage shortage still existing at the beginning of the war.

In December, 1940, Land was faced with the problem of finding personnel to run Maritime Commission-sponsored shipyards in which he proposed to build a fleet of 200 standardized emergency cargo freighters. Land attempted to get the largest shipbuilding firms on the East Coast to sponsor or staff subsidiary emergency yards, but their construction demands were so heavy that he was only partially successful. During the discussion of the staffing of an emergency yard at New Orleans with officials from The Federal Ship Building & Dry Dock Company of Kearney, New Jersey, the American Ship Building Company was mentioned as a possibility without referring to a specific site.[3]

Earlier in the month, a group of New Orleans businessmen headed by Norman O. Pedrick formed the Louisiana Shipyards, Incorporated. They leased 100 acres of swampland on the Industrial Canal from the Port of New Orleans on which to build a shipyard for the Maritime Commission.[4] On January 17, 1941, the Maritime Commission

2. *Transactions of the Society of Naval Architects and Marine Engineers*, XLVIII (1940), 276.

3. Frederick C. Lane, *Ships for Victory . . .* , p. 52, n. 28. The Maritime Commission memorandum was dated December 26, 1940.

4. Letter from Norman O. Pedrick to R. E. Anderson, Director of Finance, Maritime Commission, January 10, 1941, Records of the United States Maritime Commission, File No. 507-3-5, Part 1 (Louisiana Shipyards, Inc.), Record Group 178,

awarded a $4,841,000 contract to the New Orleans firm to build a ship-yard with six launching ways.[5] But the Louisiana firm had no experience in building ships. Within the week, Pedrick and Rudolph S. Hecht flew to Cleveland to confer with W. H. Gerhauser and other American Ship Building Company officials about staffing the shipyard. The conference went well, and the New Orleans gentlemen, who were hopeful of getting a definite commitment, returned home encouraged but empty-handed. Hecht wrote to Vickery that the Cleveland officials wanted more time to work out tax problems and that he hoped Vickery or Land could hurry their decision.[6]

Gerhauser conferred with Land two days later in Washington but again wanted more time to study the tax problems. His only concession was to agree to further negotiations with Pedrick and his group.[7] On January 30, William S. Knudsen, Chairman of the National Defense Advisory Commission, telephoned Gerhauser and stressed the importance to national defense of American Ship Building's undertaking the construction of ships at New Orleans.[8] A meeting with Pedrick and Hecht was held three days later in Cleveland in which most matters were clarified. Shortly thereafter, The Delta Shipbuilding Company was formed.[9] The corporation was a wholly-owned American Ship Building Company subsidiary with a paid-in net cash capital of $750,000. It had the right to aid in planning the yard layout but was formed solely for the purpose of building ships. A basic net fee division on a 60/40 basis was agreed upon with Delta receiving the larger and Louisiana Shipyards the smaller portion.[10] On

---

National Archives. Hereafter cited as USMC Records. The firm was incorporated on December 7, 1940, with an authorized capital of $1,500,000 divided into 150,000 shares of $10 par value common stock. The firm also made tentative banking arrangements through Rudolph S. Hecht, chairman of the board of a New Orleans bank, for an additional equal amount of capital should it be required.

5. *Ibid.*, Memorandum from E. S. Land to W. S. Knudsen, January 21, 1941.

6. *Ibid.*, Letter from Rudolph S. Hecht to Howard L. Vickery, January 21, 1941.

7. *Ibid.*, Letter from Norman O. Pedrick to Howard L. Vickery, January 25, 1941.

8. Board of Directors' Meeting, February 6, 1941, Minutes, ASBCo.

9. *Ibid.*, Report of Committee on Operation of a Shipyard at New Orleans.

10. *Ibid.*, Outline of Plan for Construction and Operation of a Shipyard, and the Building of Ships in It, at New Orleans, All for the U.S. Maritime Commission.

March 14, 1941, the Maritime Commission awarded a cost-plus-fixed-fee contract to Delta for the construction of twenty-five "Liberty-type" cargo vessels at an estimated base cost of $1,500,000 per vessel.[11]

Construction on the new yard was started immediately. John Steinman of American Ship Building was largely responsible for the design and layout of the yard.[12] It was built on marshy land. Beneath the land surface was "gumbo" mud of an indeterminate depth. Consequently, the shipways and buildings were built on an estimated 30,000 piles driven down more than sixty feet and held by friction alone. The shipways were held together by reinforced concrete slabs laid over the pilings.[13] Three building berths were constructed along either side of a narrow slip, and the vessels were launched sideways. An electro-mechanical launching-trigger arrangement with cutting ropes and guillotines was installed to insure coordinated and smooth launchings. This arrangement had been devised a few years earlier at the Lorain plant by William R. Douglas and perfected by Edgerton B. Williams.

The yard was designed to use fully a new technique known as "downwelding" which permitted the sub-assembly and welding of large sections on the ground.[14] Each building berth was incorporated with a large fabrication shop and steel storage yard directly behind it. By keeping crane movements to a minimum, this system effected a great savings in time and expense.[15] Before the yard was com-

11.   Memorandum from E. S. Land to Office of Production Management, April 1, 1941, USMC Records, File No. 507-4-5, Part 1 (Louisiana Shipyards, Inc.); "Permanent Report of Completed Ship Construction Contracts, Report B-1" ((Construction Division, United States Maritime Administration, Washington, D.C., n.d.), p. 4A. (Mimeographed.)

12.   *The American Ship Builder*, I (November, 1942), 6.

13.   E. B. Williams, "The Delta Shipyard," *Marine Engineering & Shipping Review*, XLVIII (April, 1943), 194.

14.   H. Gerrish Smith, "American Shipbuilding and Shiprepairing Industry at War," *American Merchant Marine Conference Proceedings, New York, October 15 and 16, 1942*, pp. 24-25.

15.   Layout Plan of the Delta Shipbuilding Company in F. G. Fassett, Jr. (ed.), *The Shipbuilding Business in the United States of American* (2 vols.; New York: Society of Naval Architects and Marine Engineers, 1948), I, 221.

pleted, two more building ways were added, giving it a total of eight.[16]

Inasmuch as cows were grazing on the land when it was acquired, the entire yard had to be built from scratch. When the necessary buildings were completed, men were hired and operations begun. As soon as the first building way was completed, on October 1, 1941, the keel plate was laid for the first vessel, the *William C. C. Claiborne*. She was launched on March 28, 1942, the first of 188 ships that this emergency shipyard produced. The yard was staffed with a nucleus of about twenty-five shipbuilders from the American Ship Building Company yards on the lakes. Most of the workers and many of the supervisory personnel came to work in the yard with no prior shipbuilding experience. Yet in the peak month of the yard's existence, in June, 1943, over 19,400 persons were employed there.[17] R. B. Ackerman oversaw the running of the yard, John Steinman was in charge of production, and Edgerton B. Williams was head of the engineering department.

The all-welded Liberty ships were designed by William Francis Gibbs of the New York naval architectural firm of Gibbs & Cox. Actually, Mr. Gibbs' modified plans brought sixty "Ocean" class cargo vessels from England to be constructed in this country for the British Ministry of War.[18] Hull sheer was kept to a minimum to exclude the necessity of furnacing plates. The Liberties measuring 7,176 gross tons were all 441 feet 6 inches overall in length with few deck obstructions other than the midship houses and fore and aft gun tubs. The Liberty program, which was extended through 1945, called for the construction of more than 2,600 such vessels.[19] Parts for the ships were manu-

16. Frederick C. Lane, *Ships for Victory . . .* , p. 62.

17. Gerald J. Fischer (comp.), *A Statistical Summary of Shipbuilding Under the U.S. Maritime Commission During World War II* (Washington: U.S. Maritime Commission, 1949), p. 126.

18. Frederick C. Lane, *Ships for Victory . . .* , pp. 72-79. The Canadian firms of Davie Shipbuilding & Repairing, Ltd., Burrard Dry Dock Company, Ltd., and Canadian Vickers, Ltd. built twenty-six "Fort" class vessels which were identical to the "Ocean" class except for their riveted construction.

19. U.S., Department of Labor, *Wartime Employment, Production, and Condi-*

factured by over 800 plants in thirty-two states.[20] The vessels, the yard, and the personnel were truly hybrid!

The Delta yard took 242 days from keel-laying to deliver the *Clairborne*. In May, 1943, the Delta yard delivered eight ships with an average construction time from keel-laying to delivery of 51 3/8 days.[21] The *George Poindexter* was launched in thirty-one days and delivered twelve days later for a total construction time of forty-three days!

The company received the Maritime Commission "M" pennant, an incentive efficiency award, on January 7, 1943, for delivering a "round" of eight ships in under 105 days total construction time. For W. H. Gerhauser, who came down from Cleveland, it was a double ceremony as he was celebrating his sixty-second birthday. The steady rain did little to dampen the spirits of several thousand shipyard workers and guests as they watched the launching of the *Leonidas Polk* and listened to laudatory speeches by Louisiana Governor Sam Jones and Rear Admiral Howard Vickery.[22] The Delta shipyard band, in their new uniforms, culminated the day's activities by playing the national anthem.

The Delta Shipbuilding Company turned out many Liberties bearing names of prominent Americans: *Abraham Lincoln, David G. Farragut, Robert M. LaFollette*, but one, the *Lafcadio Hearn*, gave company officials a few twinges of embarrassment. The vessel's Greek-born namesake, a well known Cincinnati and New Orleans writer and political cartoonist in the 1880's, later renounced his adopted country and died a Japanese citizen. The New Orleans newspapers received many letters from the local citizenry who were shocked to learn that the Maritime Commission would honor a "renegade and an apostate" such as this. "World War I" mustered his indignant patriotism and de-

---

tions of Work in Shipyards, Bulletin No. 824 (Washington: Government Printing Office, 1945), p. 37.

20. U.S., Maritime Commission, *Report to Congress for the Period Ended June 30, 1942* (Washington: Government Printing Office, 1943), p. 16.

21. President's Report, Board of Directors' Meeting, June 14, 1943, Minutes, ASBCo.

22. *New Orleans Times-Picayune*, January 8, 1943.

plored the fact that "thousands of others in that war and in the present one, will not meet the specifications demanded by the twisted reasoning of this great body of government bureaucrats. . . . What price glory?"[23] But the *Hearn* outlived her clouded beginning, later "returned" to Greek registry, and is sailing today under the Liberian flag.

In the fall of 1942, the savage submarine offensive seriously depleted the nation's tanker resources. The alarmed Maritime Commission searched for emergency solutions, and Admiral Vickery approached Ed Williams about the feasibility of converting Liberty ships to tankers. Ed advised him that it would be better to build the vessels as regularly designed tankers, but he thought that the basic Liberty design could be followed.[24] Both the Delta people and William Francis Gibbs went to work on plans and came up with a Liberty hull that carried the same outboard profile but whose "innards" were those of a tanker.[25] Delta received contracts for fifty-two and the California Shipbuilding Corporation contracts for fifty Liberty tankers, though both firms later had twenty contracts cancelled. Delta laid the keel to its first tanker, the *John Stagg*, on May 18, 1943, and she was launched on July 7, fifty days later.

Production was held back on the tankers by the dire shortage of steel and by the inability of the Maritime Commission to supply pumps, valves, and other equipment.[26] Production was also slowed on both tankers and standard Liberties by the lack of welders sufficiently trained for production work. In May, 1943, the firm lost 301 welders, mostly to the armed forces. The yard employed about 3,000 welders, but most were not sufficiently skilled. Although a training program was conducted, it took from six to eight weeks to turn out a good welder.[27] As a solution, the company hired women and trained many

23. *New Orleans States*, August 2, 1943.

24. Telephone interview with E. B. Williams, Winter Haven, Florida, March 20, 1968.

25. Frederick C. Lane, *Ships for Victory* . . . , p. 588. The maintenance of the Liberty profile was important because tankers were priority targets for U-boat commanders.

26. President's Report, Board of Directors' Meeting, July 20, 1943, Minutes, ASBCo.

27. *Ibid.*, April 20, 1943.

of them as welders. In September, 1944, the peak for the employment of women, "Wilma Welders" comprised 8.8 per cent of the 15,800 wage earners at Delta.[28] But the problems of the draft and lack of skilled labor continued throughout the war. Labor notwithstanding, the company had the honor of delivering the 1,000th vessel of the national Liberty program, the *Robert Lowry*, in May, 1943.[29]

In January, 1944, the Maritime Commission contracted with the Delta yard to begin preparation of plans to convert Liberty hulls to colliers.[30] Delta built twenty-four colliers and was the only yard in the country to build this type of modified Liberty. Moving the machinery aft, and thus dispensing with the propeller shaft tunnel, gave greater bulk carrying capacity in the after cargo holds. The pilothouse was retained amidships, as were the "ugly duckling" Liberty hull lines. The vessels were cheaper to build than the standard Liberties, and the Delta officials and Maritime Commission agreed on a flat fee per ship of $55,000 above construction costs.[31] They were good carriers and about half of them are still in commission today under a half dozen different flags spread across the face of the globe.

The colliers were the last vessels built at the Delta yard. The firm entered into a stand-by agreement with the Maritime Commission, while the latter decided what would be done with the $10,912,000 facility.[32] The agreement expired on April 30, 1946, and the yard was turned over to the Maritime Commission.

During the four years the yard was in operation, there were many exciting and pleasurable moments. Labor fell generally under the jurisdiction of the American Federation of Labor. There were few work stoppages. Most of these, surprisingly, were of a minor nature

28.   Gerald J. Fischer (comp.), *A Statistical Summary of Shipbuilding* . . . , pp. 126 and 129.

29.   President's Report, Board of Directors' Meeting, June 14, 1943, Minutes, ASBCo.

30.   *Ibid.*, January 18, 1944. This was part of the Maritime Commission's long-range planning program.

31.   *Ibid.*, Board of Directors' Meeting, October 11, 1945.

32.   Letter from Review Committee (Cost Construction) to Maritime Commission, November 30, 1945, USMC Records, File No. 507-3-5, Part 17 (Louisiana Shipyards, Inc.).

and were quickly settled, considering the hot, humid temperatures of the summer and the torrential downpours of the winter that made the work of building ships difficult. Often, the steel plates were hot enough to fry the proverbial eggs. The only serious slowdown occurred on January 1, 1944, when the Maritime Commission stopped all Sunday work. This involved the loss of a double-time pay day and 1,500 workers, including 300 welders, simply quit and did not return.[33] Some time was lost until more labor could be hired and trained.

One reason for the good work record at Delta was R. B. Ackerman, an advocate of recreational programs. Extensive athletic and social activities aided in developing the harmonious spirit. Even though launchings were common, they always generated momentary apprehensions and excitement. More excitement, however, was promoted by the races and wagers between the crews of the various building ways. Thousands of dollars changed hands among the workmen with each launching, and sometimes production slowed as "friendly" skulduggery was employed to gain a few hours in a hotly-contested building race. More than one launchway foreman was called on the carpet for the well-intentioned actions of his crew. But, despite the drawbacks and slowdowns, the yard made a valuable contribution to the war effort.

While the Delta Shipbuilding project had the aura of romance about it by creating a shipyard from a cow pasture, the lake shipyards of the American Ship Building Company picked up tempo in a more unobtrusive manner. Early in 1941, the company signed a $900,000 contract to build four deep sea trawlers for the General Sea Foods Corporation for delivery in November of that year.[34] Meanwhile, the net tenders under construction for the Navy Department created problems.

The company's engineering department was unfamiliar with navy requirements, and the navy inspectors ordered a multitude of minor

33. President's Report, Board of Directors' Meeting, February 15, 1944, Minutes, ASBCo.

34. *Ibid.*, Board of Directors' Meeting, January 21, 1941.

changes—all requiring drawings. Then the company manufacturing the diesel engines went on strike causing further delay.[35] All of the vessels were launched between February and April. In the latter month, two shipyard workers were overcome, one of them fatally, by cement fumes while they were applying cork insulation aboard one of the net tenders.[36] More time was lost in May when a wildcat strike by 700 shipyard workers closed the Lorain plant.[37]

The work was done under the sharp eye of Naval Supervisor Captain R. P. Schlabach. With reference to the workmanship, one navy officer made the seldom-heard remark that "it's a good job," but the superintendents at Lorain and Cleveland must have broken out in smiles when the last of the horn-bowed ships left company yards that fall.[38]

On February 11, 1941, W. H. Gerhauser attended a Washington conference with Secretary of Navy Knox and Chief Naval Constructor Rear Admiral Samuel M. Robinson to discuss the proposed construction program of a number of small type ships required by the Navy.[39] Two months later, the firm received a $13,700,000 contract to build eight 220-foot minesweepers.[40]

The company had been anticipating government contracts since the previous fall. Gerhauser's expectations were exceeded in May, 1941, however, when he not only announced the minesweeper contract but also signed contracts to build two 620-foot ore carriers for the Pittsburgh Steamship Company and still another with the Maritime Commission for the construction of fifteen steam engines for the Liberty program.[41] The company even sold the tug *T. L. Durocher* to

35. *Ibid.*, President's Report, June 18, 1941.

36. *Ibid.*, Board of Directors' Meeting, April 18, 1941; *Cleveland Plain Dealer*, April 7, 1941.

37. *Cleveland News*, May 19, 20, and 21, 1941.

38. *Cleveland Plain Dealer*, May 24, 1941.

39. Board of Directors' Meeting, February 6, 1941, Minutes, ASBCo.

40. *Ibid.*, President's Report, May 21, 1941.

41. *Ibid.* The ore carrier contract was for $4,251,000 and the Maritime Commission contract was for $1,650,000.

the Quartermaster Department of the United States Army at a handsome profit![42]

With the prospect of rising wages and inflationary conditions, the Office of Production Management, the Navy Department, and the Maritime Commission called for a conference of all lake shipbuilders at Chicago in April, 1941. Its purpose was to stabilize wages and hours. The meeting ended in an impasse when labor representatives demanded a closed shop and double the wage increase offered by the shipbuilders.[43] The company had signed an agreement with the Amercan Federation of Labor in April, 1940, that maintained the open shop, but granted concessions on wages and working conditions.[44] The failure of the Chicago Stabilization Conference prompted the wildcat strike mentioned earlier in the chapter. The Congress of Industrial Organizations noted the unrest and attempted to take advantage of the situation to make inroads into the lake shipbuilding industry.[45] American Ship Building met the situation by promising to make any wage increases arising from a reconvened stabilization conference retroactive to May 19, 1941, the date of the wildcat strike by the A.F. of L.[46]

The conference arrived at a decision in July, and the standards adopted there were accepted by the labor representatives. The open shop was maintained, and wages for standard skilled mechanics were set at $1.12 per hour.[47] In a union election held at Lorain in August, the A.F. of L. defeated the C.I.O. by a substantial margin. The C.I.O. immediately went on strike and remained out for twelve days. Fists flew when A.F. of L. members tried to return to work, after which a court injunction limited the C.I.O. to six pickets at a time.[48] No effort was made to enforce the ruling, but it served to check further violence. An appeal by Sidney Hillman, of the Office of Production Management,

---

42. *Ibid.*, Board of Directors' Meeting. The sale price was $160,000.
43. *Ibid.*, President's Report.
44. *Ibid.*, Board of Directors' Meeting, April 24, 1940.
45. *Ibid.*, President's Report, June 18, 1941.
46. *Ibid.*
47. *Ibid.*, July 23, 1941.
48. *Cleveland Press*, September 6 and 8, 1941.

and arbitration by Walter Pollard ended the strike with the A.F. of L. remaining the victor in the union struggle.[49] But labor unrest continued as the company refused to recognize the closed shop. The problem finally went before the National Labor Relations Board in Washington, and only the seriousness of the national situation in December forced the two parties into a membership-maintenance agreement.[50]

The labor unrest, combined with difficulty in obtaining steel, caused delays in the construction of the two giant Pittsburgh Steamship Company ore carriers. Gerhauser reported in December, 1941, that there was not any "apparent increase in labor efficiency and progress is not as rapid as I would like to see it."[51] On the brighter side, the company received contracts from the Maritime Commission to build six ore freighters for Great Lakes service.

Commander Vickery had conducted negotiations with representatives from the Lake Carriers' Association for several months without receiving an acceptable proposal. Finally, on October 7, 1941, the Association president, Alexander T. Wood, advised him that the vessel operators had abandoned their efforts to formulate a construction program. Vickery considered the construction of the ore carriers essential to the National Defense Program. He recommended that "in view of the urgent need for these vessels, together with the apparent inability of the operators to furnish a satisfactory proposal," the Maritime Commission contract to build them.[52] At a conference held with American Ship Building Company officials at Lorain on October 11, the company agreed to construct six ore carriers for $1,972,000 each.[53] The Great Lakes Engineering Works of Detroit received contracts for sixteen ore carriers. The American Ship Building Company-built vessels would receive the first Lentz engines built in this country.

49. *Cleveland News*, September 15, 1941.

50. President's Report, Board of Directors' Meeting, December 16, 1941, Minutes, ASBCo.

51. *Ibid.*

52. Memorandum from Commander Vickery, October 8, 1941, Minutes, U.S. Maritime Commission, LXIV, 19237-38.

53. Special Meeting, October 11, 1941, Minutes, U.S. Maritime Commission, LXIV, 19297.

After Pearl Harbor all energies of lake shipbuilders were employed in the war effort. The Superior, Buffalo, and Chicago yards of American Ship Building were used primarily to keep the iron ore fleet in good operating condition. Because of the critical demand for ore the navigation season opened early and ran late which imposed added burdens on the dry dock and repair facilities of the company. The company converted some automobile carriers, including the *Coralia* and *Penobscot*, back to bulk carriers for the War Shipping Administration. The Chicago yard drydocked the steamer *Sparta*, wrecked in the Armistice Day Storm in 1940, but her small size did not justify the expense of repairs.[54] She was ultimately sold and converted to a dock at Sturgeon Bay, Wisconsin. The Chicago yard also had the responsibility of readying several vessels for transit down the Illinois Waterway-Mississippi River System to the Gulf of Mexico.

Strong pressures from the governor of Illinois and lake shipbuilders caused the Navy Bureau of Yards and Docks to make a survey of the waterway in March, 1942. Eighteen bridges were raised to provide the necessary clearances at a cost of $2,500,000.[55] Under a procedure devised by Philip Furlong, a civilian employee with the Bureau of Ships, vessels that were to make the trip were fitted with pad-eyes at Chicago, their superstructures and draft lowered. After the vessels had passed through the Illinois system, pontoons were attached to the pad-eyes for the remainder of the voyage.[56]

The package freighters *W. J. Conners, P. E. Crowley, Duluth, Daniel Willard,* and the bulk freighter *William F. Fitch* made the journey successfully, and most of them saw action in the Pacific as repair ships for the Army.[57] Two Ford Motor Company barges, former World War I "Laker" hulls, also were readied. Engines taken out of the old passenger steamers *Missouri* and *Illinois* were carried on their

54.   Board of Directors' Meeting, April 28, 1942, Minutes, ASBCo.

55.   Lieutenant Commander Edmond S. Meany, Jr. (comp.) "Administrative History of the Ninth Naval District" (2 vols.; Historical Section, United States Navy Department Library, Washington, D.C., 1946), I, 33-35. (Type-written.)

56.   *Ibid.,* p. 338.

57.   Production Division, Shipyard Facilities File, American Ship Building Company, USMC Records, Box 839, File No. QM 50-P (QM-L11-3).

decks until they could be installed at the Gulf end of the trip.[58] The Chicago yard workers never knew what would be in their dry dock next. Everything from submarines to landing craft were drydocked. One of the trickiest jobs was docking the *Eugene J. Buffiington.* The 580-foot ore carrier struck Boulder Reef, Lake Michigan, in June, 1942 and broke her back in two places. John Steinman supervised the drydocking successfully, and the *Buffiington* returned to her important role of carrying ore within a few months. This was the largest repair job that president Gerhauser could remember the company's ever doing.[59]

The most romantic conversion job ever done on the Great Lakes fell to the Buffalo-Lake Erie plant of American Ship Building. With the U-boat campaign raging off the eastern seaboard in 1941-42, the Navy had to assign valuable escort vessels to convoy aircraft carriers used in training pilots. A former lake man, Captain John J. Manley, was struck with the idea of converting a Great Lakes sidewheel passenger liner to a training aircraft carrier. He thought the job could be done with more safety and economy on the lakes. Manley approached Captain William Amsden of the Ninth Naval District, who took the suggestion to Commander Richard Whitehead, later the "godfather" of the project.[60] In March, 1942, the American Ship Building Company was awarded a contract to convert the big, broad Cleveland & Buffalo Transit Company's *Seeandbee* into an aircraft carrier.[61] The big ship was shorn of her elaborate adornments at East Ninth Street Pier in Cleveland. The recent *Normandie* fire disaster prompted bringing aboard a Cleveland Fire Department pumper for the trip to Buffalo. In May, 1942, when the stripped hull was nudged into the Michigan Avenue slip at Buffalo, she was greeted by George Haug, Norm Rossfelder, Chris Stellrecht, and six riggers. The fire engine was unloaded

58. President's Report, Board of Directors' Meeting, September 3, 1942, Minutes, ASBCo.

59. *Ibid.*

60. Captain John J. Manley, "Great Lakes Lady Bares Her Fangs," *Inland Seas,* XIV (Spring, 1958), 58, reprinted from *Inland* (Autumn, 1956).

61. Board of Directors' Meeting, March 28, 1942, Minutes, ASBCo.

—and found to be inoperative—and within a short time, the old hull was swarming with workers.[62]

The Navy Department assigned a 14A preference rating to the project at a time when such a high rating was virtually impossible to obtain. The contract, on a cost plus 6 per cent basis, called for completion by September 1, 1942, but the Navy wanted it finished by August 1.[63] Lieutenant Commander E. A. Eisele, the BuShips representative, cut red tape whenever he could, sometimes when it seemed impossible. When fire extinguishers were needed, he and his sailors jumped into their jeep and commandeered them. When carloads of steel had to be moved, he called the Pennsylvania Railroad power foreman on Sunday—an unheard of action—and got his needed locomotive.[64] When freighters arriving at Buffalo grain elevators prevented shipyard workers from getting to work on time, Eisele personally kept the bridges from raising, then worked out bridge hours with the Buffalo city counsel.[65] Buffalo Purchasing Agent Chris Stellrecht obtained steel from local sources instead of waiting for mill shipments. The plates were moved on antiquated wooden rollers. A momentary holdup occurred when the wrong type of welding machines were shipped to the plant. A severe shortage of electricians threatened delay in June, but the company advertised widely and soon built up a competent force.[66] The great steel girders supporting the flight deck were welded into place, and a navigating island took shape on the starboard side of it. Three-inch teakwood covered the broad expanse where airplanes would land. No catapults or elevators were installed because the ship was to operate out of Chicago on a daily basis, but a

62. Interview with Christian J. Stellrecht, Orchard Park, New York, March 8, 1968. Haug and Rossfelder were company office managers at Cleveland and Buffalo respectively. Stellrecht was Buffalo purchasing agent, though later he was office manager there.

63. President's Report, Board of Directors' Meeting, March 26, 1942. Estimated cost of the project was $1,500,000.

64. Interview with Christian J. Stellrecht.

65. Telephone interview with Norman E. Borowske, Cleveland, Ohio, April 1, 1968.

66. President's Report, Board of Directors' Meeting, June 17, 1942, Minutes, ASBCo.

makeshift arresting gear to stop the forward momentum of the landing aircraft had to be provided.

With no established way of simulating the landing of planes to test
the arresting cable, the shipyard engineers resorted to Yankee ingenu-
ity. They determined mathematically that the shipyard's truck,
loaded with steel punchings and run at a speed of thirty-five miles per
hour, would approximate the landing of an airplane. Norm Borowske
and a volunteer helper donned football pads and helmets and baseball catchers' shin guards. The arresting cable was attached to the
rear of the "GMC." When the 1½-ton truck reached the required
speed, with both doors wired open, the helper nudged Norm, who
blew the horn and held on. The arresting cable brake was thrown, and
the truck, Norm and his helper, and the punchings were supposed to
come to a sudden, jolting stop. The first time they tried it, the carbure-
tor of the truck was torn loose from the manifold, and, since they had
neglected to put a canvas over the punchings, a major clean-up job
was in order. But after the first trial, the tests proceeded just as the
engineers said they would![67]

Renamed the U.S.S. *Wolverine*, her sea trials were completed on
August 11, and she was placed in full commission at Chicago on
August 21. On her shakedown cruise, a company engineer wrote that
"the crew still needs considerable experience in throwing coal the full
length of the furnace, as the after end of the grate bars are very
lightly covered."[68] Lake firemen would have laughed at the antics of
the Navy "stokers" as they stumbled over one another in the crowded
firehold. The boilers were stoked by hand, and one man was assigned
to each of the vessel's twenty-four boiler doors.[69] After the Navy boys
became accustomed to their new sidewheel home, the *Wolverine* was
acclaimed a success.

On January 19, 1943, the Lake Erie Plant of the American Ship
Building Company received the coveted Army-Navy "E" for its

67.   Telephone interview with Norman E. Borowske.

68.   Commander John D. Alden, "When Airpower Rode on Paddle Wheels,"
United States Naval Institute Proceedings, LXXXVII (May, 1961), 182.

69.   Captain John J. Manley, *Inland Seas*, XIV (Spring, 1958), 59.

achievement in converting the old sidewheeler.[70] Even as the award
was made, the work of converting another sidewheeler, the *Greater
Buffalo*, was going on. Construction was held up on her so that two
new designs of steel flight decking, laid in alternate checkerboard sections, could be applied with eight different types of commercial non-
skid coatings.[71] She was commissioned as the U.S.S. *Sable* on May 8,
1943. American Ship Building received notice of the awarding of a
contract to similarly convert the *Greater Detroit*, but it was cancelled
before demolition was started.[72] The company's Chicago yard converted the lighter *Commerce* to serve as a tender for the two grand old
ladies of the Ninth Naval District Fleet in September, 1942, and she
was used to ferry personnel, supplies, and wrecked aircraft between
ships and shore.[73]

As the romantic reconstructions were going on in Buffalo, the Lorain and Cleveland yards were suffering from the same material shortages felt by most shipyards across the nation. Vice Admiral Samuel
Robinson, Chief of the Office of Procurement and Material, noted that
the "expansion of facilities to produce ships' components has proved
to be more onerous than that of providing the ship ways themselves."[74]
A critical shortage developed in high pressure bronze valves and in
turbines and gears. This shortage, together with a shortage of steel,
necessitated cancellation of some navy construction contracts.[75] As a
result of these national shortages American Ship Building lost a
$1,700,000 contract for twelve 220-foot minesweepers and a promised

70.   Letter from L. H. Reynolds to Buffalo yard employees, February 1, 1943,
ASBCo. Papers. Reynolds was superintendent of the Buffalo plant at the time of the
award.

71.   Commander John D. Alden, *United States Naval Institute Proceedings*, p.
182.

72.   Board of Directors' Meeting, September 3, 1942, Minutes, ASBCo.

73.   *Ibid.*, President's Report.

74.   Memorandum from Vice Admiral Samuel M. Robinson to Chief of Naval
Operations, September 4, 1942, in "An Administrative History of the Bureau of
Ships During World War II" (4 vols.; Historical Section, Bureau of Ships, United
States Navy Department Library, Washington, D.C., 1946), II, 179. (Type-writ-
ten.)

75.   *Ibid.*, pp. 179-85.

contract for sixteen net tenders to be built at the Chicago yard.[76] Delivery of the eight minesweepers, then under construction at Cleveland and Lorain, was delayed by the shortages as was that of the two ore carriers for the Pittsburgh Steamship Company.

In May, 1942, the company received a Maritime Commission contract to build an additional seventeen steam engines for the Liberty program.[77] A contract for seven more followed. Most of the government contracts let during this period were on a cost-plus-fixed-fee basis, with a forty-hour work week as the standard. The fee usually was set at 6 per cent of the estimated cost and then adjusted accordingly. There were also bonus and penalty clauses, but American Ship Building was able to justify its few late deliveries.

In the summer and fall of 1942, the Maritime Commission found it necessary to increase the speed of Liberty ships because of a shortage of escort vessels. The need for speeded-up administrative action was essential for quick production, and the Commission turned to the Lentz engine as a possible solution.[78] Paul Miedlich, who originally brought the Lentz franchise and patent rights to American Ship Building, was still with the company and retained some rights to its manufacture.[79] Following talks between President Gerhauser and Maritime Commission officials, a second Lakeside Engineering Company was formed to work with the Lentz project.[80] While technical legalities were being overcome regarding American Ship Building's franchise and patent rights, and while arrangements were being made to build a pilot engine, the Maritime Commission and the War Production Board became involved in a bitter argument over the type of ship that would be propelled by the engine. The outcome of the vessel

<hr>

76.   President's Report, Board of Directors' Meeting, April 28, 1942, Minutes, ASBCo.

77.   *Ibid.*, May 26, 1942.

78.   Memorandum from Commissioner H. L. Vickery, September 18, 1942, Minutes, U.S. Maritime Commission, LII, 23012-13.

79.   Frederick C. Lane, *Ships for Victory* . . . , p. 584.

80.   Board of Directors' Meeting, October 14, 1942, Minutes, ASBCo. The Lakeside Engineering Company was formed with an authorized capital of $500,000 divided into 500 shares of par value $100 common stock.

design argument was the Victory Ship. Admiral Vickery announced that he was planning the construction of about 524 such ships of which 347 would be propelled by Lentz engines.[81] There was much opposition to the untried Lentz engine, particularly by William Francis Gibbs, who favored the turbine engine. The pilot Lentz engine was built by the General Machinery Corporation at Hamilton, Ohio, and assembled for testing at the Naval Boiler and Turbine Laboratory at Philadelphia in September, 1943. The engine withstood eighty-five hours of tests, but when the tests were only four hours from completion, a "local" fracture occurred in the casting. Examination showed that the cast iron did not have the nodular distribution of free carbon required of high strength cast irons, and the engine was rejected.[82] American Ship Building was on the verge of becoming one of the major suppliers of engines for the hundreds of Victory ships built in 1944-45, but missed by a scant four hours! Lentzifying the engines for some of the colliers being built by the Delta firm was considered in 1944, but the idea was rejected because of the excessive costs involved in the change.[83] The pilot Lentz engine was ultimately scrapped. The Lentz program consumed the better part of a year before it was rejected. During that time, much happened in the Lake Erie plants of American Ship Building.

Early in 1941, the Buffalo Chamber of Commerce called attention to that city's shipbuilding advantages and urged that it be included in the proposed small boat program of the Navy.[84] Two firms, The Bison Shipbuilding Company and The Niagara Shipbuilding Corporation, began operations on the basis of navy contracts. The latter firm received a $558,540 contract in July, 1941, to build six steel tugs.[85] The new company later received contracts for four self-propelled ammunition lighters but, overcome by production and financial problems, was prevented from completing the contracts. The Navy Department

81.   Frederick C. Lane, *Ships for Victory* . . . , p. 593.
82.   *Ibid.*, pp. 586-87.
83.   Interoffice Memorandum from C. H. Johnson to H. L. Vickery, June 9, 1944, USMC Records, File No. 606-41-1, Part 2 (Engines & Parts—Lentz Engines).
84.   *Buffalo Courier-Express*, January 12, 22, and 24, 1941.
85.   *Ibid.*, July 2, 1941.

asked American Ship Building to take over operation of the yard and complete the vessels. Gerhauser was reluctant to make such a move, but, inasmuch as "our relations with the Navy have been cordial," he felt that "this appeal could not be ignored."[86] The company entered into a contract with The Niagara Shipbuilding Company and the Navy Department to finish the ships for a flat fee of 4 per cent over construction costs, which were estimated to be $1,000,000.[87] The company took over the yard on December 22, 1942, and by August of the following year it had launched all of the vessels and closed down the yard. The lighters were completed at the Michigan Avenue-Lake Erie plant of American Ship Building.[88]

Beginning in November, 1942, the six ore carriers under construction for the Maritime Commission were launched. One of them, the *Belle Isle*, split across the deck and down each side through the sheer strake while lying at the fitout dock in Cleveland. This happened at the same time as a few Liberties, including the Delta-built *Henry Wynkoop*, and some tankers suffered fractures. They were welded ships and sensational newspaper accounts magnified the seriousness of the casualties.[89] The *Belle Isle* differed from the all-welded ships in that the Maritime ore carriers had riveted seams. After several conferences with the American Bureau of Shipping and the Maritime Commission, Gerhauser ordered all "Union-Melt" machine welding on the vessels replaced with hand welding and the gunwale construction on all six ships changed from a welded to a riveted connection.[90] This second change was later adopted by the Maritime Commission for all of its welded ships.

Two other "Maritimers," the *Thomas Wilson* and *Sewell Avery*, developed serious engine trouble when the high pressure piston rings broke and the high pressure cylinders of their Lentz engines became

86.   President's Report, Board of Directors' Meeting, December 16, 1942, Minutes, ASBCo.

87.   *Ibid.*, Board of Directors' Meeting.

88.   *Ibid.*, President's Report, July 20, 1943.

89.   Frederick C. Lane, *Ships for Victory . . .* , pp. 544-47.

90.   Board of Directors' Meeting, March 19, 1943, Minutes, ASBCo.

scored.[91] After costly machining, the difficulties were rectified and the country's first Lentz engines resumed their work in a more than satisfactory manner.

During the summer of 1942, while the Battle of the Atlantic was being waged, government officials determined to build "baby flattops" and escort vessels, similar to British corvettes, to counteract the submarine. On December 8, 1942, the Maritime Commission awarded contracts for the construction of sixty-nine frigates, as the American counterparts of the corvettes were called. One of the underlying reasons for awarding these contracts was the utilization of space that would soon open in Great Lakes shipyards, but for some reason the largest number of contracts went to West Coast builders. Kaiser Cargo, Incorporated, was given the contract to develop plans and specifications.[92] American Ship Building received contracts for seven frigates on a cost-minus basis with fees ranging from $30,000 to $90,000 per vessel. The estimated cost of each vessel was $1,723,000.[93] The 285-foot frigates were too long for the Canadian canals and had to be taken to the ocean via the Illinois Waterway and Mississippi River perched in an unlady-like manner on pontoons.

As more steel became available, ten more frigate contracts were awarded to American Ship Building in May, 1943, on the same basis as the original contracts.[94] The company ran considerably behind schedule in its frigate construction because of the demands for gunwale bar construction on the six "Maritime" ore carriers and because of a shortage of skilled labor.[95] There were also difficulties with West Coast designers who produced the drawings, but who had no concept of lake shipbuilding methods or problems. By the late fall of 1943, it became apparent that the company was not going to fulfill the contracts on

91. *Ibid.*, President's Report, July 20, 1943.

92. Frederick C. Lane, *Ships for Victory . . .* , p. 614.

93. Maritime Commission Meeting, December 8, 1942, Minutes, U.S. Maritime Commission, LIV, 236898-99; Board of Directors' Meeting, December 12, 1942, Minutes, ASBCo.

94. Maritime Commission Meeting, May 28, 1943, Minutes, U.S. Maritime Commission, LVII, 25285.

95. President's Report, Board of Directors' Meeting, October 14, 1943, Minutes, ASBCo.

time, and, since the Navy Department no longer urgently needed that type of vessel, the last four frigate hulls were cancelled.[96] The contracts were converted to a lump-sum basis of $16,200,000 for thirteen completed frigates and four that were cancelled.[97] Construction had already begun on the cancelled hulls, and they had to be disassembled and the parts shipped to a Maritime Commission storage yard.

Shortly before the frigate cancellations in September, 1943, President Gerhauser announced to his board of directors that the company had been awarded a Navy Department contract for construction of ten additional 180-foot minesweepers.[98] Later, because of an amendment to the contract, he would have serious doubts about them. The contract was on a cost-plus-fixed-fee basis, but, since it had originally been granted to the Tampa Shipbuilding Company, all the parts were in Tampa, Florida! The Tampa company was considerably behind on its delivery date with no hope of catching up, and its business and financial affairs were in a muddle. Eight of the vessels were already under construction and had to be cut apart in pieces small enough to be carried on flat-bed railroad cars and to fit through tunnels on their way north. Sam Meader and young Bill Gerhauser, the president's son, were sent to Tampa to expedite the movement. The transfer of purchase orders, which involved Navy red-tape, was a never-ending mess. All of the parts had to be numbered before shipment, and putting them together at Lorain was like assembling a jigsaw puzzle. The piping, valves, and other intricate machinery was in an even worse condition. Only four vessels were completed before the contracts were cancelled. One former employee recalled that cancellation was a "God-send because there probably were not enough parts to complete more anyhow!"[99]

96.   Maritime Commission Meeting, December 30, 1943, Minutes, U.S. Maritime Commission, LXI, 27200.

97.   Telegram from J. A. Honsick to Hugo E. Nelson, October 4, 1944, USMC Records, File No. 506-20-7, Part 8 (Corvettes—Design S2-S2-AQ1). Honsick was assistant finance director of the Maritime Commission.

98.   President's Report, Board of Directors' Meeting, September 2, 1943, Minutes, ASBCo.

99.   Telephone interview with Samuel Meader, St. Louis, Missouri, March 19, 1968.

That same September, the company received its last Navy contract. This $16,600,000 contract called for construction of eight 220-foot minesweepers. The last of them, the U.S.S. *Wheatear*, was the last vessel built by the company in its Cleveland yard and the last naval vessel delivered by the company for the war effort. American Ship Building also built eight 85-foot tugs for the U.S. Army in its Ganson Street dry dock at Buffalo in 1943, merely floating them when they were completed.

During the last two years of the war, the company kept its building ways filled but was able to shift hulls from one yard to another without maintaining the frantic pace of the first two and a half years. In some cases, it even towed incomplete hulls from Lorain and Cleveland to the Chicago yard to complete and deliver after the lakes were frozen over. Late in 1944, the Chicago yard completed one Duluth-built cargo vessel, the *Joe P. Martinez*, so that the ship might be delivered during the winter months. A secondary reason was that the Maritime Commission suspected the vessel's builder of prolonging construction to keep its yard open longer.[100] When the Lorain yard had finished vessel construction shortly before the end of the war, it turned to the assembly of tank treads and army truck frames, but not on a large scale.[101]

The labor situation during 1942 and 1943 was tense, but, although there were several strikes of short duration, it never seriously erupted. The Cleveland yard presented the most problems because of an "outlaw element in the yard which . . . assumed control in defiance of the terms of the [labor] agreement and the international officers who signed it."[102] Much of the difficulty went back to the rivalry between the A.F. of L. and the C.I.O. The company continued to uphold its policy of membership-maintenance and backed the A.F. of L. Late in 1943, it was able to subdue the "outlaw element" in the Cleveland

100. Completion of C1-M-AV1 Vessels, Memorandum from L. R. Sanford, November 7, 1944, Minutes, U.S. Maritime Commission, LXVIII, 30295-300. Sanford was director of the Gulf-Great Lakes Region for the Maritime Commission.
101. President's Report, Board of Directors' Meeting, March 5, 1945, Minutes, ASBCo.
102. *Ibid.*, November 17, 1943.

yard, and the remainder of the war saw few labor disputes in which production time was lost.

In an effort to raise yard morale and create a spirit of "togetherness" the company sponsored extensive recreation programs. Bowling leagues and softball teams provided relaxation and instilled competitiveness essential to maintaining a war effort. A company monthly, *The American Ship Builder*, carried positive propaganda aimed at increasing production. It was liberally sprinkled with photographs of employees and departmental athletic teams. Company-sponsored picnics and departmental holiday parties were highlighted. Charts were kept and large billboards erected to show whether the Cleveland or Lorain yard was ahead on controlled construction races. Many of the launchings were broadcast over local radio stations. The "ol' redhead," Tom Manning, was a regular narrator for such events, and often locally prominent citizens or mothers who had lost sons in the war sponsored the ships. All of this served as tremendous incentive to the shipyard workers.

Between 1941 and 1945, the company and its subsidiaries delivered 275 ships of all classes, built thirty-eight marine engines, converted two passenger ships to aircraft carriers, and repaired countless vessels engaged in the vital iron ore and grain trades on the lakes. Yet, despite the union rivalries, hard work under adverse weather conditions, and the demanding pace required of the war effort, employees of that era, when asked, look back fondly on their shipyard experiences as "good years."

The *Merton E. Farr* was one of four 12,000 ton lake freighters built on speculation in 1920. *Dwight Boyer.*

American Ship Building also built ten ocean type vessels in 1920, including the *Baccarat*, that it operated as the Independent Steamship Company. *American Ship Building Company.*

The tug *T. L. Durocher*, built in 1930 at Lorain, under charter in 1933 to Great Lakes Towing Company to tow oil barges *L. T. C. 8* and *L. T. C. 9*. *Richard D. Bibby*.

On June 28, 1924, a tornado struck Lorain, Ohio, killing seventy-eight people and doing severe damage to the shipyard. *American Ship Building Company*.

Construction of the sidewheelers *Greater Buffalo* (shown being launched at Lorain on October 2, 1923) and *Greater Detroit* (below) were fitting tributes to designer Frank E. Kirby. *Above, American Ship Building Company; below, Author's Collection.*

The self-unloader *Carl D. Bradley* was the largest ship on the Great Lakes when she was built at Lorain in 1927. *C. Patrick Labadie.*

The *Harry Coulby* was the flagship of the Interlake Steamship Company when she sailed on her maiden voyage from Lorain in 1927. *Author's Collection.*

Delta Shipbuilding Company at New Orleans, showing the eight building ways. Most of the ships in the fit-out dock at the top of the photograph are colliers. *Gordon Stafford.*

A new "down welding" technique at Delta permitted the sub-assembly and welding of large sections in a prefabrication process. *Gordon Stafford.*

Standard Liberty *Laurence J. Gallagher* was launched by Delta in thirty-nine days. The yard record was thirty-one days. *Gordon Stafford.*

Amship received a Navy contract in 1940 to build twelve net tenders such as the *Palm. American Ship Building Company.*

The *Seeandbee*, launched in 1912, was the largest sidewheeler ever to sail the lakes. *Author's Collection.*

In 1942 the *Seeandbee* was rebuilt as the training carrier U.S.S. *Wolverine*. *Steamship Historical Society of America.*

U.S.S. *Sustain* (AM-119), a 220-foot minesweeper built at the Cleveland yard in 1942. *American Ship Building Company.*

U.S.S. *Jubilant* (AM-255), a 180-foot minesweeper built at the Lorain yard in 1943. *American Ship Building Company.*

U.S.S. *Huron*, built at Cleveland in 1943, was typical of the frigates built by the company during World War II. *American Ship Building Company.*

The *Belle Isle* was one of six ore carriers built for the Maritime Commission in 1943 by Amship. She later became the *Champlain. American Ship Building.*

Eight tugs were built in the dry docks at Buffalo for the Defense Plant Corporation in 1943 and simply floated. *American Ship Building Company.*

Amship took over the operation of the Niagara Shipbuilding Company at Buffalo in 1943 and completed Navy tug and ammunition lighter contracts, including *YF-415. American Ship Building Company.*

Left to right: John Craig, George Craig, Craig Ship Building Company, Trenton-Gibraltar-Toledo. *Author's Collection*. C. B. Calder, Toledo Shipbuilding Company. *Author's Collection*.

Main office of the Toledo Shipbuilding Company on Front Street during a World War I Liberty Loan bond rally. The venerable John Craig is on the platform. *Author's Collection*.

Craig Ship Building Company pioneered design of the Lake Michigan carferries with the construction of the *Ann Arbor No. 1* in 1892. *C. Patrick Labadie.*

The Craig-built *Indianapolis* was the first lake passenger ship "of any pretensions" built for an Indiana Company. Several "handsome Hoosier belles" helped to launch her in 1904. *Frank E. Hamilton.*

The *Wilfred Sykes* was the first American ore carrier built after World War II.
Her lines provided a model for most ore vessels built in the next decade.
American Ship Building Company.

The *Sykes'* namesake with Mrs. Sykes and American Ship Building president
William H. Gerhauser at launching festivities at Lorain on June 28, 1949.
American Ship Building Company.

One of the biggest of the "whales" built by Amship in the fifties was the
George M. Humphrey. C. Patrick Labadie.

Amship president R. B. Ackerman with Secretary of the Treasury and Mrs.
George M. Humphrey at the christening of the *Humphrey* in 1954.
American Ship Building Company.

Left: Edmund Q. Sylvester, president of Amship, 1957-1962. *American Ship Building Company*. *Right*: William H. Jory, president of Amship, 1962-1967. *Madison Geddes Studio*.

The forward half of the ore carrier *Charles M. Schwab* was joined to the stern of the tanker *Gulfport* and jumboized in 1960. The unusual aspect was a four-foot difference in the beams of the halves. *Author's Collection*.

Left: Dr. Jacob O. Kamm has played a major role in developing Amship into a miniconglomerate corporation. *American Ship Building Company. Right*: George M. Steinbrenner III became president of Amship in October, 1967. *American Ship Building Company.*

U.S.C.G. *Steadfast*, third of seven Coast Guard cutters built at Lorain, strikes the water in a perfect launching in 1967. *American Ship Building Company.*

Artist's conception of the 858-foot bulk carrier now under construction at Lorain for the United States Steel Corporation. *American Ship Building Company.*

The beginning of the end of a cycle. The 437-foot bow section of the new "fresh-water whale" is floated from its Lorain building berth on December 21, 1968. *American Ship Building Company.*

12.

The Cycle Is Now Complete

The period immediately after World War II was, like that following World War I, one of consolidation and retrenchment for the American Ship Building Company, but for different reasons. Following World War I, the company consolidated its physical holdings and sold those yards that were operating on a marginal or sub-marginal basis. In 1945, company officials noted a steady decline in the amount of damages sustained by the Great Lakes fleet resulting from collisions, strandings, and other accidents. Channels had been widened and deepened to permit a twenty-four foot draft. Navigation had constantly been improved, particularly by the gyro-compass, radio direction finder, and radiotelephone.

The gyro-compass was first introduced to Great Lakes shipping aboard the Hanna freighter *Daniel J. Morrell* in 1922.[1] It rapidly

1. O. B. Whitaker, "Recalling How the Gyro-Compass First Came to the Great Lakes," *The Bulletin*, XXXVII (September, 1948), 1.

proved its worth to vessel operators plagued by the inherent errors of magnetic compasses. By 1941, almost every Great Lakes vessel carried a gyro-compass. About 1924, the Navy Department began to construct radio compass stations on the Great Lakes.[2] By the close of the 1927 navigation season, nineteen radio beacons were in operation and 262 ships were equipped with radio direction finders. An additional 100 vessels were expected to have sets installed by the following spring.[3] The first ship-to-shore radiotelephone on the lakes was installed on the Wilson steamer *William C. Atwater* in 1934. In 1936, the Lake Carriers' Association adopted and began to coordinate a radio-telephone system. By 1945, almost every lake vessel carried the device as standard navigational safety equipment.[4] The introduction of radar, in its commercial infancy in 1945, foretold of the reduction of the danger of fog.

After a careful study of the probable repair facilities required to service the existing Great Lakes fleet, American Ship Building decided to concentrate all of its yards on the lower lakes. Company officials felt they would effect substantial operating economies with this move.[5] The small Buffalo-Lake Erie plant, most of the old Globe yard in Cleveland, the Goose Island property in Chicago, and the Superior shipyard were declared expendable and put up for public auction.

The six-acre Buffalo plant was sold to Ranahan & McCarthy Marine Terminal, Incorporated, and was used for a number of years to receive shipments of new automobiles from Detroit.[6] A part of the old Globe property in Cleveland was sold to a trucking operator and, later in the

2. *Annual Report of the Lake Carriers' Association, 1924* (Detroit: P. N. Bland Printing Co., 1925), p. 107.

3. *Annual Report of the Lake Carriers' Association, 1927* (Detroit: P. N. Bland Printing Co., 1928), p. 199.

4. John W. Manning, "Safety and Radiotelephone Communications on the Great Lakes," Paper presented to the Marine Section of the National Safety Council at the 55th National Safety Congress and Expositions, Chicago, Illinois, October 24, 1967.

5. Forty-Sixth Annual Report of The American Ship Building Company for the Fiscal Period Ended June 30, 1945.

6. *Buffalo Courier-Express*, April 20, 1945; Board of Directors' Meeting, June 26, 1945, Minutes, ASBCo.

year, the remainder went to the Nottingham Steel Company.[7] The shipbuilding firm continued to maintain its main offices at the shipyard site at the foot of West 54th Street until 1963. At that time, they were moved to a new building at the Lorain shipyard. The Goose Island bid was rejected as being inadequate.[8] The Superior yard, sold to the Knudsen Brothers of Duluth, would continue to provide vessel operators with adequate dry dock facilities on Lake Superior. The yard is still in operation, under different management.

During the consolidation movement in 1945, American Ship Building was presented with an opportunity to purchase one of its major competitors, The Toledo Shipbuilding Company. Early in 1945, W. G. Bartenfeld, agent for Leathem D. Smith Shipbuilding & Dry Dock Company of Sturgeon Bay, Wisconsin, approached J. Burton Ayers, president of the Toledo firm, about the sale of the shipyard. The Smith company was interested in expanding its operations. Ayers was receptive to the sale because he feared that modern aids to navigation would cut too deeply into the ship repair business upon which his firm depended.[9] By May, 1945, American Ship Building was also interested in purchasing the Toledo firm, and Ayers was able to use his position to good advantage.[10] American Ship Building succeeded in purchasing the yard for over $1,000,000. The sale was consummated through The Delta Shipbuilding Company, which took formal possession on September 24, 1945.[11] This company was dissolved in 1947, and the yard came into possession of the parent firm.

When Delta Shipbuilding purchased the Toledo yard, it acquired a tradition in shipbuilding that extended back into lake history as a contemporary of the parent firm's predecessors. The founder of the Toledo yard, John Craig, came to the lake region from New York in 1866. He was born in the Dry Dock section of New York of Scottish

---

7. Board of Directors' Meeting, June 26, 1945 and June 25, 1946, Minutes, ASBCo.

8. *Ibid.*, June 26, 1945.

9. Interview with W. G. Bartenfeld, naval architect, Cleveland, Ohio, February 12, 1968.

10. Board of Directors' Meeting, May 22, 1945, Minutes, ASBCo.

11. *Ibid.*, October 11, 1945.

immigrant parents in 1838. John, closely attached to his deeply religious father, found at an early age that he did not care for the rough life of a sailor and resolved to learn the ship carpentry trade in New York. During the Civil War, he helped to lay out the lines for the Union gunboat *Winona*. Shortly afterwards, he entered into a partnership with an old New York shipbuilder named Simonson. John's half of the partnership cost only $600, so the firm was not founded with grandiose plans. The partners purchased two schooners that had been seriously damaged by fire and rebuilt them in 1864 at Keyport, New Jersey as the *Edwin Kirk* and *James H. Seguine*. Craig soon became acquainted with a cousin of the governor of New Jersey who had purchased 1,000 acres of timberland in Somerset County, Maryland. John Craig began construction of a schooner for him on Wicomico Creek. The job took two years and the vessel, the *Amelia G. Ireland*, was not completed until 1866. John sailed her to New York, but the owners refused to pay him. The war was over and there was no demand for ships. When he was unable to sell the ship, the owners passed the hat and collected $250 for his sixteen months of labor.[12] Shortly after this time, his infant son died. He found himself with one hundred dollars, a wife to support, and no prospect of a job.

Just at this time, Craig's brother-in-law, Alexander R. Linn, a Detroit merchant, told him of an uncle in Gibraltar, Michigan, who wanted a vessel built from timber on his land. John travelled to the small community at the mouth of the Detroit River. What he found was not encouraging—about fifty farm families, 200 "skedaddlers" from the Union army, and several former escaped slaves. A job was a job, nevertheless, and John Craig, in company with Cleveland ship carpenter Roderick Caulkins, built the schooner *Jane Ralston* for the uncle, Robert W. Linn. Craig received $500 and the promise of a partnership.[13]

Business went well for Linn & Craig for a few years as Robert Linn

---

12. John Craig, *Episodes of My Life, as Told in My Ninetieth Year to My Granddaughter, Ruth Craig Merrell and Compiled by Her* (Long Beach: private publication, 1928), p. 24.

13. *Ibid.*, p. 25.

supplied the timber and looked after his general store and mills while John Craig built ships. Then the Panic of 1873 descended upon the region. The firm had just completed three vessels and found itself with about $40,000 in assets but little cash. Linn & Craig made the unfortunate decision to build its first ship on builder's account. Prior to this, the partners' vessels had been built on contract. At the height of hard times, Craig had a new house, built just before the panic, a schooner on the stocks, and no money. When circumstances looked darkest, Craig received a telegram from W. W. Bates, agent for W. L. Baker, a Chicago vessel owner, that he was coming to inspect the schooner for possible sale. By this time, the schooner, the *Rutherford B. Hayes*, had been on the stocks for two or three years. Craig's nine-year old son George was as delighted as his father about the sale of the ship. He had been responsible each day after school for sprinkling the frame with water and salt to help preserve it from rotting. By Thanksgiving, 1877, the sale was completed and Craig was out of debt.[14]

John Craig and Robert Linn could not get along as partners. Both men were headstrong Scotsmen, and each was suspicious of the other's interests. Craig wanted to enlarge the shipbuilding portion of the partnership while Linn wanted to improve the activities of the store and mills.[15] As the partners' fortunes rose in the small town, Annie Craig wanted to run the Sunday School and Mrs. Linn "wanted to be queen of that and the whole town and she was jealous that I [Craig] was getting to be head of the firm."[16] The partners' business relationship deteriorated so badly that they were "so different from most other men and cannot talk without almost fighting. . . ." But when the women took up cudgels, it was more than time for a change.[17] In October, 1878, the partnership was dissolved and Craig entered the shipbuilding business for himself.[18]

14. *Ibid.*, p. 34.

15. Memorandum of conversation between John Craig and Robert Linn, n.d., in possession of George L. Merrill, Toledo, Ohio. Mr. Merrill is John Craig's grandson.

16. John Craig, *Episodes of My Life . . . ,* p. 43.

17. Letter from John Craig to Robert W. Linn, March 4, 1878, in possession of George L. Merrill.

18. Notice of dissolution, partnership of Linn & Craig, October 1, 1878, *Ibid.*

GENEALOGY OF THE TOLEDO SHIPYARD

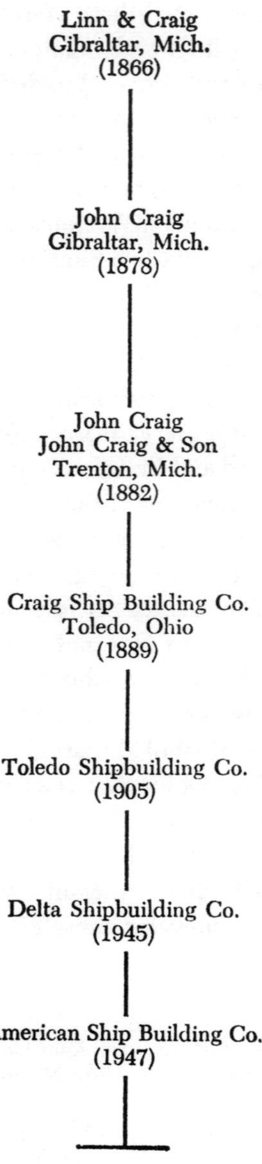

Having built five more vessels in Gibraltar, John Craig decided, in 1882, to move a few miles upstream to Trenton, Michigan, in order to enlarge his operations. He stayed there until 1889 and built sixteen wooden hulls. During his stay in Trenton, his son, George L. Craig, joined him to form the firm of John Craig & Son. George learned the shipbuilding trade from his father and supplemented his knowledge by studying drafting and vessel design under Frank E. Kirby.[19]

One of the severest drawbacks faced by the Craigs at Trenton was a lack of skilled labor. Family legend tells of Craig's purchasing government land in the area at a favorable price and using it as an inducement to attract a more stable class of laborer to the shipyard. John would hire immigrants to work in the shipyard if they would agree to buy his land at a dollar an acre. He would deduct a dollar a month from their pay envelopes. Thus he hoped to tie them to his shipyard by tying them to the land.[20] John Craig enjoyed telling how he ran afoul of contract labor laws while at Trenton by importing ship carpenters from Montreal and Quebec. He was faced with a federal court judgement amounting to $43,000. "I crawled out of a hole then," he recalled, "got every big Republican in Michigan from the governor down to file a petition which let me off with the payment of the costs."[21]

The labor shortage at Trenton, coupled with the desire to start a steel shipbuilding plant, prompted the Craigs to purchase a site in Toledo, at Front and Craig Streets on the east bank of the Maumee River in 1888. A new firm, The Craig Ship Building Company, was formed and another son, John F. Craig, who had been sent to Scotland to study steel shipbuilding methods, joined his father and older brother. George L. Craig occupied the position of general manager and consulting engineer. The company's first steel ship, the *John W. Moore*, was launched in 1890. The firm built a few bulk freighters but gained its reputation by building many specialized craft such as lightships, passenger ships, and small ocean cargo vessels.

19.   Frank E. Hamilton, "Notes . . . On Shipbuilding . . . ."
20.   Interview with George L. Merrill, Toledo, Ohio, February 16, 1968.
21.   *Toledo Blade*, January 15, 1934.

Several of the latter class were built by the Craig firm at the turn of the century. They included the *Mae, Buckman, Redondo*, and *Toledo*. One of the hardest jobs the Craigs tackled was building the first trans-lake car ferry. The Ann Arbor Railroad wanted to start a service across Lake Michigan to connect with railroads on the west side of the lake. The Craigs made several drawings, all showing the bow open. But this design was not suited to the rough weather that was sure to be encountered on the open lake. Suddenly, George Craig conceived the idea of housing in the bow but leaving the stern open for loading and discharging railroad cars.[22] The steamers *Ann Arbor No. 1* and *Ann Arbor No. 2* were built on this design in 1892. It has been followed ever since.

The Craig company was most noted for passenger ship construction. Some of the best-remembered ships were the *City of Benton Harbor, City of South Haven, Lakeside, Chippewa*, and *Iroquois*. The *Indianapolis*, built in 1904, had a dual honor. She was the first passenger steamer "of any pretensions" built for an Indiana company. The general manager of the Indiana Transportation Company dreamed up a "ladies' launching." Several "handsome Hoosier belles" were selected to name, christen the steamer, and pull the launching trigger which would send the largest white-hulled lady at the festivities down the greased ways into the slip. The *Toledo Blade* commented that the full significance of such an undertaking being entrusted to feminine hands excited more than passing interest by experienced marine men.[23]

Feminine hands notwithstanding, the Craigs left the Toledo shipbuilding scene in 1905. John Craig retired to a life filled with civic service and responsibilities. The sons moved to Long Beach, California, where they started another shipbuilding company. In November, 1905, The Toledo Shipbuilding Company was organized. Lyman C. Smith, of the Smith Premier Typewriter Company, originated the idea as an investment.[24] He interested Horace S. Wilkinson, general man-

22. John Craig, *Episodes of My Life . . .* , p. 39.
23. *Toledo Blade*, April 30, 1904.
24. *Marine Review*, XXXII (December 14, 1905), 16.

ager of the United States Transportation Company, and together, they sought out Alexander McVittie and Charles B. Calder of American Ship Building's Detroit plant. The friction that existed between McVittie, Calder, and their former employer was caused by the arbitrary manner in which the Cleveland office of the company decided how much alteration and repair work to steamers operated by the D & C and C. & B. lines should be done without cost to the vessel owners.[25]

The new corporation paid an estimated $550,000 for the shipyard, and it was incorporated for $1,000,000.[26] McVittie was elected president; Smith, vice-president and treasurer; Wilkinson, secretary; and Calder, general manager and superintendent. Frank E. Kirby was consulting engineer. Calder brought two other Detroit employees, William G. Henderson and Howard L. Shepherd, with him.[27]

The Craig Ship Building Company had built a dry dock at Toledo in 1894.[28] The new company immediately announced plans for the construction of a new dry dock. It was first used on April 22, 1907, when the island passenger steamer *Lakeside* was floated into it.[29] The company also added three electric cantilever gantry cranes to facilitate the handling of steel plates.[30]

For the first three years the Toledo Shipbuilding Company constructed bulk freighters—largely for the Wilkinson-Smith steamship interests—then reverted to building specialized craft. In 1917, the company built two "Laker" type freighters for French buyers and had seven under construction for the British when the Shipping Board req-

25. *Toledo Blade*, November 25, 1905.
26. *Ibid.*
27. *Ibid.*, November 27, 1905.
28. John M. Killits (ed.), *Toledo and Lucas County, Ohio, 1623-1923* (3 vols.; Chicago: S. J. Clarke Publishing Co., 1923), I, 529. The dry dock was originally 425 feet long on the blocks, 55 feet wide at the gate, and had 16 feet of water over the sill. In about 1904, it was enlarged to 525 feet on the blocks and 57 feet wide at the gate. It was lengthened again in 1907 to 625 feet on the blocks and 70 feet wide at the gate.
29. *Marine Review*, XXXV (May 2, 1907), 33. The new dry dock was 550 feet long on the blocks, 77 feet wide at the gate, and had 14 feet of water over the sill.
30. *Toledo Blade*, July 6, 1907.

uisitioned them. Counting the requisitioned ships, the Toledo firm built thirty vessels for the Shipping Board. It also completed, on builder's account, three ships whose keels were already laid when the Shipping Board cancelled the contracts. After the war, the company turned to the repair business for its principal livelihood. It built fourteen hulls between 1922 and 1930. During the Depression, the company existed solely on repair business. Yet between 1935 and 1940, the yard showed a net yearly average income of $86,700.[31] But by 1941 the firm was looking forward to receiving extensive government contracts.

The first company "war contract," announced on January 27, 1941, by the Navy Department, was for the construction of the 200-foot Coast Guard cutter *Storis*. The contract was considered to be "of an educational nature" to prepare the yard for others of a similar type.[32] The $1,500,000 vessel was christened with a bottle of Ohio champagne in April, 1942. If President J. Burton Ayers and Superintendent Joe Rawlinson were expecting many more government contracts to follow, they were doomed to disappointment.[33] Only one other Navy contract was forthcoming during the war. This was for the world-famous Coast Guard lake ice breaker *Mackinaw*, launched in March, 1944. The 290-foot ship, with the displacement of a light cruiser, was the heaviest vessel of its size ever built in a Great Lakes shipyard.[34] To round out its war record, the Toledo firm built several 2,500 and 1,350 horse-power steam engines for the Maritime Commission. However the yard did yeoman service in keeping its share of the iron ore fleet in repair. Prior to the yard's sale in 1945, it was expected to resume operations "without any important departure from prewar practices."[35] For the parent American Ship Building Company, however, there were postwar adjustments.

31.   Calculations by the author from Annual Report(s) of The Toledo Shipbuilding Company, Inc., for the Fiscal Year Ending December 31, 1935-40, in possession of the author.

32.   *Toledo Times*, March 30, 1941.

33.   *Toledo Business*, XX (April, 1942), 3.

34.   Annual Report of The Toledo Shipbuilding Company, Inc., for the Fiscal Year Ending December 31, 1944.

35.   *Ibid.*

The only major construction work that American Ship Building did in 1946 was the conversion of the Inland Steel Company freighter *E. J. Block* to diesel-electric drive. This was a pioneer effort on the lakes. Jewel Dean, marine writer for the *Cleveland Plain Dealer*, was aboard for her sea trials. He was accustomed to the noise and "monkey-motion" of the typical "up-and-down" lake steam engine. After the trip, he sadly commented that the "two engines just sit there, two large blocks of seemingly solid metal. . . ."[36] The high cost of labor and materials deterred lake vessel owners from contracting for new vessels. President Gerhauser thought that if ship operating costs continued to increase, vessel owners would be forced to build larger and more efficient ships; but until then the shipbuilding firm had to find supplementary work.[37]

For a few years, the Toledo yard manufactured domestic heating boilers and stokers. Delivery of stokers was delayed until 1947 because small electric motors had not been available. The sale of boilers, stokers, storage tanks, and other fabricated steel products developed into a profitable sideline, but when steel became difficult to obtain during the Korean conflict, the business was discontinued.

In 1948, the shipbuilding company received its first order for new ship construction since the end of the war. The Inland Steel Company ordered a 678-foot ore carrier which would be the largest vessel on the Great Lakes. She was launched on June 28, 1949 at Lorain, and named the *Wilfred Sykes*. Her refined lines were a departure from the traditional Great Lakes ore carrier and provided the model for most of the large freighters built in the fifties. She had a "kettle-back" or cruiser stern whereas most lake freighters had elliptical sterns. The cruiser stern was first used on the six "Maritimers" built by American Ship Building in 1943 with gratifying results. The ship's resistance was materially reduced, and better flow conditions to the propeller contributed to a higher propulsive efficiency. These two factors combined to

36. *Cleveland Plain Dealer*, September 18, 1946.
37. Forty-Eighth Annual Report of The American Ship Building Company for the Fiscal Period Ending June 30, 1947.

provide a substantial savings in power, particularly when the vessel was operated in shallow water.[38]

The *Sykes* had full stern lines to accommodate the largest propeller possible. The propeller was mounted on a bulbous skeg that not only aided in the flow of water past the contra-guide rudder but also gave added strength to that critical area of the hull.[39] The general appearance of the vessel was given much attention. It was modernized as far as the practical arrangement of cabins and hull lines would allow. The stem was given considerable rake, the cabins were streamlined, and the stack was designed to balance the picture of the rakish, massive forward cabins.

One vesselman facetiously referred to the early 1950's as the "coming of the whales." The construction of the *Wilfred Sykes* and the need for iron ore prompted by the Korean conflict triggered a flurry of new vessel construction. The five ships built by American Ship Building followed the same basic hull design of the *Sykes*. One, the *Ernest T. Weir*, went beyond her in size. Four of them were built at Lorain; the fifth, the *Edward B. Greene*, at Toledo.

Construction ran considerably behind schedule because of labor shortages and late delivery of materials. With building berths filled on the lakes, vessel owners turned to East Coast shipyards for help. Four ore carriers were built at the Sparrows Point, Maryland, yard of the Bethlehem Steel Corporation and towed up the Mississippi River–Illinois Waterway System with deckhouses and stacks lashed to their decks. Several C-4 class cargo vessels and a Victory ship were purchased, lengthened, and converted to ore carriers. They followed the same route, and all were completed at the South Chicago yard of American Ship Building. One of the converted ships, Hanna's *Joseph H. Thompson*, was 696 feet long!

Gerhauser's prediction had come true, but the lake shipyards were unable to cope with the suddenness of the demand for new ships.

38. E. B. Williams, Kent C. Thornton, W. R. Douglas, and Paul Miedlich, "Design and Construction of Great Lakes Bulk Freighter Wilfred Sykes," Pamphlet reprinted from *Marine Engineering & Shipping Review* (June, 1950), 10.
39. *Ibid.*, p. 13.

Only the national emergency justified the great expense of towing the hulls from the East Coast. Despite a lack of building berths, the American Ship Building Company, with its South Chicago yard, was able to benefit materially from the influx of salt water-built or converted ships. As the demand for ships ran high, so did the demand for skilled shipbuilding labor.

Wages had increased as the cost of living rose, but the company was handicapped by the semi-depressed lake trade following the busy war years. With the return of wartime conditions in the early 1950's, the company had to obtain permission from the Wage Stabilization Board to increase wages beyond the established 10 per cent ceiling set by that body. Even this raise failed to attract all the needed manpower.[40] The Lorain yard was in a particularly poor situation because it had to compete with the area's steel mills for labor. A few strikes marred the scene, but generally the company enjoyed a good employer-employee relationship. Contracts were negotiated between the A.F. of L. and the company about every two years, and the closed shop had been in effect since September, 1948. In 1954, the standard hourly rate for skilled labor reached $2.13. In 1955, a supplemental agreement boosted it to $2.28 an hour.[41] But the man who guided the company through this period of amicable relations with the unions was not there to witness its results.

Harry Gerhauser became ill in 1951 but came regularly to his desk until October, 1952. He died on November 23, 1952. Gerhauser had come to Cleveland from Detroit in 1917 to assist his father-in-law, Merton E. Farr, in the wartime production of the company. In 1928, at the age of thirty-nine, he had assumed the presidency of the company. Tall, white-haired, and dignified, with urbane geniality and a good sense of humor, Harry Gerhauser had commanded the respect of business colleagues and shipyard workers alike. The company would miss the strong hand of leadership he had displayed through the Depres-

40. Fifty-Second Annual Report of The American Ship Building Company for the Fiscal Period Ended June 30, 1951.

41. Agreement Between The American Ship Building Company and Unions Affiliated with the American Federation of Labor, Dated August 1, 1954; Supplemental Agreement Effective August 27, 1955.

sion and Second World War. Robert B. Ackerman succeeded him as president. Ackerman had been vice-president of the Delta Shipbuilding Company during the war and later filled the same position with the parent firm.

Ackerman was president of the firm during its most difficult period since the Depression years. Prolonged strikes in 1954, 1955, and 1956 cut deeply into expected profits from new construction. The company built another "whale," the Hanna freighter *George M. Humphrey*, in 1954. She was 710 feet long overall, had a molded breadth of 75 feet, and could carry 23,600 tons of iron ore in a single trip. She was so big that company engineeers decided to build her in the dry dock at Lorain rather than risk plate damages caused by a side launching. In 1955, the company was awarded a Navy contract for $16,263,540 to build two Landing Ship Tanks.[42] Complications arising from this contract would contribute to Ackerman's death.

The slight recession that blanketed the nation following the Korean conflict was reflected on the lakes in less hauling of iron ore and as a result, in fewer repairs for the shipbuilding company. Union difficulties, complications with the LST contract, as well as the recession, placed the company in a serious financial position.

The LST contracts were made on a competitive basis with little room left for error. The usual shortages of skilled labor and steel plates contributed to the late delivery of the vessels, and the company lost almost $1,000,000 on each of them.[43] The acceptance trials of one of them, the U.S.S. *Wood County*, symbolized the story of their construction. Plans were made to beach the 442-foot ship on the sandy shores of Kelleys Island in May, 1959. As the vessel was run ashore, her stern anchor was dropped so that she could pull herself off the beach. On board were 250 guests and technicians, including two rear admirals and top company executives. When the windlass began to reel in the stern cable, the anchor failed to catch in the clay bottom.

Furthermore, the ship was high and dry on a slight sand ridge. A harbor tug was dispatched from Sandusky but was unable to render assistance. The day was unseasonably warm, there was little breeze, and the "provisions" soon ran out aboard the *Wood County*. The arrival of the ship attracted most of the islanders, and as the situation became more awkward to those on board, the not-too-gentle taunts of the islanders became unsettling. Fortunately, the big tug *John Roen IV*, passing by the scene, was called in. After an eight hour imprisonment, the big LST was pulled off. The incident was embarrassing to those on board but did neither seriously damaged the ship nor impaired its acceptance by the Navy. Today, the participants smile when the episode is mentioned, but there were few smiles that May day aboard the *Wood County*!

Neither were there smiles at American Ship Building when the amount of the loss sustained by the company on the contracts became apparent. The firm was also awarded Navy contracts for the construction of two destroyer-escorts which also loomed as large financial losses. The pressures became too great for Ackerman who resigned in 1957 and died the following year at the age of seventy-four. It was a sad ending of forty years of dedicated shipbuilding with the company.

Edmund Q. Sylvester, a distinguished research engineer and inventor of a revolutionary pressure pouring technique for casting steel, became the third president of American Ship Building in five years. One of his first moves was to subcontract construction of the destroyer-escorts to Avondale Marine Ways in New Orleans. Since the latter firm was familiar with naval construction, American Ship Building hoped to reduce the expected losses from the contract. The prefabricated steel and plate in the Lorain yard was transferred to Chicago on the steamer *W. C. Richardson* and taken to New Orleans on barges.[44] The company was saved from further loss when the Navy Department cancelled the contracts in an economy move.[45]

Meanwhile, construction continued on two giant ore carriers that

44. *Lorain Journal*, May 27, 1958.
45. *Ibid.*, June 10, 1958.

the company had contracted while Ackerman was still president. They followed the lines of the *George M. Humphrey* and were built at the Toledo yard. The vessels, *Shenango II* and *John Sherwin*, were 690 keel feet long. Since the Toledo dry dock was only 640 feet long on the keel blocks, each ship was constructed as far forward as the collision bulkhead, then floated back so that the stern extended about 100 feet out from the dry dock. The stern was ballasted, and the forepeak was added to complete the hull!

While the Toledo shipyard struggled with ships that were too big for the dry dock, and while company officials curtailed shipyard operations to reduce operating expenses in 1958, tragedy of another sort struck the Lorain yard. In 1957, the Buffalo yard began construction on the gatelifter *Grasse River* for the St. Lawrence Seaway Development Corporation. The barge was to be used to raise gates of the Seaway locks, should they become damaged. The *Grasse River* was towed to Lorain in May, 1958, to be fitted with an A-frame, boom, and lifting beam. On July 3, final lifting tests were being conducted under the surveillance of shipyard and Corps of Engineers officials when something went wrong with the lifting mechanism. The full weight of 300 tons of steel suddenly shifted to the frame supports of the boom. The supports buckled, and the great weight pinned one end of the barge to the bottom of the Black River.[46] Two shipyard workers were drowned, and five others hospitalized with injuries.

Despite financial and shipyard tragedies, Edmund Sylvester maintained an optimistic outlook. The cancellation of the destroyer-escort contract came in the nick of time. The company's work force was slashed to half its former size, and, after seventy-one days of strike, a three-year labor agreement was signed with the A.F. of L. Modernization and conversion work on older ore freighters also helped to ease the situation. The major contracts began to pick up.

In 1960, American Ship Building received a contract to lengthen the Pickands-Mather steamer *Charles M. Schwab*. The steamship company purchased the laid-up ocean tanker *Gulfport*. The Lorain shipyard cut both vessels in half. The stern half of the tanker was

46. *Ibid.*, July 4, 1958.

joined to the forward end and new midbody of the *Schwab*. The unusual aspect of the job was that the *Gulfport* was sixty-four feet wide and the *Schwab* was only sixty! The shipyard converted the 586-foot *Schwab* into a 664-foot ore carrier at a much reduced cost. She proved to be a good carrier despite her somewhat unorthodox dimensions!

The *Schwab* experiment started a trend by lake vesselmen to "jumboize" vessels, much as they had shortly after 1900, because of a loophole in custom laws. While it was unlawful for foreign-built ships to be registered under the flag of the United States, midbodies constructed in foreign shipyards were not defined as "ships." Accordingly, lake firms purchased ships laid up in the mothball fleet and had them cut in half. By joining the forward and after ends of the American-built vessels to the foreign-built midbodies, a savings of several million dollars was effected. This operation was performed on four ships —two by East Coast shipyards and two by American Ship Building. In 1961, the 483-foot tanker *Chiwawa* became the 716-foot ore freighter *Walter A. Sterling*, and the 504-foot *Atlantic Dealer* became the 710-foot ore carrier *Paul H. Carnahan*. The midbodies, built at Hamburg, Germany, were towed through the St. Lawrence Seaway to Lorain. It did not take the government long, however, to plug the hole in the dam.

In 1962, Edmund Sylvester was elevated to chairman of the board of directors of the shipbuilding company. William H. Jory, of the Maryland Shipbuilding & Dry Dock Company, was elected president. The change occurred under conditions similar to Sylvester's election to the presidency. The lake shipping industry had experienced a depressed condition the year before, the company had no new construction or conversion jobs, and another lengthy strike occurred in the late summer of 1961. Jory tried to reduce operating expenses by disposing of surplus property.

In 1961, one of American Ship Building's chief competitors for almost sixty years, the Great Lakes Engineering Works, with plants at Ecorse, Michigan, and Ashtabula, Ohio, began liquidation proceedings. American Ship Building purchased the firm's patterns and drawings, a large floating dry dock, and the Ashtabula shipyard. The Ashtabula yard was dismantled and later sold to the City of Ashtabula. Plans for the floating dry dock never materialized and it was moored at Toledo for several years awaiting a buyer. Because of the high cost of labor in Buffalo and lack of ship repairs, the Ganson Street yard was closed down in 1962 and sold at public auction the following year.[47] The auction failed to draw a bid and the property remained idle until 1966 when buyers were found.[48]

The shipbuilding company also began to diversify its interests. The trend began under Sylvester's guidance in 1959 when the firm purchased Automobile Transport, Incorporated, a common carrier owning trucks and piggyback automobile trailers. The following year, American Ship Building began to manufacture Biogest, a sewage disposal unit designed for ships and underground mines. In 1960, the parent firm entered the bowthruster field and, in 1964, adopted the trade name of "Amthrust."[49] Using Sylvester's innovations of pressure casting, the company manufactured equipment to make steel slabs directly from the furnace. The process enabled steel manufacturers to by-pass the costly ingot, blooming, and slabbing stages. In the same period, American Ship Building purchased the American Submarine Company, manufacturers of two-man submarines.[50] A large testing tank was built at the Chicago yard, a few submarines were sold, and then the subsidiary collapsed. In 1959, American Ship Building formed a business association with the Doran Company of Mobile, Alabama, and began the production and repair of ships' propellers under the firm name of the American Propeller Company. The propellers were cast in Mobile and shipped to Toledo where the firm balanced and finished them. The work in Toledo was done in a building adjacent to the Toledo shipyard.[51]

The subsidiary companies and sideline ventures entered into by American Ship Building were in most instances unsuccessful. The pri-

47.   *Buffalo Courier-Express*, August 8, 1962.
48.   *Ibid.*, October 23, 1963; *Buffalo Evening News*, September 22, 1966.
49.   Bowthrusters are propellers recessed in tunnels on the bow to aid in steering the vessel by use of powerful jet streams of water.
50.   *Cleveland Plain Dealer*, July 18, 1964.
51.   *Toledo Blade*, July 19, 1959, and April 5, 1964.

mary business of the company was still dependent on the vagaries and whims of the lake shipping industry. Many smaller, older vessels in the lake fleet, uneconomical to operate, were being scrapped. New ship construction brought revenue into the coffers of the shipbuilding company, but it also displaced older vessels that formerly provided a substantial repair business. American Ship Building turned aggressively, though unwisely, to new salt water fixed price construction contracts.

In the spring of 1963, the company was the second lowest bidder for a $26,000,000 construction contract for three ocean freighters. The ships were to be built for the Gulf & South American Steamship Company. Because of the government subsidies involved, the Maritime Commission awarded the contracts. Avondale Marine Ways of New Orleans was the lowest bidder, but it had a backlog of orders amounting to more than $100,000,000, including ten cargo ships and five destroyer-escorts. Jory argued that American Ship Building should have received the contracts because its building ways were empty and the firm was assured of union support to complete the ships.[52] He exerted congressional pressures on Secretary of Commerce Luther Hodges, but Hodges remained adamant.[53] Within a month, however, American Ship Building received a government contract.

In May, 1963, the Navy Department awarded a $6,500,000 construction contract to American Ship Building for an oceanographic survey vessel, the *Silas Bent*.[54] This contract was followed in the fall by Navy contracts for the conversion of a Victory ship to a polaris missile supply tender and the jumboizing of three Navy tankers.[55] In the next three years, the company also received government awards for the

---

52. *Cleveland Plain Dealer*, April 20, 1963. American Ship Building's bid of $8,791,364 for each ship was only 2 per cent higher than that of the New Orleans firm, which was $8,613,000 per ship.

53. *Ibid.*, April 30, May 4, and June 11, 1963.

54. *Ibid.*, May 24, 1963.

55. *Ibid.*, November 25, 1963; *Toledo Blade*, September 6, 1963. The contract for conversion of the polaris missile supply ship, the *Furman Victory*, amounted to $3,400,000, and was done at Toledo. The three Navy tankers were the U.S.S. *Mispillion*, *Passumpsic*, and *Pawcatuck*, and the contract amounted to $25,185,000. The first named was lengthened at Toledo and the others at Lorain.

SIDELINES & SUBSIDIARIES
1941-1968

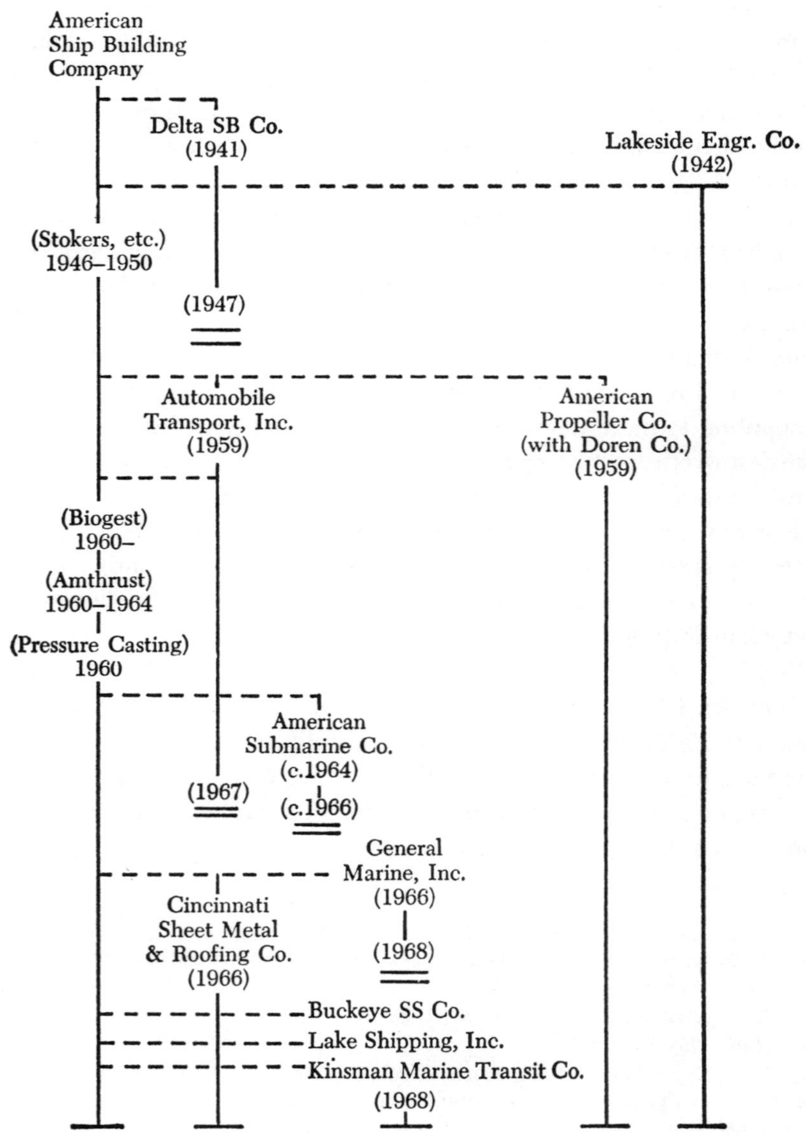

construction of seven Coast Guard cutters and a fisheries research ship as well as for the conversion of a Liberty ship to a "special" minesweeper. All proved to be monumental financial detriments to the company.

The ship building company performed a neat bit of nautical surgery in connection with the Navy oilers. In 1966, American Ship Building contracted with Hudson Waterways, Incorporated, a New York shipping firm, to jumboize three tankers. The tankers were cut in half, and the midsections taken from the Navy oilers were inserted.[56] An old-time lake veteran remarked that the shipbuilding business was becoming a cross between a tailor shop and a game of musical chairs!

As company fortunes remained static, Bill Jory explored possible sideline investments. "A business that doesn't have a definite growth pattern can only have lean management," he said.[57] In April, 1966, the company purchased General Marine, Incorporated, a Rockford, Illinois, firm engaged in the production of small, jet-propelled fire boats which resembled pleasure cruisers.[58] In December, American Ship Building made its first solid acquisition, the Cincinnati Sheet Metal & Roofing Company, manufacturer of rain disposals, furnace fittings, roofing, and siding equipment. The price was said to be in excess of $3,000,000, but the southern Ohio firm's annual sales exceeded $8,000,000.[59]

The desire to diversify company interests in 1966 is understandable in light of what was again developing in connection with some of the government contracts. On June 15, 1965, the *Cleveland Plain Dealer* headlines screamed news of a $13,000,000 contract awarded to the Lorain firm for the construction of five Coast Guard cutters. Two additional cutter contracts, to be awarded within sixty days, would boost the total value of the work to $18,076,770.[60] By 1967, rumors were heard within the lake shipping fraternity to the effect that American

---

56. The three commercial tankers were the *Transhuron, Transerie,* and *Bladensburg.* The latter ship was completed at Toledo as the *Transsuperior.*

57. "Takeover on the Lakes," *Business Week,* August 26, 1967, p. 30.

58. *Cleveland Plain Dealer,* April 19, 1966.

59. *Ibid.,* December 31, 1966.

60. *Ibid.,* June 15, 1965.

Ship Building was in very serious financial difficulty because of the Coast Guard contracts. President Jory confirmed them in part in his annual message to stockholders:

> While our company suffers from the hazards of large fixed price contracts, the present Management group is considered well qualified to cope with the situation and can be trusted to maintain the company's sound condition.[61]

The well worded message attempted to allay stockholders' fears, not only of the Coast Guard cutter dilemma, but of two other threats that had appeared on the horizon. In 1966, the giant and diversified Litton Industries attempted to gain a controlling interest in the Lorain-based shipbuilding firm. Failing in this, Litton turned its attentions to wooing the City of Lorain to aid in backing a second shipbuilding concern in that town through tax and bond inducements. Finally, Litton went to Erie, Pennsylvania, where it successfully began construction of a shipyard.

As a result of the rumors of financial instability and Litton threats, a proxy battle appeared to be shaping up at the annual meeting of stockholders scheduled for October, 1967. A group of Clevelanders, headed by George M. Steinbrenner III, youthful president of The Kinsman Marine Transit Company, were interested in keeping the firm in local hands.

They sent their representative, Thomas Roulston of Roulston & Company, a Cleveland member of the New York Stock Exchange, to meet with the shipbuilding company's board of directors. Roulston approached them as representing 38 per cent of the company's shareholders, or about $9,000,000 worth of stock. After the meeting, Roulston commented that he went to the meeting with the assurance that his group would be given their fair representation. He said that the meeting "was a complete waste of time. They didn't even look at our affidavits."[62] In June, rumors persisted that the Cleveland group was being backed by Litton money, but Roulston denied it.[63] On July 26, Jory an-

---

61.   The American Ship Building Company, 68th Annual Report, 1967, p. 5.
62.   *Cleveland Plain Dealer*, May 20, 1967.
63.   *Cleveland Press*, June 2, 1967.

nounced that he had offered five seats on the ten-seat board of directors to the Cleveland-based group. Roulston said that "this action as-
sures retention of control of an old Cleveland-area company with
Cleveland interests."[64] Bill Jory summed up his position by saying that
"as a salt-water man I guess I wasn't as popular as the fresh-water people."[65]

On October 11, 1967 the new management assumed control of
American Ship Building with thirty-six year old George M. Steinbrenner III as president. Immediately, things began to happen. On October 26, the shipbuilding firm was awarded a $20,000,000 contract for
construction of a revolutionary self-unloading bulk vessel to be built
for the United States Steel Corporation. The new ship was to be 850
feet long and 105 feet wide. Steinbrenner, who looked for from five to
seven similar orders in future years, referred to "Round One" by saying that "the shipyard that gets the first order for a new class of ships
has a huge head start in the competition to land more orders, and now
we are off and running."[66]

But before much running could be done, a dry dock large enough to
accommodate the new bulk carrier had to be built. On December 20,
1967, the Lorain Port Authority announced that it would issue
$7,000,000 in industrial revenue bonds to finance modernization of the
Lorain shipbuilding facilities, including a new dry dock scheduled for
completion in 1970.

With regard to other critical matters, Steinbrenner announced that
the company was trying to renegotiate the inherited Coast Guard cutter contracts in an attempt to reduce those losses.[68] The company sold
its trucking subsidiary in November, 1967, and the jet-propelled fire-
boat company the following spring. The American Submarine Company was simply dropped.

But the new management's activities were not limited to the disposal of its subsidiary holdings. It took a page from the defunct Inde-

64. *Cleveland Plain Dealer*, July 27, 1967.
65. "Takeover on the Lakes," p. 30.
66. *Ibid.*, October 26, 1967.
67. *Ibid.*, December 21, 1967.
68. *Ibid.*, November 17, 1967.

pendent Steamship Company when it began to acquire a fleet of bulk carriers. In February, 1968, American Ship Building acquired the Buckeye Steamship Company, one of the few independent American steamship companies still operating on the lakes. The four-vessel fleet was acquired through an exchange of shipbuilding company stock. Steinbrenner felt strongly that acquisition of the Buckeye fleet was a positive step toward "the goal of successful bulk carrier operation as a part of American Ship."[69]

In June, the shipbuilding company purchased the steamer *Joseph Block*, which had run aground at Death's Door, Green Bay, the month before. She suffered extensive bottom damage and was surrendered to the underwriters. The *Block* was taken to Chicago for repairs and formed the nucleus of another new subsidiary, Lake Shipping, Incorporated.[70] The same month, Buckeye Steamship Company purchased the 600-foot steamer *William J. Olcott*.

On June 28, 1968, a special meeting of stockholders was called to approve purchase of The Kinsman Marine Transit Company.[71] The eight vessel fleet was another "independent" which, with its antecedents, was established in 1842 by Steinbrenner's ancestors.

George Steinbrenner's great-great-grandfather, Philip Minch, was one of the imaginative men who gambled with the construction of the *Onoko* in 1882. Minch was also one of the founders of the Cleveland Ship Building Company in 1887. Captain Peter Minch and most of his family were lost in the *Western Reserve* disaster. The Kinsman Marine Transit Company received its name from the family homestead on Kinsman Road in Cleveland.

It is fitting that the Kinsman corporate name should be drawn into a shipbuilding business headed by an imaginative ex-football coach, with a Minch heritage, named Steinbrenner. That the Minch tradition, which helped to begin a revolutionary construction trend in 1882, should be involved in the construction of a ship which again promises to revolutionize the Great Lakes vessel industry fits a historical pattern. The cycle is now complete . . . .

69. *Ibid.*, February 14, 1968.
70. *Ibid.*, June 11, 1968.
71. *Ibid.*, June 29, 1968.

Epilogue

The corporation's historical development has changed only slightly over the years. The prosperous years for the lake shipping industry have likewise been the profitable years for the shipbuilding company. The national recessions and depressions that affected the steel industry were reflected in the profit and loss accounts of the company. Yet the company emerges as the major concern of its kind on the Great Lakes and, as in 1900, enjoys a favorable position on the American side of the lakes.

The historical cycle of a family heritage is now complete, as is also that of the evolution of the bulk lake freighter. The problems that faced the vesselmen in the 1880's are still relatively the same, and the basic ship design conceived by naval architects in that early era is also unchanged. Deeper and wider channels permit the construction of deeper, longer ships. Unloading equipment has been refined although the hulett unloading machine is still the basic tool. Some new ports have appeared on the upper lakes that utilize conveyor belt

loading. The crushing and shipping of taconite iron ore in pellet form
has given new life to the northern iron ore regions, but the use of grav-
ity loading devices is still basic.

The greatest changes have occurred in the engine rooms of lake
freighters. Today's giants are propelled by turbines or by diesel engines. The introduction of refined hull designs and new propeller and
rudder innovations, adding as much as ten miles per hour to the speed
of ships, mean added trips and a more economic operation. Light
weight, high-tensile steel permits the building of larger ships with less
relative weight.

The overall operation and role of the company has also been refined.
The new management now has a year of hard work and experience
under its belt. It has suffered from the very unwise management decisions of its immediate predecessors and has rid itself of the sore spots.
With a determination exemplified by the enthusiasm and imagination
of George Steinbrenner and the financial acumen of his brother-in-
law, Dr. Jacob O. Kamm, the company yards are beginning to take on
new life. Part of this revival is the result of a clean-up program which
includes much fresh paint. But largely it revolves around a three-fold
plan to utilize the available resources of the company to the utmost.

The most important phase is still the shipbuilding and repair business with an added operational branch, that of lake transportation. A
second phase includes building materials and steel fabrication. The
company has the technical skill and machinery to carry out the production of a wide range of products. The third phase, relatively new to
the lake industrial scene, is that of marine technology, water pollution
control, and oceanography, including both research and development. This phase will call for added emphasis on the Biogest branch of
American Ship Building. Steinbrenner likens future operations to a
"laser" concept in which company interests represent colors in the
spectrum. The total goal is a diversified, conservative, conglomerate,
corporate mold that is closely correlated to management expertise—all
designed to increase present earnings. But, with past company experiences fresh in mind, Steinbrenner cautions that "two and two must
equal five" before moves are made toward diversification.

Yet, despite the fresh and progressive wind that blows throughout

American Ship Building's corporate structure, the same basic design demanded of the *R. J. Hackett* and the *Onoko* is still to be seen in the profiles of the newly emerging freighters—these long, modern "freshwater whales."

Bibliography

PRIVATE PAPERS & CORPORATE RECORDS

Agreement Between The American Ship Building Company and the Unions Affiliated with the American Federation of Labor, Dated August 1, 1954, with Supplemental Agreement Effective August 27, 1955.

American Ship Building Company. Annual Reports of the American Ship Building Company, 1899-1967. In possession of author.

———. Corporate and Miscellaneous Records. In possession of author.

———. Corporate Minutes, 1899-1947. 9 vols. Lorain, Ohio.

American Steel Barge Company. Warranty deed to The Superior Ship Building Company, April 14, 1899. Land deed in possession of Fraser Shipyards, Inc., Superior, Wisconsin.

Beauchamp, George A. Letter to Wesley R. Harkins, August 18, 1964, Superior, Wisconsin.

Buffalo Dry Dock Company Papers. In possession of Christian J. Stellrecht, Orchard Park, New York; microfilm copy in possession of author.

Burton, Clarence M. Clarence M. Burton Papers. Burton Historical Collection, Detroit Public Library, Detroit, Michigan.

[Calder, Charles B.] Daily Journal, 1895-1918. Hand-written. In possession of author.

Chicago Ship Building Company Papers. In possession of author.

Coffinberry Family Papers. Western Reserve Historical Society Library, Cleveland, Ohio.

Detroit Ship Building Company Papers. In possession of author.

Independent Steamship Company. Minutes of the Independent Steamship Company, 1920-37. In possession of author.

Linn & Craig. Papers in possession of George L. Merrill, Toledo, Ohio.

McDonald, William A. William A. McDonald Great Lakes Collection. Dossin Great Lakes Museum, Belle Isle, Detroit, Michigan.

McDougall, Alexander. Expense Account Book. Handwritten notebook in possession of Alexander McDougall, Cleveland, Ohio.

McMillan, James. James McMillan Correspondence. Burton Historical Collection, Detroit Public Library, Detroit, Michigan.

Milwaukee Dry Dock Company. Minutes of the Milwaukee Dry Dock Company, 1891-1930. In possession of Edmund Fitzgerald; on loan to Marine & Local History Room, Milwaukee Public Library, Milwaukee, Wisconsin.

"Record of Engines Built by Globe Iron Works." Hand-written index in possession of author.

Ship Owners' Dry Dock Company (Chicago). Minutes, 1900-1912. In possession of author.

Toledo Shipbuilding Company. Annual Report of the Toledo Shipbuilding Company, Inc., 1935-44. In possession of author.

Wheeler, Frank W. Frank W. Wheeler Papers, Michigan Pioneer & Historical Collection, Ann Arbor, Michigan.

PUBLIC DOCUMENTS & PAPERS

State of New York. Department of State. Letter to the author, 1968.

U.S. *Congressional Record*. Vol. XXII.

U.S. Department of Labor. *Wartime Employment, Production, and Conditions of Work in Shipyards*. Bulletin No. 824. Washington: Government Printing Office, 1945.

U.S. Maritime Administration. "Permanent Report of Completed Ship Construction Contracts, Report B-1." Construction Division, Maritime Administration, Washington, D.C. (Mimeographed.)

U.S. Maritime Administration. United States Maritime Commission Minutes, 1940-45. Maritime Administration, Washington, D.C.

U.S. Maritime Commission Records. Record Group 178, National Archives (Suitland Records Center).

U.S. Maritime Commission. *Report to Congress for the Period Ending June 30, 1942, 1943, 1944.* Washington: Government Printing Office, 1943, 1944, 1945.

U.S. Shipbuilding Labor Adjustment Board. *Decisions as to Wages, Hours and Other Conditions in Atlantic Coast, Gulf and Great Lakes Shipyards, October 1, 1918.* Washington: Shipbuilding Labor Adjustment Board, 1918.

U.S. United States Shipping Board Records. Record Group 32, National Archives (Washington, D.C.).

U.S. Vessel Customs Enrollments (Buffalo, New York and Milwaukee, Wisconsin). Record Group 41, National Archives (Washington, D.C.).

UNPUBLISHED MATERIAL

"An Administrative History of the Bureau of Ships During World War II." 4 vols. Historical Section, Bureau of Ships, United States Navy Department Library, Washington, D.C., 1946. (Typewritten.)

"Dedication of Carnegie Library, Girardin Notes, no date." Shipbuilding Notes, Notebook II, Wyandotte Public Library, Wyandotte, Michigan. (Typewritten.)

Gardiner, Charles E. Rare Book List No. 320, Bayside, New York, 1968. Rare book catalog. (Mimeographed.)

Hamilton, Frank E. "Notes and Lists on Shipbuilding in Great Lakes Ports." Unpublished manuscript, Kelleys Island, Ohio.

Harkins, Wesley R. "Head of the Lakes Shipbuilding Industry; Steel Vessels Built." Unpublished manuscript, Superior, Wisconsin, 1963. (Mimeographed.)

———. "Notes on Duluth-Superior Shipbuilding History: American Steel Barge Company." Unpublished manuscript, Superior, Wisconsin.

Harkins, Wesley R., and Barstow, Barney B. Tape-recorded interview with Mr. Louis Dahlgren, Superior, Wisconsin, May 10, 1960. (Typed transcription.)

Kirby, Frank E. Scrapbooks. 3 vols. Burton Historical Collection, Detroit Public Library, Detroit, Michigan.

Knowlton, Ralph S. "A Short History of the Improvements of Duluth-Superior Harbor." Address given before the St. Louis County Historical Society, Duluth, Minnesota, March 24, 1959. (Mimeographed.)

Manning, John W. "Safety and Radiotelephone Communications on the Great Lakes." Paper presented to the Marine Section of the National Safety Council at the 55th National Safety Congress and Expositions, Chicago, Illinois, October 24, 1967.

Meany, Lieutenant Commander Edmond S., Jr. (comp.). "Administrative History of the Ninth Naval District." 2 vols. Historical Section, United States Navy Department Library, Washington, D.C., 1946. (Typewritten.)

Wright, Richard J. "Great Lakes Vessels with Second-Hand Engines." Notebook compiled by the author.

Wyandotte Public Library. "Local History, Industrial/Shipbuilding" folder, Pamphlet & Miscellaneous file, Wyandotte, Michigan.

PERSONAL INTERVIEWS

Barstow, Barney B. Interview, Superior, Wisconsin, September 18, 1967.

Bartenfeld, W. G. Interview, Cleveland, Ohio, February 12, 1968.

Borowske, Norman E. Telephone interview, Cleveland, Ohio, April 1, 1968.

Fitzgerald, Edmund. Telephone interview, Milwaukee, Wisconsin, February 25, 1968.

Meader, Samuel. Telephone interview, St. Louis, Missouri, March 19, 1968.

Merrill, George L. Interview, Toledo, Ohio, February 16, 1968.

Stellrecht, Christian J. Interview, Orchard Park, New York, March 8, 1968.

Williams, Edgerton B. Telephone interview, Winter Haven, Florida, March 20, 1968.

NEWSPAPERS

The newspapers listed below are those that have been examined for purposes of this study. The dates indicated are inclusive, but not all years within the inclusive period have been used for a particular newspaper. The researcher is referred to the individual footnote citations for a more specific reference.

Bay City Daily Post. 1890.
Bay City Daily Tribune. 1885-1905.
Bay City Evening Press. 1888.
Bay City Times. 1898.
Bay City Times-Press. 1898-1899.
Buffalo Commercial Advertiser & Journal. 1878-1883.
Buffalo Courier-Express. 1941-1962.
Buffalo Daily Courier. 1900.
Buffalo Evening News. 1966.
Buffalo Morning Express. 1863-1905.
Buffalo Sunday Times. 1901.
Chicago Herald. 1891.
Chicago Inter Ocean. 1890.
Chicago Sunday Tribune. 1895.
Chicago Tribune. 1890.
Cleveland Leader. 1872-1873.
Cleveland News. 1930-1945.
Cleveland Plain Dealer. 1876-1968.
Cleveland Press. 1941-1968.
Cleveland Weekly Herald. 1847.
Detroit Journal. 1903.
Detroit News. 1880.
Detroit Tribune. 1861-1867.
Grand Rapids Leader. 1890.
Lorain Journal. 1924-1958.
Lorain Times Souvenir. April 13, 1898.
Milwaukee Sentinel. 1863-1901.
New Orleans States. 1942-1943.
New Orleans Times-Picayune. 1942-1943.
Saginaw Courier-Herald. 1891-1895.
Superior Daily Call. 1890-1891.
Superior Evening Telegram. 1890-1945.
(Superior) *Inland Ocean.* 1891-1899.
Toledo Blade. 1904-1964.
Toledo Times. 1941.
Wyandotte Herald. 1880-1945.

BOOKS

Abrams, Richard M., and Levine, Lawrence W. *The Shaping of Twentieth-Century America*. Boston: Little, Brown & Co., 1965.

Baker, Ralph W. (comp.). *Annual Report to the Duluth Board of Trade of the Trade and Commerce of Duluth for the Year Ending December 31, 1885*. Duluth: Rossiter & Evans, 1886.

Baxter, Henry A., and Heyl, Erik. *Maps Buffalo Harbor, 1804-1964*. Buffalo: Lower Lakes Marine Chapter of Buffalo & Erie County Historical Society, 1965.

Bowen, Dana Thomas. *Lore of the Lakes*. Daytona Beach: Published by the author, 1940.

———. *Memories of the Lakes*. Daytona Beach: Dana Thomas Bowen, 1946.

Bugbee, Gordon P. *The Lake Erie Sidewheel Steamers of Frank E. Kirby*. Detroit: Great Lakes Model Shipbuilders' Guild, 1955.

Burton, Clarence M. (ed.). *The City of Detroit, Michigan, 1701-1922*. 5 vols. Detroit: S. J. Clarke Publishing Co., 1922.

Chicago Ship Building Company, Ship Builders and Engineers. Published catalog. Philadelphia: Armstrong & Fears, 1899.

Craig, John. *Episodes of My Life, as Told in My Ninetieth Year to My Granddaughter, Ruth Craig Merrell and Compiled by Her*. Long Beach: private publication, 1928.

Deep Waterways Convention Held at Detroit, Michigan, December 17 and 18, 1891. Detroit: Free Press Printing Co., 1892.

De Kruif, Paul. *Seven Iron Men*. New York: Harcourt, Brace & Co., 1929.

Dorr, E. P. (ed.). *Rules for the Construction, Inspection and Characterization of Sail and Steam Vessels*. Buffalo: International Board of Lake Underwriters, 1876.

Dowling, Rev. Edward J. *The "Lakers" of World War I*. Detroit: University of Detroit Press, 1967.

Elliott, James L. *Red Stacks Over the Horizon; the Story of the Goodrich Steamboat Line*. Grand Rapids: William B. Eerdmans Publishing Co., 1967.

Evans, S. M. *A Discussion of Conditions Affecting Ship Production; Together with an Estimate of Ship Deliveries (Steel and Wood), April to December, 1918*. Washington: Government Printing Office, 1918.

Fassett, F. G., Jr. (ed.). *The Shipbuilding Business in the United States of America.* 2 vols. New York: Society of Naval Architects and Marine Engineers, 1948.

Fischer, Gerald J. (comp.). *A Statistical Summary of Shipbuilding Under the U.S. Maritime Commission During World War II.* Washington: U.S. Maritime Commission, 1949.

Flower, Frank A. (ed.). *The Eye of the Northwest; Report of the City Statistician for the Year 1892.* Superior: By authority of the city statistician, 1892.

Gasser, Augustus H. (ed.). *History of Bay County, Michigan, and Representative Citizens.* Chicago: Richmond & Arnold, 1905.

Hall, J. W. (comp.). *Hall's Record of Lake Marine Embracing: The Marine Casualties of 1877, Rules of Navigation-Collisions-Insurance-Courses and Distances-Steamboats and Propellers; also, the Names of Deceased Captains, Etc., Etc.* Detroit: William Grahams Steam Presses, 1878.

Harger, Charles B. (ed.). *Milwaukee Illustrated; Its Trade, Commerce, Manufacturing Interests, and Advantages as a Residence City.* Milwaukee: W. W. Coleman, 1877.

Havighurst, Walter. *Vein of Iron, the Pickands Mather Story.* Cleveland: World Publishing Co., 1958.

Heyl, Erik, *Early American Steamers.* 5 vols. Buffalo: Erik Heyl, 1953-67.

History of Bay County, Michigan, with Illustrations and Biographical Sketches of Some of its Prominent Men and Pioneers. Chicago: H. R. Page & Co., 1883.

Hurley, Edward N. *The Bridge To France.* Philadelphia: J. B. Lippincott & Co., 1927.

The Industries of the Bay Cities. Bay City: A. N. Marquis & Co., 1889.

Kelly, Roy W., and Allen, Frederick J. *The Shipbuilding Industry.* Boston: Houghton Mifflin & Co., 1918.

Killits, John M. (ed.). *Toledo and Lucas County, Ohio, 1623-1923.* 3 vols. Chicago: S. J. Clarke Publishing Co., 1923.

Lane, Frederick C. *Ships for Victory, A History of Shipbuilding Under the U.S. Maritime Commission in World War II.* Baltimore: Johns Hopkins Press, 1951.

Larned, J. N. *A History of Buffalo Delineating the Evolution of the City.* 2 vols. New York: The Progress of the Empire State Co., 1911.

Mansfield, J. B. (ed.). *History of the Great Lakes.* 2 vols. Chicago: J. H. Beers & Co., 1899.

Mattox, W. C. *Building the Emergency Fleet.* Cleveland: Penton Publishing Co., 1920.

Mills, James Cooke. *Our Inland Seas.* Chicago: A. C. McClurg & Co., 1910.

Nute, Grace Lee. *Lake Superior.* Indianapolis: Bobbs-Merrill Co., 1944.

Official Directory and Legislative Manual of the State of Michigan for the Years 1889-1890. Lansing: Darius D. Thorp, 1889.

Orth, Samuel P. *A History of Cleveland, Ohio.* 3 vols. Chicago: S. J. Clarke Publishing Co., 1910.

The Pennsylvania Railroad's Cleveland Docks. Cleveland: Ohio & Western Pennsylvania Dock Co., 1946.

Report of the Harbor Committee in Relation to an Increase of Harbor Facilities at the City of Buffalo. Buffalo: Jewett, Thomas & Co., Printers, 1847.

Rockefeller, John D. *Random Reminiscences of Men and Events.* New York: Doubleday, Page & Co., 1909.

Runeberg, Robert. *Steamers for Winter Navigation and Ice-Breaking.* ("Excerpt of Minutes of Proceedings of The Institution of Civil Engineers"; Vol. CXL, Session 1899-1900, Part ii) London: The Institution of Civil Engineers, 1900.

The Sault Ste. Marie Canal and Hay Lake Channel. Necessity of their Speedy Improvement. Proceedings of the Waterways Convention Held at Sault Ste. Marie, Michigan, July 20, 1887. Duluth: Daily News Print, 1887.

Welch, Samuel M. *Home History, Recollections of Buffalo During the Decade from 1830 to 1840, or Fifty Years Since.* Buffalo: Peter Paul & Brother, 1891.

Williams, Ralph D. *The Honorable Peter White; A Biographical Sketch of the Lake Superior Iron Country.* Cleveland: Penton Publishing Co., 1907.

PERIODICALS & ANNUALS

The dates indicated below are inclusive although not all of the years within the periods have been used in this study.

American Bureau of Shipping. *Record of American Bureau of Shipping.* Annual. 1935-1964.

————. *Record of American Bureau of Shipping—Great Lakes Department.* Annual. 1914-1932.

American Ship Building Company. *The American Ship Builder.* Monthly. 1942-1954.

————. *Live Wire.* Monthly. 1915.

Annual List of Merchant Vessels of the United States. 1874-1965. Washington: Government Printing Office.

Emergency Fleet Corporation. *Emergency Fleet News.* Monthly. 1918-1919.

Great Lakes News. Monthly. 1934-1945.

Great Lakes Red Book. Annual. Cleveland: Penton Publishing Co., 1921-1968.

Lake Carriers' Association. *Annual Report of the Lake Carriers' Association,* 1905-66.

Marine Record. Weekly. 1894-1902.

Marine Review. Weekly. 1890-1908.

Ship Masters' Association Directory. Annual. 1902-1966.

Statistical Report of Lake Commerce Passing Through Canals at Sault Ste. Marie, Michigan and Ontario, 1904-1920. Bound annual reports. Washington: Government Printing Office, 1904-1921.

Toledo Business. Monthly. 1942.

Transactions of the Society of Naval Architects & Marine Engineers. Annual. XXV-XLVIII (1917-1940).

ARTICLES & PAMPHLETS

Alden, Commander John D. "When Airpower Rode on Paddle Wheels," *United States Naval Institute Proceedings,* LXXXVII (May, 1961), 180-83.

Allen, Frederick Lewis. "Building the Bridge to France; Why the Government is Calling for United States Shipyard Volunteers," *The Outlook,* CXVIII (February 20, 1918), 284-86.

"American Promise and Performance in Regard to Ships and Aeroplanes," *Current Opinion,* LXIV (May, 1918), 301-04.

"America's Shipbuilding Resources," *Living Age,* CCXCIII (June 17, 1917), 699-701.

Beard, Alexander H. "The Fabricated Ship; How American Ship-Building Is Being Revolutionized," *The Outlook,* CXVIII (April 10, 1918), 581-83.

"British and American Shipbuilding," *Living Age*, CCXIX (November 2, 1918), 315-16.

Browne, Lewis Allen. "Rivets," *The Forum*, LX (July, 1918), 24-35.

Carden, Godrey L. "Ship-Building on the Great Lakes," *Harpers' Weekly*, XXXVI (July 23, 1893), 705-08.

Cooke, Douglas H. "S.O.S.—Send Out Ships! How the Spirit of Adventure Has Been Put Into Industry," *The Outlook*, CXX (September 4, 1918), 28-29.

Cowles, Walter C. "Queen of the Lakes," *Inland Seas*, XX (Spring, 1964), 54-57.

Dowling, Rev. Edward J. "Milwaukee's Freighter Fleets," *Inland Seas*, XV (Summer, 1959), 117-19.

Duncan, Francis. "The Story of the D & C," *Inland Seas*, serially, VII-XIV (1951-58).

Fawcett, Waldron. "The Most Remarkable Year in the History of the Great Lakes," *Harpers' Weekly*, XL (September 29, 1900), 915.

Ferguson, Homer L. "The War's Effect on Merchant Shipbuilding, The Standard Ship and Momentous Problems of Production," *Scientific American Supplement*, LXXXIV (December 1, 1917), 338ff.

"Finance: Fortunes of the Shipping Industry," *The Nation*, CII (March 9, 1916), 294-95.

Foord, John. "The Great Lakes and Our Commercial Supremacy," *North American Review*, CLXVII (November 17, 1898), 155-64.

Gregory, W. M. "Steel Shipbuilding on the Great Lakes," *Journal of Geography*, VI (March, 1908), 255-61.

Greusel, John Hubert. "Frank E. Kirby, Designer of Vessels," *Detroit Free Press*, January 7, 1906.

Hendrick, Burton J. "Can We Build Those Ships in Time?" *The World's Work*, XXXV (December, 1917), 172-86.

Holt, Hamilton. "Ships Will Win," *Independent Magazine*, XCIII (March 23, 1918), 486ff.

"Houses for Shipyard Workers," *Survey*, XXXIX (January 5, 1918), 399.

"How and Why We Are Making Good as Shipbuilders," *The American Review of Reviews*, LVIII (September, 1918), 309-10.

"How the Ships Are Built," *The Nation*, CVI (April 25, 1918), 496-97.

"How the Shipyards Are Speeding Up to Challenge the U-Boats," *Current Opinion*, LXIII (September, 1917), 210-12.

Hungerford, Edward. "America's Armada in the Making," *Harper's Magazine*, CXXXVI (January, 1918), 188-91.

——. "Building Ships!," *Everybody's Magazine*, XXXVII (July, 1917), 114-25.

Hurley, Edward N. "Bridging the Atlantic with Ships; The Fight for Our Line of Communications with the United States Shipping Board," *Scientific American*, CXVIII (April 6, 1918), 304-05.

Johnson, Alvin. "Tonnage Situation," *The New Republic*, CII (May 26, 1917), 102-04.

"July Fourth in Our Shipyards," *Scientific American*, CXIX (July 6, 1918), 3.

Laut, A. C. "Where Are the Ships Coming From?," *The Forum*, LIX (February, 1918), 153-64.

"The Limitations of Standardized Shipbuilding," *Scientific American Supplement*, LXXXIII (May 26, 1918), 334.

Lomax, Alfred L. "Whalebacks Promised a Shining Future for Early-Day Everett," *Seattle Times*, November 11, 1962.

Manley, Captain John J. "Great Lakes Lady Bares Her Fangs," *Inland Seas*, XIV (Spring, 1958), 58-60. Reprinted from *Inland* (Autumn, 1956).

Marvin, Winthrop L. "American Shipbuilding—A Real Renaissance," *The American Review of Reviews*, LVI (July, 1917), 63-72.

Mason, George Carrington, "McDougall's Dream: The Whaleback," *Inland Seas*, IX (Spring, 1953), 3-11.

McDonald, William A. "Composite Steamers Built by the Detroit Drydock Company," *Inland Seas*, XV (Summer, 1959), 114-16.

McDougall, Alexander. "The Autobiography of Captain Alexander McDougall," *Inland Seas*, serially, XXIII-XXIV (1967-68).

McKellar, Norman L. "Steel Shipbuilding Under the U.S. Shipping Board, 1917-1921," *The Belgian Nautical Shiplover*, serially, Nos. 270-96 (1962-63).

"Mobilizing the Shipyards," *The Nation*, CIV (April 12, 1917), 423-24.

"Our Answer to the U-Boat; Our Great Shipbuilding Victory," *Literary Digest*, LVIII (July 13, 1918), 11.

"Our National 'Breakdowns'," *The Nation*, CVI (February 21, 1918), 199.

P.T.C. "A Labor View of the Shipbuilding Programme," *The New Republic*, XIV (February 23, 1918), 111-12.

"The Progress of the World," *Review of Reviews*, IV (September, 1891), 125-36.

"Rivets for Ships," *Scientific American Supplement*, LXXXIV (September 22, 1917), 181.

Schwab, Charles M. "The Shipbuilder's Job," *The Forum*, LIX (June, 1918), 667-75.

"Shipbuilding in the West," *The Graphic*, X (June 16, 1894), 468-69.

"The Shipping Situation," *Scientific American*, CXVIII (February 16, 1918), 142.

"Ships and Organized Labor," *The New Republic*, XIV (March 2, 1918), 132-33.

"The Significances of the Changes in the Shipping Board," *The Outlook*, CXVII (November 21, 1917), 446.

Smith, H. Gerrish. "American Shipbuilding and Shiprepairing Industry at War," *American Merchant Marine Conference Proceedings, New York, October 15 and 16, 1942*, 24-27.

"Some Achievements of the Original Shipping Board," *The New Republic*, XII (September 1, 1917), 123-25.

"The Spectator on the Great Lakes," *The Outlook*, LIV (September 26, 1898), 544-45.

"Speeding Up the Shipbuilding Program," *New York Times Current History*, VII (February, 1918), Part 2, 254-56.

"Takeover on the Lakes," *Business Week*, No. 1982 (August 26, 1967), 29-30.

Turnbull, George B. "General Cargo Ships—Single-Deck Type," *Great Lakes Engineering Works, Detroit, Michigan*. Published catalog. Battle Creek: Gage Printing Co., c.1916, 90-93.

"Turning Our Sky-Scrapers into Fleets of Cargo Ships," *Current Opinion*, LXV (November, 1918), 337-38.

"The United States and the Starvation of England," *Scientific American*, CXVI (March 31, 1917), 325.

Vaughan, Crawford. "The Shipyards of the Great Lakes," *The Outlook*, CXIX (June 9, 1917), 381-82.

Walker, Augustus. "Early Days on the Lakes, with an Account of the Cholera Visitation of 1832," *Publications of the Buffalo Historical Society*, V (1902), 287-318.

Waterbury, George. "Memories of the Steamer *Maritana*, 1892-3-4-5," *Inland Seas*, VI (Spring, 1950), 54-55.

"What the 'Fabricated' Ship Is and Some Secrets of its Construction," *Current Opinion*, LXIV (May, 1918), 436.

Whitaker, O. B. "Recalling How the Gyro-Compass First Came to the Great Lakes," *The Bulletin*, XXXVII (September, 1948), 1-4.

Wildman, Edwin. "Edward N. Hurley—Shipbuilder to Uncle Sam," *The Forum*, LIX (April, 1918), 411-23.

Williams, E. B. "The Delta Shipyard," *Marine Engineering & Shipping Review*, XLVIII (April, 1943), 192-202.
Williams, E. B., Thornton, Kent C., Douglas, W. R., and Miedlich, Paul. "Design and Construction of Great Lakes Bulk Freighter Wilfred Sykes." Pamphlet reprinted from *Marine Engineering & Shipping Review* (June, 1950).

Index

GENERAL

SHIP INDEX

Above: the American Ship Building's Toledo, Ohio, plant. *American Ship Building Company. Below*: the South Chicago, Illinois, plant. *American Ship Building Company.*